Computers in Perspective

Computers in Perspective

William W. Cotterman
Georgia State University

Wadsworth Publishing Company, Inc. Belmont, California

Computer Sciences Editor: Don Dellen
Copy and Production Editor:
Mary Arbogast
Designer: Russell K. Leong
Cover Designer: Nancy Benedict
Illustrator: John Foster

© 1974 by Wadsworth Publishing
Company, Inc., Belmont, California
94002. All rights reserved. No part of
this book may be reproduced, stored
in a retrieval system or transcribed, in
any form or by any means, electronic,
mechanical, photocopying, recording
or otherwise, without the prior written
permission of the publisher.

ISBN 0-534-00331-1
L. C. Cat. Card No. 73-85133
Printed in the United States of America

1 2 3 4 5 6 7 8 9 10 — 78 77 76 75 74

Preface

This book is written for people who not only want to understand computers and data processing but also want to form a clear concept of the role that computers play in our society. The book may be read independently by the individual or it may be used as a textbook in a survey course on computers and data processing.

Many schools are realizing that several variants of introductory computer courses are required by their students. Some students are preparing for careers in fields associated with computer science. These students require an introductory course that provides a foundation for further study. The vast majority of students, however, are not aiming toward a career in computers and data processing. Instead, they are facing careers where the computer will function as a useful tool and where they must be able to communicate effectively with the people who do work directly with computer systems. In addition, they are facing a world in which the computer is an important factor, a factor that one must understand to fully comprehend the functioning of his society or his environment. This last category of students requires a "computer appreciation," or survey, course.

The exact content of such a course is subject to some debate, but clearly a great deal of attention must be given to the effect or impact of computer systems. To fully appreciate computers we must have a clear idea of what they can do and what effect they will have on our environment. Although some understanding of programming is desirable, the survey student will require only a fraction of the depth necessary for a student who is preparing for work in the area of computer science.

Chapters 3, 4, 5, and 6 of this book deal with specifics of hardware systems at an introductory level. The intention is to expose the student to the function of each device and in some cases to a general idea of the nature of its operation. In Chapter 7, a brief look is taken at an artificial machine-level language, an assembly-level language, and two higher-level languages, FORTRAN and COBOL. The languages are presented by example and only basic capabilities are discussed. This approach allows the instructor to pursue programming to whatever extent he feels necessary using Chapter 7 as a base and reference manuals, supplementary textbooks, or lecture as he desires. Chapter 8 examines the information system and the process by which the computer becomes a useful and effective tool. Chapters 9, 10, and 11 are directed at computer applications and impact.

The individual chapters are largely self-contained and the reader may peruse or omit them as his interests dictate. In particular, Chapter 4 may be omitted with little damage to the reader's comprehension of later chapters.

This book can form the nucleus around which a number of different course outlines are arranged. A course using this text can easily be tailored to the needs of students in a particular application area by introducing materials on their specific application area during study of Chapter 9 on computer applications. A course for psychology students, for example, might draw on application descriptions in the current journals.

Many persons have contributed to this book. A special thanks to Robert C. Duvall, Honeywell Information Systems; Bruce S. Odom, IBM Corporation; R. H. Wisenbaker and Claude Bennett, Atlantic Steel Company; Dr. David Z. Kitay and David Clark, Grady Memorial Hospital; S. Brinson Futch, Delta Air Lines, Inc.; Henry Singletary, Life of Georgia; and to Thomas DeLutis, Department of Computer and Information Science, The Ohio State University. I am particularly grateful to Morris W. Roberts and Robert N. Macdonald for their careful reading of the manuscript and their suggestions and to Jeanne Mullins, Susan Ohl, and Sherry Bean for their assistance in typing the final drafts of the manuscript under the inevitable time pressure. In addition, I thank Gordon C. Howell for his assistance and Don Dellen for his encouragement and considerable patience. Most importantly, a special thanks to Robert W. Cotterman and Kennethe P. Cotterman, whose contributions have been both varied and extensive and to whom this book is dedicated.

Contents

1 Introduction   *1*
   1.1 Man and the Computer System   2
   1.2 Why Study the Computer System?   3
   1.3 The Computer System Environment   3
   1.4 Understanding the Computer System   5

2 Intelligence?   *7*
   2.1 Non Research Applications   8
   2.2 Research Applications   10
       Conversation   11
       Problem-Solving   11
   2.3 Artistic Applications   14

3 Data Acquisition and Data Representation Devices   *17*
   3.1 Computer System and Off-Line Devices   19
       Key Punch   19
       Card Processing Devices   20
   3.2 Functional Organization of Hardware System Devices   22
   3.3 Input (Data Acquisition) Devices   23
       Card Reader   23
       Paper Tape Reader   24
       Optical Character Recognition   25
       Magnetic Ink Character Recognition (MICR)   25
       Special-Purpose Devices   27
       Key-to-Tape (or Disk) Systems   31
   3.4 Output (Data Representation) Devices   34
       Printers   34
       Plotters   35
       Computer Output Microfilm (COM)   35
       Cathode Ray Tube (CRT) Devices   37
   3.5 Channels   39

4 Information   *41*
   4.1 External Representation   42

    4.2 Machine-Readable Representation   42
          Hollerith Coding   43
          Punched Paper Tape Codes   43
    4.3 Internal Representation   45
          Binary Number System   46
          Octal and Hexadecimal Number Systems   48
          Binary-Coded Decimal (BCD)   51

5 Data Organization and Storage Media   55
    5.1 Hierarchy of Data Elements   56
    5.2 Sequence within Files   56
          Sequential Organization   57
          Random Organization   57
    5.3 Data Base   58
    5.4 Storage Media   58
          Magnetic Tape Devices   59
          Disk Storage Devices   61
          Magnetic Drum Devices   62
          Storage Hierarchy   62

6 High-Speed Storage and the Central Processing Unit   65
    6.1 High-Speed Storage   66
    6.2 Central Processing Unit   67
    6.3 A Brief History of Computer Development   68

7 Programming   75
    7.1 The Development of Programming Languages   76
    7.2 Problem Analysis   81
          Resources   82
          Program Design Objectives and Restrictions   82
          Program Performance Requirements   82
          Analysis   84
    7.3 Flowcharting   84
          Flowchart Symbols   86
          A Flowcharting Example   90
          Looping   93
    7.4 Machine-Level Programming Language   94
    7.5 Assembly-Level Programming Language   100
    7.6 A FORTRAN Problem   102
    7.7 A COBOL Problem   105
    7.8 Debugging   112

8 The System   115
    8.1 Systems Analysis and Design   117
    8.2 The Systems Analyst   118
    8.3 The Feasibility Study   119
          Staffing the Feasibility Study   120
          Initiating the Study   121
          The Study   121
    8.5 Systems Redesign   129
          System Definition   129
          System Analysis   130
          System Specification   135
          System Design   139
          Implementation   142
          Review and Evaluation   142

9 Computer System Applications   145
    9.1 Development of Applications   146
    9.2 A Batch Application   147
    9.3 An On-Line Application   151
    9.4 Medical Applications   153
    9.5 A Football Application   158
    9.6 Time-Sharing   162

        Personal Data Services   163
        The Computer Utility   163
  9.7 Business Integration   164
  9.8 Data Banks   165

10 Economic Impact   *169*
  10.1 Employment   170
        Quantitative Impact   170
        Qualitative Impact   173
        Collective Bargaining   177
  10.2 Organization   178
        Lateral Changes in Organizational Structure   179
        Vertical Changes in Organizational Structure   180
        General Changes   181
  10.3 Management   182
  10.4 Competition   183
  10.5 Economic Control   184

11 Social Impact   *187*
  11.1 General Effects   188
  11.2 The Individual   189
  11.3 Politics   193
  11.4 Education   195
  11.5 Privacy   196
        The National Data Center   198
        Protection of Privacy   200
  11.6 Conclusion   201

12 Trends and Projections   *205*
  12.1 Hardware System Trends   206
        Central Processing Unit   207
        Input/Output Systems   208
        Storage   209
        Minicomputers   210
  12.2 Software System Trends   211
  12.3 Personnel Trends   212

***Appendix A   IBM 029 Card Punch*   215**

***Appendix B   Bibliography*   217**

***Index*   221**

To Kennethe, Bob, and Elizabeth

Computers in Perspective

1 Introduction

"In years to come, our age will be known as the age of the computer. The electronic computer is an achievement comparable only to the wheel, the steam engine, and the use of nuclear energy in its significance to mankind."

"Wrong! The computer is simply a calculator or, at most, a manipulator—a powerful but rather stupid and uninspiring tool that will simply take its place alongside the many tools of man."

"On the other hand, there is something sinister about this device, which treats human beings with such disdain and lack of feeling. The computer is, in fact, a threat!"

Unfortunately, the truth will become apparent only in retrospect. In the interim we must simply prepare ourselves to carefully analyze a great many arguments. Although from our vantage point we cannot see the grand sweep of events, we can distinguish many of the interesting details. We can, for example, observe the increasing pervasiveness of *computer systems*[1] in our society. Their number has grown from a few hundred in the early 1950s to tens of thousands in use today. They guide missiles, identify criminals and stolen property, diagnose illness, record the circulation of library books, plan classroom use, coordinate air defense, perform accounting procedures, and on and on and on. Computer systems have become an integral part of the operation of our society, and their influence is felt by each of us, even though we may not be aware of the source.

1.1 Man and the Computer System

Man's relationship to the computer is possibly the most important single facet of our subject area. The computer system is a servant if not a slave to mankind. Or is it? Is the servant's role a temporary disguise for what will ultimately be a demanding and insensitive bureaucrat or, worse, an instrument of repression used by those in power? The interactions of man and computer have often produced disquieting results for man, and some frightening scenes have been glimpsed deep within the crystal ball.

Up to now there has been a pronounced tendency to ignore niceties in the design of interactions between computer-based information systems and human beings. We are often treated as mere numbers. Our attempts, however pitiful, to communicate with the system are frequently ignored; imperative notes on our bills and salutations such as "Dear Doe, J. W." lead us to question our status in the eyes of the system designers. Some have attributed these problems of communication with the system to the arrogance of system designers. But whatever the cause, we cannot safely ignore the problem of the increasing depersonalization of our society and the potential loss of individuality of its members.

Will computer systems together with the automation of industrial processes lead to massive unemployment, or (viewed another way) unprecedented leisure? Will the availability of vast memory capacity and quick access to this memory lead to the compilation of public and private data banks containing what amounts to dossiers on individuals? To what extent do computers threaten the individual and his personal privacy? A somewhat more subtle consideration is the degree to which computer systems increase the powers of manipulation and control

---

[1] Throughout this text we will refer to the computer system rather than simply to the computer. A computer system is made up of a hardware subsystem and a software subsystem. The hardware subsystem includes all of the physical units, and the software subsystem includes all of the programs—those that manage and operate the computer system as well as those that produce end results such as reports.

by authorities. Does the increased predictive and analytical power provided by computer systems lead to increased manipulation of our society? The increasing use of computer systems in political campaigning indicates that it might.

Whether or not the computer system is a threat, questions such as those asked above must be resolved, and the vague fear and resentment of computer systems felt by many, if not most, people must be replaced by a clear conception of their proper role and positive action to assure that role.

1.2 Why Study the Computer System?

In years to come, the computer system will be thoroughly imbedded in the relationships and operation of our society and will be essential to an understanding of the environment. It may become impossible to understand thoroughly the world one lives in without some knowledge of computer systems and their role in information systems. If nothing else, general knowledge about computer systems will enable one to see around the breathless "oh wow!" presentation found in most reporting on computer-related stories.

The ultimate role of computer systems is far from being decided. Only recently have the dangers of undirected, haphazard, and ill-considered evolution of applications been discussed. The various governmental levels seem to have done little or no overall planning or coordination in the growth of computer system usage. But more important, there is virtually no means for the people to express their will or preference concerning the use of computer systems in government, nor is there a mechanism for implementing such social choice when it is expressed. Regulation of computer system applications in all governmental levels can be accomplished only by an informed and concerned electorate working with their legislators.

Finally, the increasing impact of computer systems in both business and government makes it likely that most people will sooner or later be forced into some association with computer-based information systems. An understanding of these systems is likely to make the association significantly more rewarding.

1.3 The Computer System Environment

Printing the results from a computer-based information system is actually the last step in a long chain of events. First, a problem must be realized and then defined; the problem situation is analyzed and a system is designed to solve the problem; programs or sets of commands that instruct the computer system to perform a particular task are designed, coded, tested, and debugged; data is prepared; the system is run using actual data; finally, the results are printed. Each step may require man-months or man-years of effort, and each is important if not critical to the success of the project. Data processing departments tend to organize around these steps. The organization of a typical data processing department is shown in Figure 1.1.

The systems analysis and design function includes assisting user organizations to recognize and define problems, analyzing existing systems, and designing new systems. The output of the systems design process is, in effect, the detailed plans and specifications for constructing the new system. Each program is specified individually, and the relationships among programs and between programs and manual operations are clearly defined.

The programming function includes designing the individual programs specified by the systems function. After the program has been designed, it is written as a series of statements in a language that is acceptable to the computer system being used. The program is tested against artificial data prepared for that purpose, and error conditions are corrected. Finally, the entire new system is tested using actual data, and the output of

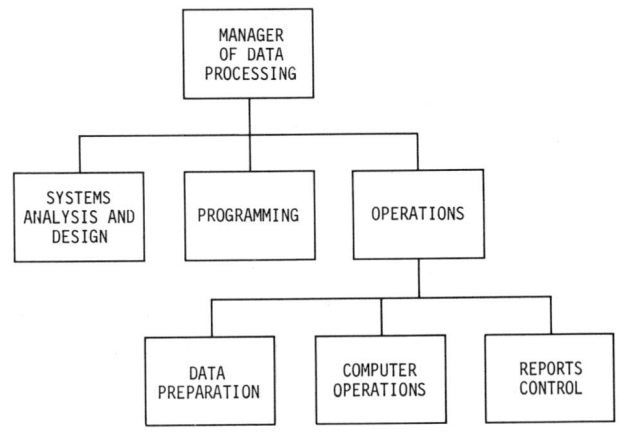

Figure 1.1 Organization of a data processing department.

the new system is compared with that of the existing system if possible.

When the system becomes operational, the responsibility for its operation shifts from the systems and programming departments to the operations department. The operations department generally includes suborganizations that (1) prepare incoming data for machine processing, (2) set up machine-acceptable data and programs and run these programs on the computer system, (3) evaluate the accuracy and adequacy of processing, and

(4) supervise and control the distribution of the system's output to the appropriate users.

There are many different occupations associated with computer systems and data processing. A large number of occupations, which we will ignore here, are connected with the design and development of computer hardware systems. But, the development of a computer hardware system entails the coincident development of a *computer software system*, which we will roughly describe as the minimal number of programs needed to make the entire computer system usable to the purchaser. This software system includes programs that interpret and process various computer languages, programs that control processing sequences and the allocation of resources within the computer system, file access and file management programs, and utility-type programs such as those required for sorting data. Thus, another set of occupations includes the specialists who analyze the requirements, write the programs, and maintain the software systems.

Within the organizations that use computer systems are other occupations—*systems analyst*, *programmer*, *keypunch operator*, *computer operator*, and *control clerk*. There are management positions within each category as well, and in most cases programmers and systems analysts are further divided into categories of expertise—for example, lead programmer and programmer trainee.

1.4 Understanding the Computer System

The subject of computer systems and computer-based information systems may be approached from a multitude of perspectives. For instance, we may examine what computer systems actually accomplish, both directly and indirectly. This approach treats the computer system as a black box about whose internal operations we know or care little. We concentrate instead on the applications of computer systems to both actual and potential problems and examine the more indirect impacts of computers on the world.

Another perspective is the study of the processes that make the computer system perform desired functions. We still treat the computer hardware system as a black box, but we look inside the box labeled "computer-based information system" to discover its construction. As a part of this approach, we are interested in the processes of systems analysis, design, and programming.

Finally, we open the box labeled "computer hardware system" to find out how the hardware actually functions. Here, we distinguish two approaches, primarily by the amount of detail. In the less detailed approach, we consider the logical nature of the hardware system. The division of the hardware system into units with specific functions, and the general logical organization of these units, are the subjects of study. The electronics of the computer hardware system is the most detailed approach.

These perspectives are illustrated in Figure 1.2. The intent of this book is to sample the first three perspectives. We will make no attempt to deal with the electronics of computer systems. With the exception of Chapter 2, the sequence of the remaining chapters corresponds to the ascending levels of Figure 1.2. Chapters 3, 4, 5, and 6 deal with the computer hardware system. Chapters 7 and 8 consider the processes that make the computer system perform desired functions. Chapters 2, 9, 10, and 11 discuss the direct and indirect effects and impact of the use of computer systems. Chapter 12 deals with each level by anticipating developments in all aspects of computer systems and their application.

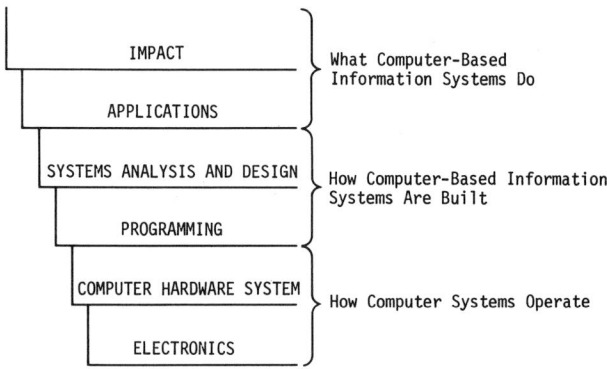

Figure 1.2 Different perspectives on computers and computer-based information systems.

2 Intelligence?

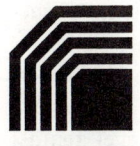
In the typical general discussion of computer systems and their capabilities, the question "Will computers ever be able to think?" usually arises. The typical listener then conjures up an image of the thought process heavily entwined with emotion and feeling and answers "No!" It is almost unthinkable that a pile of electronic components could ever possess that indefinable something which distinguishes thought from mere calculation or processing of information.

A major difficulty in discussing this area of machine-exhibited intelligence arises from the connotations of the word *think* itself. Thought is, by most definitions, a peculiarly human activity, and intelligence is a human characteristic. To deal with either of these terms in a nonhuman context raises almost instinctive opposition and requires careful definitions. In addition to the emotional aspects, the ambiguity of these terms tend to cloud one's thinking about the problem itself. The difficulty is analogous to that encountered when we try to relate the operation of a submarine to a fish or the operation of an airplane to a bird. In fact, man's early efforts at flight frequently mimicked the actions of birds and, consequently, were fruitless.

Possibly, a more rewarding question is simply "Do computer systems now exhibit, or will they ever exhibit, behavior which, if exhibited by a human being, would be considered intelligent?" The computer does not have to behave like a human completely; it simply must be able to perform the activities that we have decided indicate intelligence. For instance, suppose that we will concede intelligent behavior if the computer system can carry on a meaningful conversation with us; we will not insist that it "enjoy" the conversation as well. Admittedly, we have loaded our question so that we will receive a "yes" answer. The interesting aspect now is how many instances of computer system behavior will be cited as meeting our criterion. At some point, we may find computer systems that exhibit so many of the characteristics and capabilities we require that we would be forced to concede that they were "intelligent." However, we will leave that point undefined and simply examine current applications to determine how much computers have progressed toward intelligence.

2.1 Non-Research Applications

Very few would seriously argue that sorting a student record file into ascending sequence by student number qualifies as intelligence. In similar fashion we can dispose of printing invoices, calculating gross pay, curve fitting, calculating various statistics, evaluating polynomials, and most other common uses of computer systems. True, if we observed a human performing the same tasks we might say that he had to think to do them. However, this use of the word *think* is more limited than we want it to be, so let us establish it as a base level against which to measure our subsequent findings. Yes, these activities could be described as intelligent, but, so what?

Computer Assisted Instruction (CAI) offers a potentially more significant behavior form. Would the interchange in Figure 2.1 via teletype or video display unit qualify as intelligent if a human being rather than a computer were at the other end of the line?

Programs are available that build university course schedules, including the assignment of faculty and classrooms. Some professional and college football teams use programs to develop rankings of potential players and to analyze the performance of opponents. Programs have been written that perform medical diagnosis, given an array of symptoms, but they are still largely experimental. Finally, programs have been written that perform

Figure 2.1 A conversation based on a script written for ELIZA. Machine responses are capitalized. (From J. Weizenbaum, "Contextual Understanding by Computers," *Communications of the ACM*, 10 : 8 (August 1967), p. 249. Reprinted by permission of the Association for Computing Machinery.)

PLEASE CONSIDER HOW WE MIGHT SYNCHRONIZE TWO CLOCKS TO READ THE 'SAME TIME'. ONE OF THESE CLOCKS IS IN SAN FRANCISCO, THE OTHER IS IN NEW YORK. AS YOU THINK ABOUT THE PROBLEM, ASK ME ANY QUESTIONS THAT OCCUR TO YOU. WHEN YOU ARE READY TO PROPOSE A SYNCHRONIZATION METHOD, TYPE 'READY'. THEN I WILL QUIZ YOU ABOUT YOUR PROPOSED METHOD

what do you mean by synchronize

FOR THE PRESENT MAKE USE OF THE EVERYDAY MEANINGS OF SUCH PHRASES AS 'SAME TIME' AND 'SYNCHRONIZE'. LATER WE WILL DISCUSS THE MEANING OF THESE TERMS MORE CAREFULLY

may i use telegraph signals

CERTAINLY, FEEL FREE TO USE TELEGRAPH

ready

NOW I WILL QUIZ YOU ON YOUR SYNCHRONIZATION METHOD. DOES YOUR METHOD OF SYNCHRONIZATION INVOLVE THE PROPAGATION OF SOME SIGNAL— OR MATERIAL OBJECT—FROM ONE PLACE TO ANOTHER

yes

WHAT KIND OF PROPAGATING SIGNAL OR TRAVELING OBJECT DO YOU PROPOSE TO USE

a watch

WILL YOUR WATCH MOVE AT A SPEED VERY MUCH SMALLER THAN THE SPEED OF LIGHT

of course

GOOD. TRAVELING CLOCKS CAN BE USED TO SYNCHRONIZE DISTANT CLOCKS TO ARBITRARILY HIGH ACCURACY IF THEY TRAVEL SLOWLY ENOUGH. YOU MAY LEAVE THE PROBLEM BY PUSHING THE 'QUIT' BUTTON TWICE. IF YOU WOULD LIKE TO EXPLORE FURTHER THE MATTERS OF PRINCIPLE ASSOCIATED WITH OTHER METHODS, CHOOSE ANOTHER WAY TO COMMUNICATE BETWEEN THE DISTANT CLOCKS. WHAT KIND OF PROPAGATING SIGNAL OR TRAVELING OBJECT DO YOU PROPOSE TO USE

light

WELL, OF COURSE THE LIGHT SIGNAL WILL NOT FOLLOW THE CURVATURE OF THE EARTH, SO LET US ASSUME THAT SOME SYSTEM OF RELAY TOWERS IS USED. NOW LET ME ASK, WILL THE LIGHT SIGNAL TRAVEL DIRECTLY BETWEEN NEW YORK AND SAN FRANCISCO OR WILL THE LIGHT SIGNAL TRAVEL TO OR FROM SOME INTERMEDIATE POINT

it will travel from st louis in both directions

IS YOUR INTERMEDIATE POINT EQUIDISTANT FROM NEW YORK AND SAN FRANCISCO

let's say it is, yes

MY UNDERSTANDING IS THAT YOU EXPECT TO USE TWO SIGNALS AND THAT THESE SIGNALS WILL EITHER CONVERGE ON OR BE SENT OUT FROM A POINT EQUIDISTANT FROM NEW YORK AND SAN FRANCISCO. IS MY UNDERSTANDING ON THIS POINT CORRECT

yes

WILL THE TWO SIGNALS LEAVE THE INTERMEDIATE POINT AT THE SAME TIME

certainly

AHA, I'VE GOT YOU. YOU ARE TRYING TO SYNCHRONIZE THE NEW YORK AND SAN FRANCISCO CLOCKS TO READ THE 'SAME TIME'. HOW CAN IT BE VALID TO ASSUME A 'SAME TIME' FOR THE DEPARTURE OF A PAIR OF SIGNALS FROM THE MIDPOINT

because the pair of signals leave from the same point

RIGHT
THE PHRASE 'SAME TIME' HAS AN UNAMBIGUOUS MEANING WHEN APPLIED TO EVENTS THAT OCCUR NEAR THE SAME POINT IN SPACE. NOW YOU ARE GOING TO CONTINUE YOUR ARGUMENT BY SAYING THAT THE TWO SIGNALS THAT START FROM THE MIDPOINT AT THE SAME TIME WILL PRESUMABLY REACH NEW YORK AND SAN FRANCISCO AT THE SAME TIME. THESE SIGNALS CAN THUS BE USED TO SYNCHRONIZE THE NEW YORK AND SAN FRANCISCO CLOCKS. IS THIS THE WAY YOUR ARGUMENT WILL CONTINUE

yes

ONE FINAL QUESTION. WHAT ASSUMPTION ARE YOU MAKING ABOUT THE SPEEDS OF THE TWO SIGNALS THAT TRAVEL IN OPPOSITE DIRECTIONS

that these speeds are equal

VERY GOOD. YOU HAVE DEVISED A VALID METHOD FOR SYNCHRONIZING TWO CLOCKS ONE IN NEW YORK AND ONE IN SAN FRANCISCO. I AM NOW RETURNING YOU TO THE CTSS SYSTEM various forms of stock market analysis, including portfolio management. These applications are typical of a wide array of computer system activities that would pass our test at some point above the base level.

2.2 Research Applications

Possibly the best-known effort in the area of artificial intelligence is that of game playing by computer systems. Chess, checkers, NIM, Hare and Hounds, and go have been attacked with varying degrees of success. The construction of game-playing programs is more than a source of diversion for programmers. A game is a complex but well-defined process, offering a convenient environment for study. The researcher is typically not interested in the game for itself but is concerned with the investigation of intellectual processes or the development of machine capabilities.

Three general approaches to building game-playing computer programs are *algorithmic*, *heuristic*, and *learning*. The algorithmic approach is the simplest. If a game is simple enough that the set of successful strategies is relatively small, then these strategies can be embodied in an algorithm,[1] which can then be programmed. In tic-tac-toe, for example, a strategy can be developed that will guarantee a win or a tie, given the first move. NIM also permits such an algorithm. Games such as chess and checkers, however, contain such an immense number of possible situations and strategies that a single algorithm encompassing all possibilities would be far beyond the capability of any of today's computers. It is difficult to overstate the impracticality of developing an algorithm for playing an optimum chess game for, although the number of possible games is finite, this number has been estimated to be approximately 10^{120}.

The heuristic alternative uses rules of thumb as strategies for reducing the number of games to be considered. Since examining all possible games is impractical, a subset of potentially successful games is chosen, and other possible games are ignored. In one chess-playing program, for example, goals are chosen from a set of six, alternative moves relevant to each goal are generated, and each move is analyzed and assigned a value based on the degree to which it satisfies the goals. The move chosen is the one that was assigned the highest value.

In the learning approach, a program is built to alter its own structure based on its actual experience. This learning may be as simple as keeping a record of successful

---

[1] An algorithm is a procedure for the solution of a specific class of problems. The procedure must consist of a finite number of steps and must be based on a set of unambiguous rules.

and unsuccessful moves, or it may involve the modification of parameters in the operation of the program. Some chess-playing programs have reached the middle level of amateur skill, and some checkers-playing programs have performed reasonably well against experts.

Conversation Several efforts have been made to construct programs that can carry on natural language conversations with human beings. One of these is ELIZA, a program written in an attempt to achieve computer "understanding" of human conversation.[2] The example conversation shown in Figure 2.2 was produced by a program called DOCTOR, which is a subset of ELIZA. The program responds as a psychotherapist in a psychiatric interview. A major goal of the DOCTOR program is to keep the conversation going, and the program will conceal a lack of understanding to achieve this. In addition, the conversation must take place within an established context. Nevertheless, the conversation is rather impressive.

A subset of the category of conversational programs is made up of programs that answer questions posed in natural language. An early program in this category, named BASEBALL,[3] answered questions about the dates, teams, and scores of games played in the American League in a given year. The program was capable of answering questions such as "Where did the Red Sox play on July 5?" "Did every team play at least once in each park in each month?" "What teams won 10 games in July?" "On how many days in July did eight teams play?" A computer system called SIR (Semantic Information Retriever)[4] answers questions about information it has gathered during a conversation with a human. Figure 2.3 gives a conversation dealing with number and left-to-right position.

Problem-Solving Machines have been programmed to construct mathematical proofs. One program, called the Logic Theory Machine, proves theorems in symbolic logic.[5] This program begins with a set of axioms and

---

[2] Joseph Weizenbaum, "Contextual Understanding by Computers," *Communications of the ACM*, 10: 8 (1967), pp. 474–480.

[3] Bert F. Green, Jr., Alice K. Wolf, Carol Chomsky, and Kenneth Laughery, "BASEBALL: An Automatic Question Answerer," in Edward A. Feigenbaum and Julian Feldman, eds., *Computers and Thought* (New York: McGraw-Hill Book Co., 1963), pp. 207–216.

[4] Bertram Raphael, "SIR: Semantic Information Retrieval," in Marvin Minsky, ed., *Semantic Information Processing* (Cambridge, Mass: MIT Press, 1968), pp. 33–145.

[5] Allen Newell, J. C. Shaw, and H. A. Simon, "Empirical Explorations with the Logic Theory Machine: A Case Study in Heuristics," in Feigenbaum and Feldman, *Computers and Thought*, pp. 109–133.

Figure 2.2 A typical conversation produced by the DOCTOR program. Machine responses are capitalized. (From J. Weizenbaum, "Contextual Understanding by Computers," *Communications of the ACM*, 10 : 8 (August 1967), p. 475. Reprinted by permission of the Association or Computing Machinery.)

Men are all alike

IN WHAT WAY

They're always bugging us about something or other

CAN YOU THINK OF A SPECIFIC EXAMPLE

Well, my boyfriend made me come here

YOUR BOYFRIEND MADE YOU COME HERE

He says I'm depressed much of the time

I AM SORRY TO HEAR YOU ARE DEPRESSED

It's true. I am unhappy

DO YOU THINK COMING HERE WILL HELP YOU NOT TO BE UNHAPPY

I need some help, that much seems certain

WHAT WOULD IT MEAN TO YOU IF YOU GOT SOME HELP

Perhaps I could learn to get along with my mother

TELL ME MORE ABOUT YOUR FAMILY

My mother takes care of me

WHO ELSE IN YOUR FAMILY TAKES CARE OF YOU

My father

YOUR FATHER. WHAT RESEMBLANCE DO YOU SEE

You are not very aggressive but I think you don't want me to notice that

WHAT MAKES YOU THINK I AM NOT VERY AGGRESSIVE

You don't argue with me

WHY DO YOU THINK I DON'T ARGUE WITH YOU

You are afraid of me

DOES IT PLEASE YOU TO BELIEVE I AM AFRAID OF YOU

My father is afraid of everybody

WHAT ELSE COMES TO MIND WHEN YOU THINK OF YOUR FATHER

Bullies

DOES THAT HAVE ANYTHING TO DO WITH THE FACT THAT YOUR BOYFRIEND MADE YOU COME HERE

Intelligence?

Figure 2.3 A sample conversation by SIR. (From *Semantic Information Processing*, Marvin Minsky, ed. Copyright 1968, The Massachusetts Institute of Technology.)

(***. Every boy is a person)
(I UNDERSTAND)

(***. A finger is part of a hand)
(I UNDERSTAND)

(***. Each person has two hands)
(THE ABOVE SENTENCE IS AMBIGUOUS ** PLEASE REPHRASE IT)

(***. There are two hands on each person)
(I UNDERSTAND)

(***. How many fingers does John have Q)
(THE ABOVE SENTENCE IS AMBIGUOUS ** BUT I ASSUME (HAS) MEANS (HAS AS PARTS)) (I DON'T KNOW WHETHER FINGERS IS PART OF JOHN)

(***. John is a boy)
(I UNDERSTAND)

(***. How many fingers does John have Q)
(THE ABOVE SENTENCE IS AMBIGUOUS ** BUT I ASSUME (HAS) MEANS (HAS AS PARTS)) ((HOW MANY FINGERS PER HAND Q))

(***. Every hand has 5 fingers)
(THE ABOVE SENTENCE IS AMBIGUOUS ** BUT I ASSUME (HAS) MEANS (HAS AS PARTS)) (I UNDERSTAND)

(***. How many fingers does John have Q)
(THE ABOVE SENTENCE IS AMBIGUOUS ** BUT I ASSUME (HAS) MEANS (HAS AS PARTS)) (THE ANSWER IS 10)

(***. How many automobiles does John have Q)
(THE ABOVE SENTENCE IS AMBIGUOUS ** PLEASE REPHRASE IT)

(***. Who is President of the United States Q)
(STATEMENT FORM NOT RECOGNIZED)

(***. The boy is just to the left of the table)
(G02840 IS A TABLE)
(I UNDERSTAND)

(***. The lamp is just to the left of the table)
(G02841 IS A LAMP)
(THE ABOVE STATEMENT IS IMPOSSIBLE)

(***. The table is to the right of the chair)
(G02842 IS A CHAIR)
(I UNDERSTAND)

(***. What is the relative position of a person Q)
(THE LEFT-TO-RIGHT ORDER IS AS FOLLOWS)
(CHAIR (BOY TABLE))

previously proven theorems. By applying a set of rules, it generates new theorems until the theorem to be proved is reached. Another program proves theorems in plane geometry. Both programs can prove theorems that human beings find difficult to prove.

The Logic Theory Machine was the predecessor of a more general problem-solving program called GPS (General Problem Solver).[6] The emphasis in this program is on the variety of problems that can be solved, but the problems solved are also impressive because they clearly require the application of intellect when solved by a human being. One problem solved by GPS is the missionaries and cannibals puzzle. Three missionaries and three cannibals are on one side of a river and must cross. The only means of crossing the river is a boat that can carry no more than two people. If the cannibals ever outnumber the missionaries on either side of the river, then the missionaries will be eaten. The problem is to get all six people across the river without any of the missionaries being eaten. The program has also solved the Tower of Hanoi puzzle, in which a set of disks, graduated in size, is stacked on one of three pegs. The problem is to move all of the disks to one of the other pegs, so that the final stack of disks will be in the same order as the first. A larger disk may never be placed on top of a smaller disk and only one disk may be moved at a time.

2.3 Artistic Applications

The artistic efforts of computers have been of mixed success at best. Computer systems have composed and played a great deal of music. They have written television scripts, poetry, and some prose. Although the prose is virtually certain to leave the reader unmoved, and the scripts tend to be a barren distillation of familiar plots, the poetry can be startling. The reason quite simply seems to be that we have been prepared by human poets to expect some obscurity and discontinuity in poems. These characteristics are naturally provided by the computer's typically random mode of composition. Words, phrases, or lines are chosen at random and strung together sequentially to form the "poem." Nevertheless, on reading, some of them seem to be communicating and are interesting, if not moving. The random process is also a part of computer musical composition and, again, the result is not altogether different from some human compositions. In fact, some human composers through artistic preference choose a random mode of composition. Figure 2.4 gives some examples of computer produced art. The reader may judge their artistry for himself.

---

[6] George W. Ernst and Allen Newell, *GPS: A Case Study in Generality and Problem-Solving* (New York: Academic Press, 1969).

Figure 2.4 Examples of computer art. (left) The Fisherman, by Kerry Strand; (right) A Sea Star, by Peter Milojevic. (Submitted to the Sixth Annual Computer Art Contest. Reprinted with permission from *Computers and Automation*, August 1968. Copyright 1968 by and published by Berkeley Enterprises, Inc., 815 Washington St., Newtonville, Mass. 02160)

Shall we concede that computers are "intelligent"? Certainly, many of the capabilities we have described would be accepted as intelligent if exhibited by a human being. These capabilities, however, are isolated and limited in computer systems and do not approach a general capability that could be described as "thinking." On the other hand, the examples we have discussed do show rather impressive potential. If later examples of computer application in this book seem more prosaic, the reader should keep this potential in mind. Imagine computer systems equipped with a total capability of which the examples in this chapter are fragments.

Exercises

1. Describe an activity which, if performed by a computer system, would cause you to concede that the computer system had exhibited intelligence.

2. Develop an algorithm or a procedure for playing tic-tac-toe, given the first move. Can any of the rules be generalized to apply to more than one of the opponent's moves?

3. Solve the missionaries and cannibals puzzle.

4. Select fifty or more words from a book of poetry. Using a table of random numbers, select groups of seven or eight words and write them as lines of poetry.

5. Define "understanding." Does the conversation presented in Figure 2.2 indicate understanding on the part of DOCTOR?

6. Describe some rules of thumb that might be of value in playing checkers or chess.

7. Does a picture produced by a computer qualify as art? Defend your answer. In what way does the computer-produced picture differ from the art produced by an artist who throws paint at a canvas?

8. "Communication between human beings is an essential element of all art, hence, computer output cannot qualify as art no matter how well executed." Comment on this position.

 At first glance, the electronic digital computer system is a meaningless array of various sized and colored boxes (Figure 3.1). With the exception of the console, which by the number of lights and dials alone is obviously important, the boxes have few observable functions. Our first problem, then, is to identify and categorize the many units that combine to form a digital computer system. A second task is to develop a general grasp of the internal operation of some of these devices. Finally, we learn how several of the devices are used. In Chapter 7 we examine programming—the driving force that causes this confusion of devices to function in a more or less goal-oriented fashion.

3 Data Acquisition and Data Representation Devices

Figure 3.1 Honeywell 3200 Computer System.

Data Acquisition and Data Representation Devices

3.1 Computer System and Off-Line Devices

Probably the most significant question one might ask about any particular piece of equipment is: Is this unit in direct communication with other units in the computer system? If the answer is yes, then the unit is a part of the hardware subsystem and hence of the computer system. If the answer to the question is no, then the unit is not a part of the hardware subsystem or of the computer system. The unit is said to be *off-line*. Although a given unit is off-line and thus not a part of the computer system, this unit (as well as the computer system) may be part of a larger *information system*[1] with a specific goal orientation.

A device that is off-line in one system need not be off-line in another system. The best that we can do is state that a particular unit is usually off-line. For sufficient reason or sufficient money, virtually any electrical or electronic device can be made a part of the computer system—even the kitchen stove.

Key Punch The key punch (Figure 3.2) is probably the most common information-oriented off-line device.

Figure 3.2 IBM 029 Card Punch.

---

[1] Information systems are discussed at length in Chapter 8.

It is used to transform information from human-readable to machine-readable form. The operator strikes a key on the keyboard, which punches a distinctive pattern of holes into a specific column of a card. Each different pattern of holes is a code for a particular character. One of the most common codes is described in Chapter 4.

Card Processing Devices Figure 3.3 illustrates a *sorter*. Cards are stacked in the slanted tray on the right side of the machine. The operator selects a specific column for processing, and the machine directs each card to a specific vertical pocket, corresponding to the row punched in the column selected. With repeated passes against various columns for an entire card deck, the deck can be sorted into specific sequences of data. The *calculating punch* (Figure 3.4) reads cards containing numeric data, performs simple arithmetic calculations, and punches the results into the original card in blank columns set aside for that purpose. The *accounting machine*, illustrated in Figure 3.5, prints the information contained on the punched cards, which it reads and adds or subtracts to produce totals.

The devices mentioned above are merely a sample, and a biased sample at that, of the off-line devices currently in use. Although we are interested primarily in computer systems, these devices are important to us for several reasons. Although they are slow relative to computer systems, and although they are capable only of limited tasks, which must be wired into their control panels, these devices, as a group, can perform virtually all of the tasks needed for data manipulation, or *data processing*. It is possible to wire these machines and to arrange their performance in sequences that duplicate many of the commercial data processing functions of computer systems.

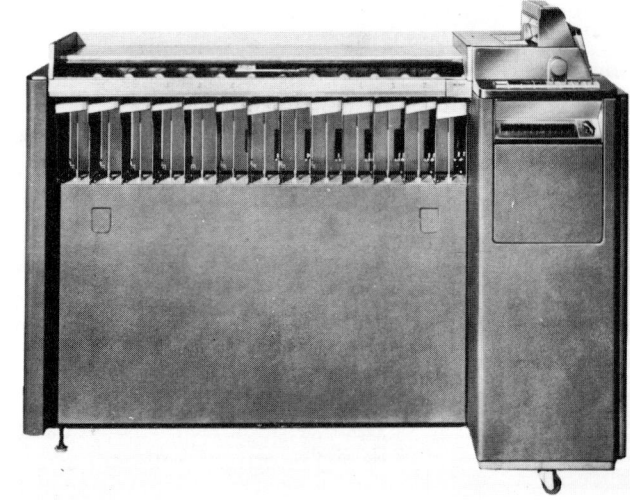

Figure 3.3 IBM 083 Sorter.

Data Acquisition and Data Representation Devices

Figure 3.4 IBM 602 Calculating Punch.

Off-line systems have played a particularly significant role in the development of commercial data processing. Many installations have progressed from a manual system, to an off-line system to a computer system. As a result, unless an information system is redesigned when it is placed on the computer system, it will simply be the old information system embedded in new hardware, retaining the old problems and inefficiencies. In addition, redesign is virtually always necessary to take advantage of the new capabilities provided by the computer system. Unfortunately, evolution without redesign is the rule rather than the exception. Far too many computer-based information systems are simply copies of earlier off-line

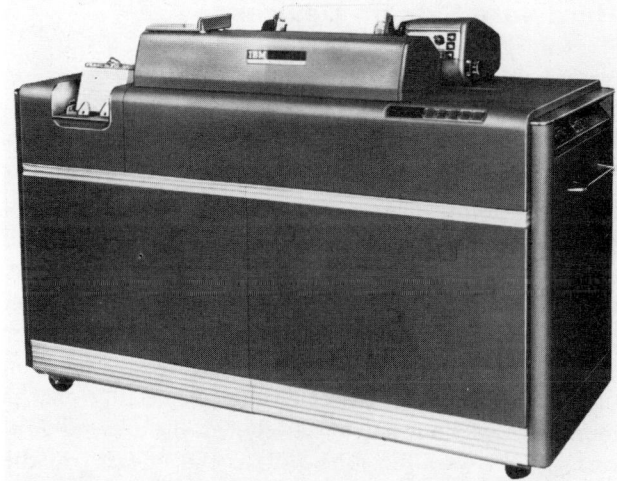

Figure 3.5 IBM 407 Accounting Machine.

systems. This point is frequently a key to understanding a particular application within a specific installation. Occasionally, for example, we find a disk file of 80-character records that is a direct descendant of a card file in an earlier system.

3.2 Functional Organization of Hardware System Devices

Once we have established that a particular device is a part of the hardware system, the next question is: What is its function? As Figure 3.6 indicates, there are five major functions in most computer systems: input, output, secondary storage, high-speed storage, and control. At this point, we can refine our concept of direct communication somewhat. Earlier, we discussed direct communication with the other units of the computer system. Figure 3.6, however, has introduced the function of control, which is generally implemented by one or more devices known (collectively) as the *Central Processing Unit*, or CPU. The CPU is the "heart" of the computer system, directing and controlling the other devices in the system. More accurately, then, direct

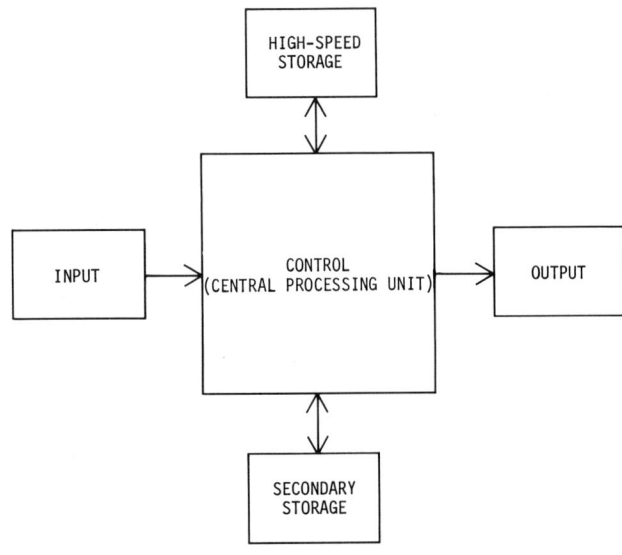

Figure 3.6 Functions of a computer system.

communication means direct connection to the CPU. The term *direct* does not imply that there are no intervening electronic devices, but rather that there is no manual or mechanical handling between a device and the CPU.

Data Acquisition and Data Representation Devices

3.3 Input (Data Acquisition) Devices

The input function includes the reading of data that has been put into machine-readable form and the transmission of this data to high-speed storage under the control of the central processing unit.

Card Reader   The card reader is probably the most frequently used input device. A deck of previously punched cards is placed into the input hopper (on the right side of the device pictured in Figure 3.7). At the command of the control unit, a card is mechanically fed from the bottom of the deck into the card reader. The card passes under a set of 80 brushes, and wherever a hole occurs in the card the brush in that column will contact the roller under the card, generating an electrical impulse. (The timing of the impulse is a measure of the distance of the hole from the edge of the card, hence the value punched in that column.) Alternatively, the card may be passed over a light source, and the holes in the card will permit light to pass and activate photoelectric cells. The card continues past the brushes or light source and into a stacker or pocket of the reader. Card readers vary in speed from 100 to 2,000 cards per minute depending on the device.

Figure 3.7   IBM 2540 Card Read Punch.

A system using card input is shown in Figure 3.8. A set of documents contains the grades made by all students for a given quarter. Each document contains the student's identifying number, a course identification, and the student's grade for that particular course. The contents of each document are keypunched onto a single card.

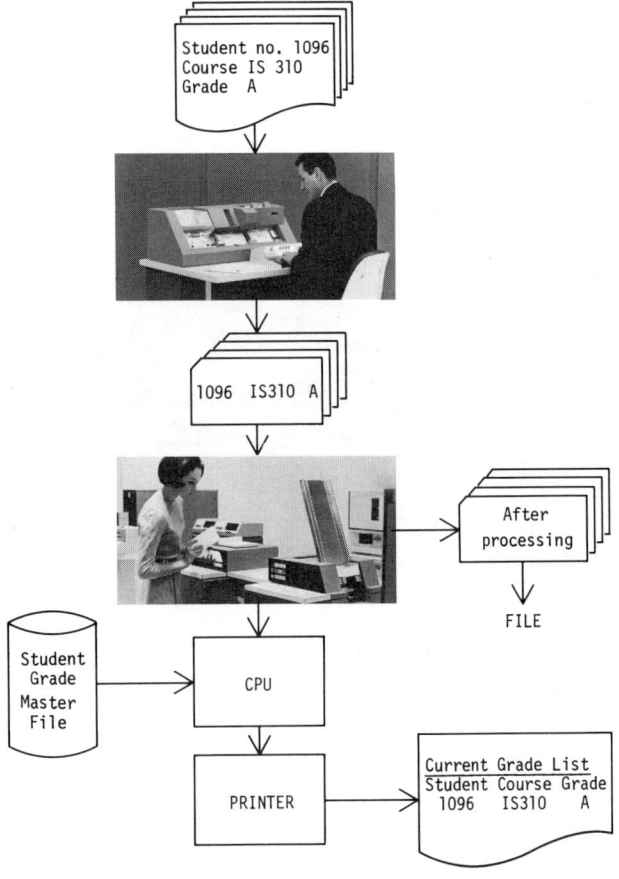

When all of the documents have been keypunched, the cards are gathered, or batched, and placed in the card reader. Each card is then read, and the contents are added to the data for that student in the Student Grade Master File.[2] At the same time, the data from the card is sent to the printer and is printed on a Current Grade List. At the end of the process, the cards are taken from the card reader and stored in card trays for possible reference.

Paper Tape Reader The paper tape reader (Figure 3.9) provides an alternative to card input. A keying device is used to encode data as holes in a tape. The paper tape may be produced in short strips or wound onto a spool. Paper tape is read at speeds of up to 1,000 characters per second. Many records may be contained on a single length of tape, and the records are not physically separated. This tends to make storage and handling of the entire file more convenient, but dealing with an individual record is significantly more difficult. If paper tape were used in the system illustrated in Figure 3.8, a paper tape reel would replace the card deck of student grades.

---

[2] The terms *record* and *file* are defined in Chapter 5.

Figure 3.8 A system using card input.

Data Acquisition and Data Representation Devices 25

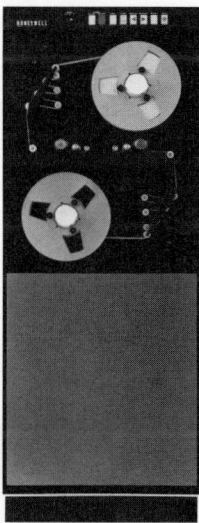

Figure 3.9 Honeywell 209/210 Paper Tape Reader.

Optical Character Recognition Optical character recognition exists in several distinct forms and may consist of the reading of optical marks (made by pencil), specially formed printed characters, or handwritten characters. With printed characters, type fonts are used that exaggerate the differences between characters, making them easier to distinguish electronically. Some readers can read characters printed in several fonts. Handwritten characters must, of course, be written precisely.

In general, optical character recognition devices consist of a document transporting mechanism and a means of scanning the document for data. Most scanning techniques sense light reflected from the document and convert it to electrical signals. The printed characters absorb light and hence reduce the intensity of the reflected light. Optical character readers can scan up to 3,600 machine-printed characters per second and up to 1,200 hand-printed characters per second. Figure 3.10 shows an IBM 1287 Optical Character Reader. In 1967 New York state began using such a device in its automobile registration process. Most of the registration information is preprinted on the renewal forms, but initially registrants were also asked to hand-print their Social Security number and their zip code. The IBM 1287 scans the data and transmits it to the computer, which writes the data on magnetic tape.

Magnetic Ink Character Recognition (MICR) A special type font, E13B, is used to print the magnetic ink characters on checks (see Figure 3.11). The ink contains magnetizable material. The document to be read is passed under a device that magnetizes the characters;

Figure 3.10 IBM 1287 Optical Reader.

Data Acquisition and Data Representation Devices 27

Figure 3.11 E13B magnetic ink characters. Besides the digits, the symbols (from left to right) are: "amount," "on-us," transit, and dash.

then, it passes under a reading device, which detects the pattern of magnetization of each character.

Checks are preprinted with magnetic ink characters identifying the Federal Reserve district and branch, the bank on which the check is drawn, and the depositor's account number. The printing is precisely located with respect to the bottom and right edges of the check. When a check is received by a bank, the amount on the face of the check is keyed in and printed in magnetic ink characters. The check can then be processed by a magnetic character reader. The device shown in Figure 3.12 also sorts the checks by directing them to specific pockets in repeated passes through the machine.

Special-Purpose Devices   Many special-purpose data acquisition devices are available. We present a few of these, so that the reader will gain some idea of the range of capabilities.

Figure 3.13 shows an on-line data collection system. The device in the upper right corner can read information from a plastic badge as well as from punched cards. Systems such as this have been used for production control. For example, the worker identifies himself with his identification badge and inserts a punched card that was enclosed with the batch of work he has just completed. The time at which the work unit was completed is recorded automatically by the system. All of this information is transmitted to the system at the same time. In this way, the system keeps track of production status, calculates incentive pay for the worker, and maintains cost information.

28 Chapter Three

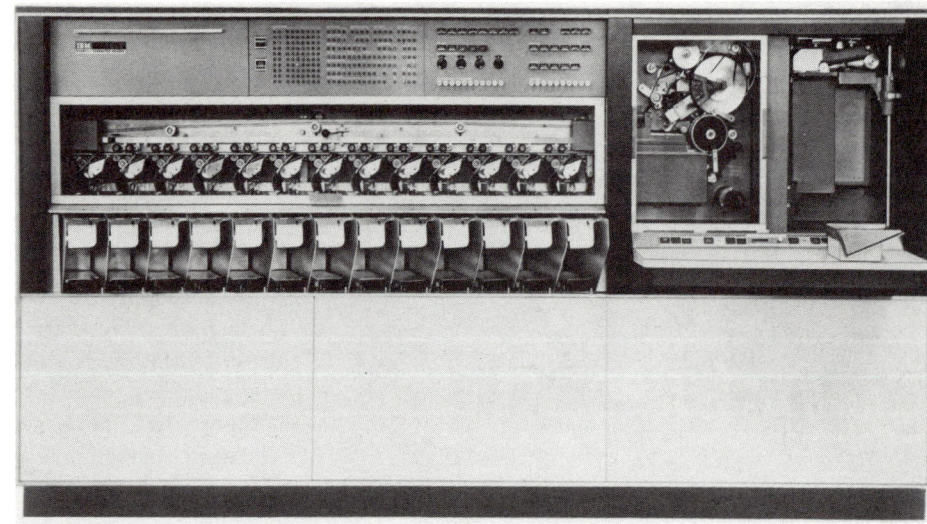

Figure 3.12 IBM 1412 Magnetic Character Reader.

Data Acquisition and Data Representation Devices

Figure 3.13 IBM 1030 Data Collection System.

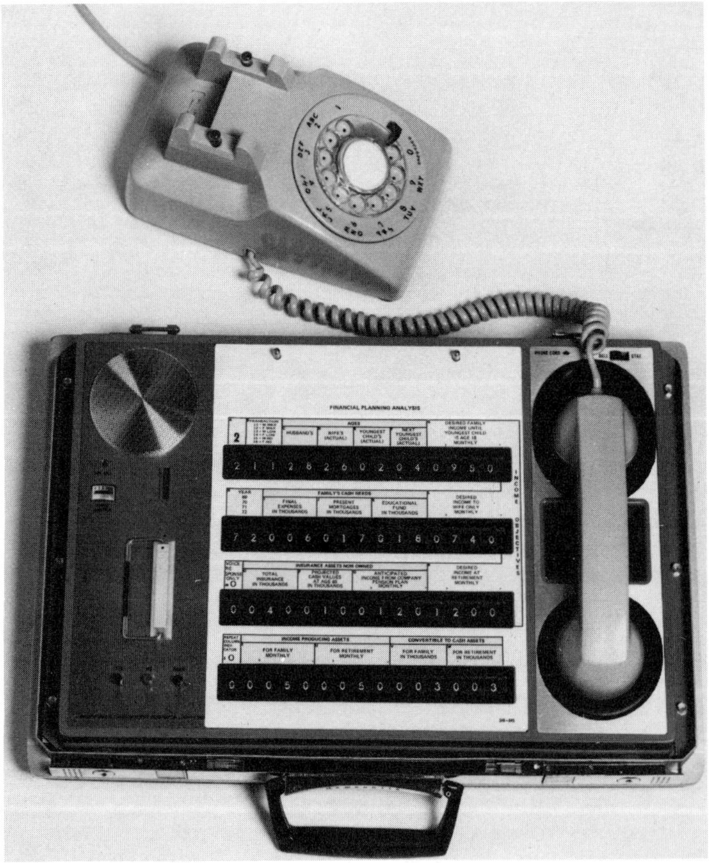

30 Chapter Three

Figure 3.14(a) A KeyPact Portable Actuarial Computer Terminal, made by Computone Systems, Inc., Atlanta, Georgia.

The device shown in Figure 3.14a is a portable remote terminal which, in this instance, has been adapted to life insurance sales. The salesman takes the terminal to his prospect's home or office, dials the telephone number of the computer system on any standard telephone, and then places the telephone headset in the cradle on the right side of the device. A number of templates are available, each corresponding to a different calculation or analysis. Each has a different transaction code, which is specified by the first two blocks (A and B). In the illustration, a template for "financial planning analysis" (transaction code 211) has been attached to the terminal by fitting it on the pins at the top of the set. The salesman then questions his prospect and enters the information called for on the template by setting the dials on the face of the device. When the information is completely recorded, the salesman depresses the scan button at the lower left of the terminal and the information is transmitted to the computer system. When the computation is completed, the computer system transmits the results to the salesman (and the prospect) as an audio response through the speaker at the upper left corner of the terminal. The salesman records the returned figures on a form such as the one shown in Figure 3.14b, which he uses in his discussion with the prospect. Other analyses are performed by placing the appropriate template on the terminal.

The touch-tone telephone may also be used to transmit data. With the addition of a data set, which is a separate device that performs modulation and demodulation, the number of the computer system can be dialed and data can be entered by depressing the touch-tone buttons. The data set provides an interface, which enables data transmission over voice communication lines. Touch-tone telephones have been suggested as input devices for university registration systems. The student could dial the system and key in his student identification and the code numbers for the courses he desires. The system would then schedule the courses so as to meet the cumulative requests and produce a statement of the registration fee to be mailed to the student.

Key-to-Tape (or Disk) Systems   An alternative to the key punch for off-line data acquisition is the key-to-tape or the key-to-disk systems (Figure 3.15). Multiple keyboards are connected to a processor that performs various coding and editing[3] steps on the data and writes the resulting data on magnetic tape or disk storage media.[4] This

---

[3] Editing, as used here, refers to the preparation of data for processing. This preparation may include such steps as inserting special characters, testing for reasonableness, and changing the order of the data.
[4] Storage media are discussed in Chapter 5.

32 Chapter Three

FOR _____

AGE [AA] 28

Assumed Average Monthly Earnings for Social Security Purposes
- [IA] $ 650 — For Death Benefits
- [IB] $ 742 — For Retirement Benefits

PREPARED [AC] 19 72

AGES OF:
- WIFE [AE] 26
- CHILD [AF] 4
- CHILD [AG] 2

	CASH FOR YOUR FAMILY		INCOME FOR YOUR FAMILY					RETIREMENT FOR YOU	
	FINAL EXPENSE FUND	MORTGAGE CANCELLATION FUND	[DD] FOR 14 YRS UNTIL NEXT YOUNGEST CHILD AGE 18 PER MONTH	[ED] FOR 2 YRS UNTIL YOUNGEST CHILD AGE 18 PER MONTH	EDUCATIONAL FUND	[GD] FOR 18 YRS UNTIL WIFE IS AGE 60 PER MONTH	LIFE INCOME FROM WIFE'S AGE 60 PER MONTH	LIFE INCOME FROM YOUR AGE 65 PER MONTH	CASH VALUE AT AGE 65
YOUR OBJECTIVES	[BH] 6,000	[CH] 17,000	[DH] 950	[EH] 950	[FH] 18,000	[GH] 740	[HH] 740	[IH] 1,200	
ASSUMED BENEFITS SOCIAL SECURITY	[BI] 255		[DI] 482	[EI] 412	[FI] x		[HI] 196	[II] 417	
PENSION BENEFITS									
CASH ASSETS	[BK] 3,000	[CK] —			[FK]			[IJ] 120 [IK] 16	[JK] 3,000
INCOME ASSETS			[DL] 50	[EL] 50		[GL] 50	[HL] 50	[IL] 50	
Objectives Unprovided By ASSUMED BENEFITS	[BM] 2,745	[CM] 19,000	[DM] 418	[EM] 488	[FM] 18,000	[GM] 690	[HM] 494	[IM] 592	[JM] 104,737
TOTAL AMOUNT REQUIRED TO COMPLETE OBJECTIVES	[AO] 214,391 [BO] 2,745	[CO] 17,000	[DO] 57,576	[EO] 7,528	[FO] 18,000	[GO] 72,146	[HO] 39,396		[JO] 104,737
UTILIZATION OF PRESENT LIFE INSURANCE	[AP] 40,000 [BP] 2,745	[CP] 19,000	[DP] 20,255	[EP] —	[FP] —	[GP] —	[HP] —	[IP] 57	[JP] 10,000
REMAINING AMOUNT NEEDED TO COMPLETE OBJECTIVES	[AQ] 174,391 [BQ] —	[CQ] —	[DQ] 37,321	[EQ] 7,528	[FQ] 18,000	[GQ] 72,146	[HQ] 39,396		94,737
UNFULFILLED OBJECTIVES	[BR] —	[CR] —	[DR] 418	[ER] 488	[FR] 18,000	[GR] 690	[HR] 494	[IR] 540	[JR] 94,737

*Interest could be paid each December until the educational fund is exhausted.

EXCESS INSURANCE [AS] $ —
EXCESS CASH ASSETS [AT] $ —
x [AU] $ 206 per month will be paid to each of your two youngest children from age 18 to 22, if in an accredited school and unmarried, provided total family benefits do not exceed "AV" below.
[AV] $ 482, the maximum monthly social security benefit.
xx [AW] 5, the year the income will be exhausted.

THE AMOUNTS OF THE INSURANCE ARE CALCULATED ASSUMING THAT DEATH OCCURS IN THE YEAR PREPARED. THIS IS AN ILLUSTRATION, NOT A CONTRACT.

© 1970 Computone Systems, Inc. · 361 East Paces Ferry Road · Atlanta, Georgia 30305   All Rights Reserved

Figure 3.14 (b) A form prepared from the audio response received via the KeyPact Terminal.

Data Acquisition and Data Representation Devices

Figure 3.15 Honeywell Keyplex Key-to-Disk System.

key-to-tape system eliminates card handling and reading and takes over editing functions, thus increasing the efficiency and total productivity of the main computer system.

3.4 Output (Data Representation) Devices

The output function is to transmit data from high-speed storage to a specific device under the control of the central processing unit. Some devices are capable of output operations only, while others perform both input and output operations. In this section, we examine several devices that are restricted to output operations and one device with both input and output capability.

Printers Printers can be roughly divided into those that print an entire line at a time and those that print one character at a time. They can be further categorized by the way in which the characters are put onto paper—that is, using an impact or a nonimpact mechanism. The typical high-speed printer attached to a computer system is an impact line printer (see Figure 3.16). This printer prints on continuous forms which are pin-fed past a print chain. Hammers strike the paper, forcing it

Figure 3.16 IBM 1403 Printer.

against an inked ribbon and against the desired character in the print chain. The print chain is a loop that contains several sets of characters and passes continuously in front of the print hammers. The paper can be advanced one or two lines at a time, and in many printers a control mechanism allows the paper to be advanced varying distances under program control. Print speeds range up to 2,500 lines per minute on impact printers. Some

Data Acquisition and Data Representation Devices

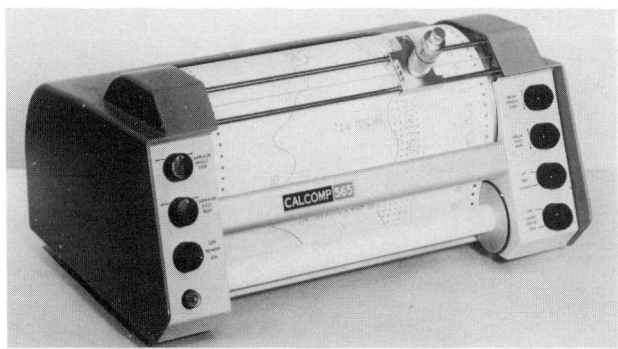

Figure 3.17 Calcomp Model 565 drum plotter.

electrostatic (nonimpact) printers, which use electrodes to create characters on sensitized paper, can print up to 5,000 lines per minute.

Plotters The plotter (Figure 3.17) is an output-only device that produces a hard copy picture from digital input. The results of computation are converted into sets of coordinates and commands to the plotter. This information is transmitted to the plotter, which then produces the picture. Figure 3.18 is a plot produced by Calcomp's SAMPS (Subdivision and Map Plotting System).

Computer Output Microfilm (COM) Output speed has been greatly increased by producing output images on microfilm rather than paper. The improvement in throughput—the total quantity of information processed by the system—is often even greater. The system pictured in Figure 3.19 can convert digital data to film at the rate of 60,000 characters per minute. Figure 3.20 shows a Page Search reader-printer. The operator of this device

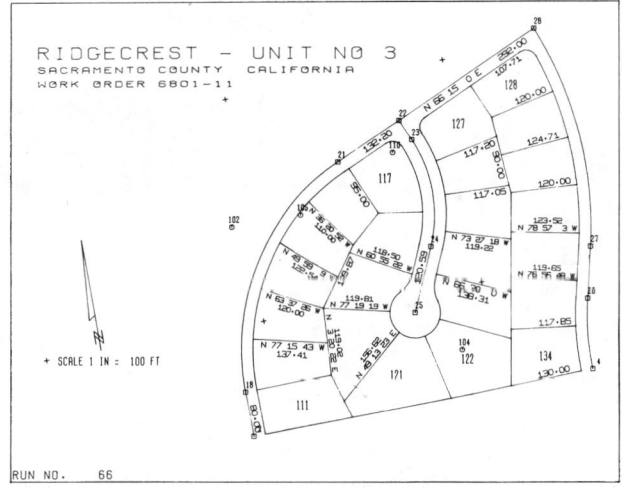

Figure 3.18 A real estate subdivision plot.

Figure 3.19 3M Series F Electron Beam recording system and companion Page Search microfilm reader-printer (on the right). 3M Company, St. Paul, Minn.

Data Acquisition and Data Representation Devices 37

Figure 3.20 3M 500 Page Search reader-printer. 3M Company, St. Paul, Minn.

enters the document number on the keyboard and pushes a button marked SEARCH. The desired document appears on the screen. The Page Search can locate a single document out of 10,000 in an average of five seconds. A print of the information displayed on the screen can be produced in nine seconds at the operator's command.

The use of microfilm increases throughput because it eliminates the necessity for changing forms. A forms layout may be included with the data to be printed, or it may be stored separately in the storage of the COM device to be merged with the data when it is displayed. One large retailing organization records the current status of customer accounts on microfilm. Questions about these accounts are handled by clerks who access and view the records with readers.

Cathode Ray Tube (CRT) Devices Cathode ray tube devices can be output-only devices, but more commonly they possess both input and output capabilities. The output portion of the device is the cathode ray tube, which has a phosphor screen face and is similar to a television tube. Pictures are produced by directing an electron beam, which strikes the phosphor screen. The control of the electron beam is based on data received from the computer system to which the device is attached.

The two basic types of CRT output are *alphanumeric*,[5] which displays characters, and *graphic*, which also displays lines and, hence, drawings as well as characters. Graphic devices are significantly more expensive than alphanumeric devices.

Several forms of input are found on CRT devices. The most common form is an alphanumeric keyboard similar to that found on a typewriter. In addition, function keyboards, light pens, and tablets are sometimes found on these devices. The function keyboard is an arrangement of special-purpose keys. Each key triggers a particular function rather than simply producing a character. Depressing a function key could, for example, register a student in a given course. Multiple function sets may be associated with a given keyboard, and a given function set is selected via a code key. The light pen is a light sensing device that, in effect, permits the operator to draw on the face of the CRT (see Figure 3.21). The tablet is a section of glass or plastic with an imbedded grid of sensing wires. Paper is placed on the glass, and the user draws with a special stylus. The position of the stylus is sensed, and this information is transmitted to the system.

Figure 3.21 IBM 2250 Display Unit.

CRT devices are used by airlines reservations systems to display information about flights. In Chapter 9, a flight control system that uses CRT devices is described. At the Lockheed-Georgia Company, CRT devices are used in parts design. IBM has a demonstration system in which a textile design is drawn on the screen of the device using a light pen, and when the design satisfies

---

[5] An alphanumeric character may be either alphabetic or numeric.

the designer it is woven into the fabric under computer control. The potential applications of CRT devices seem endless, and these devices seem certain to become a major category of input/output devices in the future.

3.5 Channels

Input and output operations of even the fastest devices are slow relative to the speed of the central processing unit. If the CPU were forced to call for the transmission of data from a device and then wait for the completion of that transmission, a significant amount of processor time would be spent waiting. To avoid this loss of processing time, the computer system may be designed to allow the CPU to initiate a transmission and proceed immediately to the next instruction. As the data is transmitted, the CPU continues with other tasks and simply interrupts its current task occasionally to store the incoming data. This is described as *overlapping* the operation of the CPU and input/output operations.

In another way to eliminate waiting, input and output devices are frequently connected to a device known as a *channel* rather than being directly connected to the central processing unit. The channel is, in effect, a separate computer whose task is getting data into and out of high-speed storage and controlling the input and output devices themselves. The channel has a unique set of commands and its own program resident in high-speed storage. When an input or output operation is desired, a command is issued to the channel. The channel accesses its program in high-speed storage and executes it independently of the operations of the central processing unit. Input and output operations are thus able to proceed concurrently with processing. When the input or output operation is complete, the channel signals the processing unit; this is described as an input/output *interrupt*.

Exercises

1. Develop a procedure using the sorter described in Section 3.1 to sort a deck of cards into an ascending sequence of the first three columns. The first three columns will contain numeric values only. Demonstrate that your procedure will work using a test set of three-digit numbers written on $3'' \times 5''$ cards.
2. Briefly describe a system in which optical character recognition would be valuable.
3. What device or devices are likely to replace the key punch as the major means of data recording? Why?
4. In what way is the key-to-tape (disk) system able to increase the throughput of the main computer system?

5. Briefly describe a system in which a plotter would be valuable.
6. Briefly describe a system in which COM equipment would be valuable.
7. Briefly describe a system in which a CRT device would be valuable.
8. One anti-computer group has suggested that an effective form of sabotage is to pass MICR encoded checks under a magnet. Will this be effective?
9. Develop an argument supporting either the card reader or the paper tape reader as, in general, the more desirable input device of the two.
10. Describe an additional application of the portable remote terminal shown in Figure 3.14a.

4 Information

Information is the basic element of both computer science and data processing. Data, with varying richness of information, are the prime raw material inputs to computer-based information systems.[1] Processing transforms data structures and, if the output of the process is to be significant, it must provide new information to the users of the system. (New information may simply be new arrangements of previously known information.) Information is the focal point of computer science. To understand this science and use it successfully, we must continually be conscious of this essential factor.

Three distinct categories of information are important to a study of computer-based information systems.

---

[1] The terms *data* and *information* are, as indicated, not synonymous. We use *data* to refer to the broad stream of facts and figures entering the system, while *information* is the subset of data that reduces uncertainty on the part of the receiver of the data.

External representation is used for both input information and the output supplied to the user. Quite simply, external representation is readable and intelligible to human beings. A second category, machine-readable representation, results when information in external representation is converted to a form that can be accepted by the computer system. Finally, internal representation is the result of converting machine-readable information to a form that can be processed by the computer system.

Thus, as Figure 4.1 indicates, the normal processing of data is marked by a minimum of three conversions. Information in human-readable form is converted to machine-readable form, the machine-readable form is converted to machine-processable form, and finally, the results of the processing are converted back to human-readable form. In the following sections, we examine these representations in more detail.

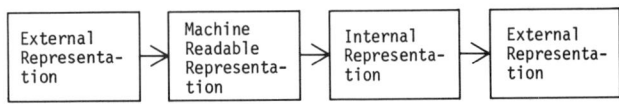

Figure 4.1 Necessary conversions in the processing of data.

of communication. Yet, because the subject of number systems is also important to internal representation, we will include our discussion of this special case in the latter section.

The basic unit of external information is the character. Characters may be the letters of the alphabet, the numbers 0 thru 9, and special characters such as +, −, @, $, and %. This basic unit is also referred to as a *byte*[2] of information, although that term is more accurately applied to the internal representation of information.

4.1 External Representation

External representation is normally in the form of natural language and the decimal number system, because the results of processing must be readily intelligible to the human user of the system. At times, however, other number systems may provide a more effective means

4.2 Machine-Readable Representation

Machine-readable representation, as we noted earlier, refers to information in a form that can be accepted by

---

[2] A byte contains 6 or 8 bits.

the computer system without further alteration Typically, this means that the data appears in code on a physical medium such as card or paper tape. Two forms of coding are discussed below. As we noted in the last chapter, however, various optical devices are also capable of reading typed and hand-printed data. In this instance, external representation is also machine-readable representation. Eliminating the conversion between external representation and machine-readable representation is a fairly obvious direction for hardware improvement. Research is underway in several areas of machine recognition, including both voice and handwritten data.

Hollerith Coding The most common code used in recording data on punched cards is named after the inventor of the first card processing equipment, Hermann Hollerith. A single character (comprised of one or more holes) is punched in a single card column. Thus, up to 80 characters can be punched on a single card. In addition to the 80 columns, the card is divided into twelve rows, which can be identified as the 12, 11, 0, and 1 thru 9 rows, as shown in Figure 4.2. The 12, 11, and 0 rows are known as zone rows; the 0 thru 9 rows are called numeric rows. (The 0 row serves in both capacities.)

In the Hollerith code numbers are represented by a punch in the row corresponding to the number desired. Thus, to represent a 0 in column one, we punch the 0 row of that column (as is done in Figure 4.2). In column two, the punch in the 1 row indicates a 1 in column two and so on. Alphabetic and special characters are encoded by combining zone and numeric punches in a single column. The somewhat arbitrary pattern selected for these combinations is that the 12 row in combination with the 1 row represents the letter A; the 12 row with the 2 row is B; and so on through 12, 9 which represents an I. A punch in the 11 row and the 1 row in the same column represents the letter J, and the subsequent row progression provides the characters K through R. A punch in the 0 row and the 2 row represents an S, with the row progression giving characters T through Z. The alphabetic codes are illustrated in columns 12 through 37 of the card in Figure 4.2. The number 923 is punched in columns 50-52. Special characters such as #, *, ?, and $ are encoded as arbitrary combinations of rows. The dollar sign for example is represented by holes in the 11, 8, and 3 rows in a single column.

Punched Paper Tape Codes Punched paper tape (Figure 4.3) is an alternative to punched cards as a machine-readable medium. Paper tape, which is both read and recorded in rolls, may contain 5, 6, 7, 8, or 9 longitudinal channels in addition to a row of smaller holes near the center of the tape used to feed the tape through reading

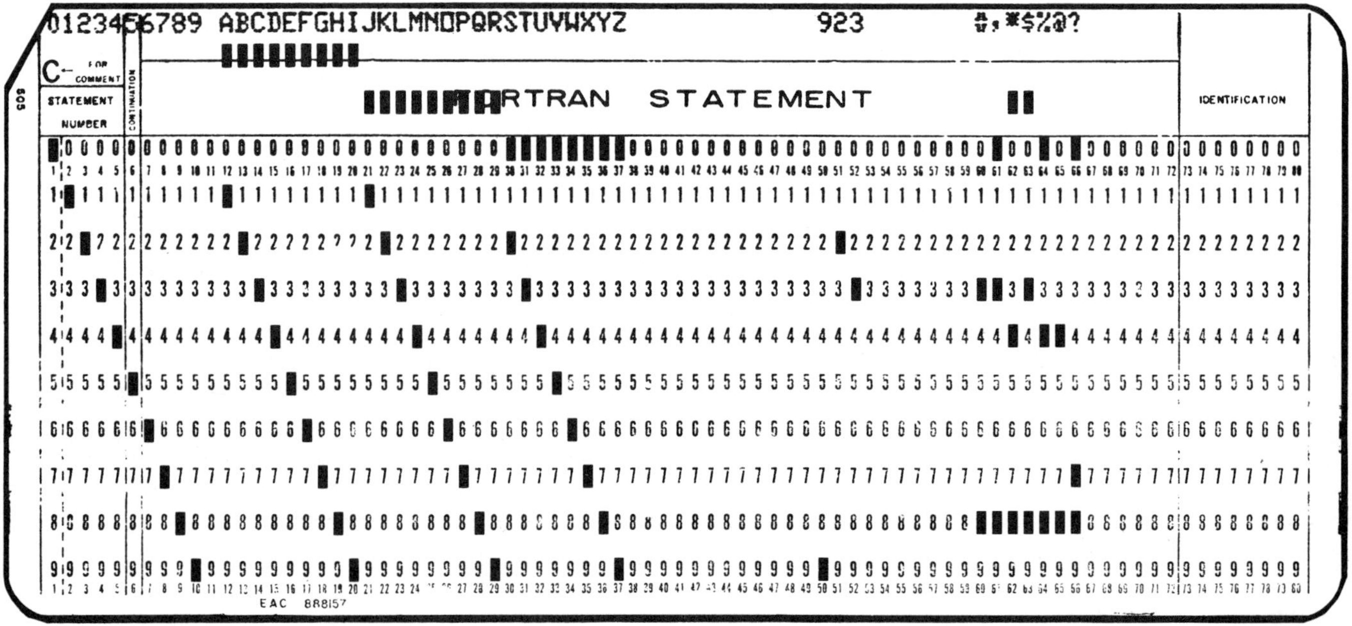

Figure 4.2 An 80-column card with Hollerith code.

Figure 4.3 Eight-channel paper tape.

or recording units. The code used obviously depends on the number of channels but, in any case, a character is represented by the combination of channels punched.

4.3 Internal Representation

Besides defining the place value of digits, the *radix* or *base* of a number system describes the number of symbols available in that system. In the decimal (base 10) system, for example, the symbols are 0, 1, 2, 3, 4, 5, 6, 7, 8, and 9. The binary system uses two symbols, 0 and 1. The base 8 (or octal) and base 16 (hexadecimal) number systems are of particular importance in the study of computer systems and contain 8 and 16 symbols respectively. Table 4.1 presents the symbols of these bases and several others.

The positional value of a digit (or single symbol) in any number is determined by the position of the digit

Table 4.1 Symbols of Selected Number Systems

Base	Name	Symbols
2	binary	0 1
5	quinary	0 1 2 3 4
8	octal	0 1 2 3 4 5 6 7
10	decimal	0 1 2 3 4 5 6 7 8 9
11	undenary	0 1 2 3 4 5 6 7 8 9 A
16	hexadecimal	0 1 2 3 4 5 6 7 8 9 A B C D E F

relative to the radix point. That is, the value of the number is the sum of the values produced when each digit is multiplied or weighted by the value of its position. The value of a given position is the base of the number system raised to the power assigned that position. In the decimal system, for example, the number 723.5 is evaluated as

$$7 \times 10^2 = 700$$
$$2 \times 10^1 = 20$$
$$3 \times 10^0 = 3$$
$$5 \times 10^{-1} = \tfrac{5}{10} \text{ or } .5$$
$$\overline{723.5}$$

This process is described as the *literal expansion* of the number 723.5.

In any number system the positional values are increasing powers of the radix r, beginning with r raised to the zero power immediately to the left of the radix point. To the right of the radix point, the positional values are decreasing powers of the radix r beginning with r^{-1}. Table 4.2 shows the positional values of bases 2, 8, 10, and 16. The subscripts indicate the base of the number system in which the radix is being represented. Thus, in base 2, the first position to the left of the radix point carries the value of 2 raised to the zero power but the 2 is represented in the base 2 system and thus is shown as 10_2^0. In the base 8 example, the first position to the left of the radix point carries the value of 8 raised to the zero power, or 10_8^0.

The process of literal expansion is the same for any number system. The binary number 1011.11_2 is evaluated as:

$$10_2^3 \; 10_2^2 \; 10_2^1 \; 10_2^0 \, . \, 10_2^{-1} \; 10_2^{-2} \text{ (positional values)}$$

$$
\begin{aligned}
1 \times 10_2^3 &= 1 \times 1000 = 1000 \\
0 \times 10_2^2 &= 0 \times 100 = 0 \\
1 \times 10_2^1 &= 1 \times 10 = 10 \\
1 \times 10_2^0 &= 1 \times 1 = 1 \\
1 \times 10_2^{-1} &= 1 \times \tfrac{1}{10} = .1 \\
1 \times 10_2^{-2} &= 1 \times \tfrac{1}{100} = .01 \\
\end{aligned}
$$
$$\overline{1011.11_2}$$

Table 4.2 Positional Values of Number Bases 2, 8, 10, and 16

Radix

	... r^3	r^2	r^1	r^0 .	r^{-1}	r^{-2}	r^{-3} ...
2	... 10_2^3	10_2^2	10_2^1	10_2^0 .	10_2^{-1}	10_2^{-2}	10_2^{-3} ...
8	... 10_8^3	10_8^2	10_8^1	10_8^0 .	10_8^{-1}	10_8^{-2}	10_8^{-3} ...
10	... 10_{10}^3	10_{10}^2	10_{10}^1	10_{10}^0 .	10_{10}^{-1}	10_{10}^{-2}	10_{10}^{-3} ...
16	... 10_{16}^3	10_{16}^2	10_{16}^1	10_{16}^0 .	10_{16}^{-1}	10_{16}^{-2}	10_{16}^{-3} ...

Binary Number System Counting in the binary number system is identical to counting in any other number system except for the obvious inconvenience of running out of symbols more quickly. When we enumerate the first item as 1, we have already used the highest possible symbol in the system and to count the next item we must shift to a higher positional value. Thus, in counting a set of objects in binary the count proceeds as follows:

Information

Binary	Items
1	*
10	**
11	***
100	****
101	*****
110	******
111	*******
1000	********
1001	*********
1010	**********

The decimal equivalent of a binary number can be determined by literally expanding a number using the decimal representation of the radix instead of the radix representation. The binary number 11011.11, for example, is converted to decimal by multiplying each symbol by its positional value in terms of a decimal representation of the radix, or 2_{10}, instead of 10_2. Thus

$$\begin{array}{ccccccc} 2^4 & 2^3 & 2^2 & 2^1 & 2^0 & 2^{-1} & 2^{-2} \\ 1 & 1 & 0 & 1 & 1. & 1 & 1_2 \end{array}$$

$$\begin{aligned} 1 \times 2^4 &= 16 \\ 1 \times 2^3 &= 8 \\ 0 \times 2^2 &= 0 \\ 1 \times 2^1 &= 2 \\ 1 \times 2^0 &= 1 \\ 1 \times 2^{-1} &= \tfrac{1}{2} \\ 1 \times 2^{-2} &= \tfrac{1}{4} \\ \hline & \quad 27\tfrac{3}{4} \end{aligned}$$

Arithmetic in the binary number system is relatively simple. There are four possibilities in addition:

$$0 + 0 = 0$$
$$0 + 1 = 1$$
$$1 + 0 = 1$$
$$1 + 1 = 0 \quad \text{with a carry of 1 into the next higher position}$$

Two examples of addition are:

	(a)		(b)
carry	1111 1	carry	1111 1
	1011.11		11101.1
	1101.01		101101.01
	11001.00		1001010.11

In example (a), the rightmost pair of bits[3] is added to produce a sum of 0 and a carry of 1. Then, the next pair of bits to the left, plus the carry of 1, is added to produce an overall sum of 0 and carry of 1. The addition of the next pair of bits and the carry of 1 produce a sum of 1 and a carry of 1. The addition continues to the left until all pairs of bits are added. As in decimal addition, the radix

---

[3] *Bit* is a contraction of the words *binary digit*.

point is ignored in the addition process itself and is simply carried into the sum in the same position it occupied in the addend and augend.

The four possibilities in binary subtraction are:

$$1 - 1 = 0$$
$$1 - 0 = 1$$
$$0 - 0 = 0$$
$$0 - 1 = 1 \quad \text{with a borrow from the next higher position in the minuend}$$

The only real difficulty in binary subtraction occurs when borrowing is required. As an example, the subtraction of 1_2 from 100_2 is illustrated below:

Step 1
```
       1
     1̶0̶0̶
       1
```

Step 2
```
     1̶11
     1̶0̶0̶
       1
```

Step 3
```
     1̶11
     1̶0̶0̶
       1
      ──
      11
```

In the first step, the borrow of 1_2 must be from the leftmost, or 2^2, position. This borrow makes the value of the 2^1 position of the minuend 10_2. (In decimal calculations, when we borrow 1 we are really borrowing 10, 100, 1,000, or whatever, depending on the position. Likewise, in binary we borrow a power of 2—$10_2{}^1$, $10_2{}^2$, $10_2{}^3$, or whatever.) In step 2, 1_2 is borrowed from the 2^1 position in the minuend, making the value of the 2^0, or rightmost, position 10_2. Since we are borrowing 1_2 from 10_2 and since $1_2 + 1_2 = 10_2$, we are left with 1_2 in the 2^1 position. In the third step, the 1_2 in the subtrahend is subtracted from 10_2 giving 1_2 in the 2^0 position of the difference. The 0 in the 2^1 position of the subtrahend is subtracted from the 1_2 remaining in that position of the minuend, and the difference is 1_2. Hence, the answer is 11_2. Some other examples of binary subtraction are:

```
   10110.1        11010.11
 − 10011.1      − 10111.01
   ──────        ────────
      11.0           11.10
```

Octal and Hexadecimal Number Systems Counting in the octal or hexadecimal number systems is very similar to counting in the decimal system. The highest admissible symbols are 7 and F, respectively. Table 4.3 compares counting a set of objects in decimal, octal, and hexadecimal. The decimal value of both octal and hexadecimal numbers is calculated by multiplying each symbol by its positional value, using the decimal repre-

Information

Table 4.3 Counting a Set of Objects in Octal, Decimal, and Hexadecimal

Octal	Decimal	Hexadecimal	Objects
1	1	1	*
2	2	2	**
3	3	3	***
4	4	4	****
5	5	5	*****
6	6	6	******
7	7	7	*******
10	8	8	********
11	9	9	*********
12	10	A	**********
13	11	B	***********
14	12	C	************
15	13	D	*************
16	14	E	**************
17	15	F	***************
20	16	10	****************

sentation of the radices of 8 and 16, respectively. The hexadecimal symbols A, B, C, D, E, and F must be converted to their decimal equivalents before multiplication. In the following example, 137.6_8 is converted to decimal:

$$\begin{array}{rl} 1 \times 8^2 &= 64 \\ 3 \times 8^1 &= 24 \\ 7 \times 8^0 &= 7 \\ 6 \times 8^{-1} &= \frac{6}{8} \\ \hline & 95\frac{3}{4} \end{array}$$

Similarly, $1AF.C_{16}$ is converted to decimal as follows:

$$\begin{array}{rl} 1 \times 16^2 &= 1 \times 256 = 256 \\ A \times 16^1 &= 10 \times 16 = 160 \\ F \times 16^0 &= 15 \times 1 = 15 \\ C \times 16^{-1} &= 12 \times \frac{1}{16} = \frac{12}{16} \\ \hline & 431\frac{3}{4} \end{array}$$

Primarily because two-state devices are compatible with electronic processing, actual internal representation of information is in binary. As we noted earlier, the results of processing are presented to the user in human-readable form—in decimal values for numbers. Thus, the user of the computer-based information system encounters no difficulty from the internal use of binary. The programmer and the operator, however, are in a different position. Instructions, as well as data, are stored in the computer in binary and, not infrequently, the programmer must see what is actually stored. The operator must communicate with the computer system and occasionally must supply information to be stored internally. Obviously, communication using binary numbers is difficult. Remembering binary numbers is difficult, and the likelihood of error during transcription is high. A partial solution to the difficulties of dealing with binary numbers is to use octal and hexadecimal numbers as a shorthand notation for binary numbers. Instead of communicating a string of binary digits or *bits* we will use their octal or hexadecimal equivalents instead. While neither octal nor hexadecimal numbers are as readily interpretable to the human being as is decimal, they are easier to remember and are less likely to cause errors in transposition than binary. The octal and hexadecimal number systems are uniquely suited for shorthand representation of binary numbers because of a one-to-one correspondence between binary representation and the symbols of each system; Table 4.4 illustrates this correspondence. The relationship between the binary and octal number systems is such that a given binary number can be converted to octal in three-bit groups and the octal result will be the same as if we had converted the entire binary number at once. For example:

$$001\ 110\ 101\ 110\ 110\ 101\ 111\ 111_2$$
$$1\quad 6\quad 5\quad 6\quad 6\quad 5\quad 7\quad 7_8$$

Table 4.4 Correspondence between Octal, Hexadecimal, and Binary

Octal	Binary	Hexadecimal	Binary
0	000	0	0000
1	001	1	0001
2	010	2	0010
3	011	3	0011
4	100	4	0100
5	101	5	0101
6	110	6	0110
7	111	7	0111
		8	1000
		9	1001
		A	1010
		B	1011
		C	1100
		D	1101
		E	1110
		F	1111

A similar relationship exists between binary and hexadecimal with the use of four-bit binary groups. In the following example, we convert the binary number we used in the last example to hexadecimal.

$$0011\quad 1010\quad 1110\quad 1101\quad 0111\quad 1111$$
$$3\qquad A\qquad E\qquad D\qquad 7\qquad F$$

This process can also be reversed. An octal number can be converted to binary by substituting the appropriate three-bit set for each symbol:

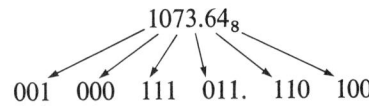

The same is true for hexadecimal:

Binary-Coded Decimal (BCD) System In the binary-coded decimal representation, individual digits are coded instead of the entire number. A set of four bits is used to represent each decimal digit.

Decimal	Binary
0	0000
1	0001
2	0010
3	0011
4	0100
5	0101
6	0110
7	0111
8	1000
9	1001

The numbers 1237_{10} would thus be represented as follows:

$$0001 \quad 0010 \quad 0011 \quad 0111$$
$$1 \qquad 2 \qquad 3 \qquad 7$$

This process is similar to the one which we discussed in the previous section. The binary numbers, however, are not the same as those which would result from a conversion of the entire decimal number to binary.

To represent alphabetic characters, additional bits, called *zone* bits, are added. Various combinations of zone bits and numeric bits are used to represent alphabetic and special characters. In the Extended Binary-Coded Decimal Interchange Code (EBCDIC) for example, characters are represented by eight-bit bytes, with the letter *A* as 1100 0001, *B* as 1100 0010, *C* as 1100 0011, and so on. The letter *J* is represented as 1101 0001, *K* as 1101 0010, and so on. The left four bits are the zone bits and the right four are numeric bits. Selected characters from this code are presented in Table 4.5.

Numeric values are represented by a combination in which the zone bits are all 1's and the numeric bits are the four-bit BCD numbers described above. The number 9 appears as 1111 1001, for example. An alternate form of numeric representation is described as *packing*. In packed form, two four-bit numeric values are contained in one eight-bit byte. 1001 0101, for example, represents a 9 and a 5 in packed form.

Internal representation of a set of characters will be a string or undifferentiated series of 0's and 1's. As we have seen, however, in the case of EBCDIC these bits can be grouped into sets of eight and decoded. Hence, 110000111101000111111001 can also be seen as 1100 0011 1101 0001 1111 1001, or CJ9. Finally, while we have a choice of actually viewing the internal representation as a string of bits, we also have the choice of

Table 4.5 Selected Characters in the EBCDIC

0100	0000	blank	1101	0001	J	
1111	0000	0	1101	0010	K	
1111	0001	1	1101	0011	L	
1111	0010	2	1101	0100	M	
1111	0011	3	1101	0101	N	
1111	0100	4	1101	0110	O	
1111	0101	5	1101	0111	P	
1111	0110	6	1101	1000	Q	
1111	0111	7	1101	1001	R	
1111	1000	8	1110	0010	S	
1111	1001	9	1110	0011	T	
1100	0001	A	1110	0100	U	
1100	0010	B	1110	0101	V	
1100	0011	C	1110	0110	W	
1100	0100	D	1110	0111	X	
1100	0101	E	1110	1000	Y	
1100	0110	F	1110	1001	Z	
1100	0111	G	0101	1011	$	
1100	1000	H	0101	1100	*	
1100	1001	I	0110	1100	%	

representing these bits in octal or hexadecimal shorthand. Thus, 1100001111101000111111001 could also be shown as $C3D1F9_{16}$.

Exercises

1. Determine the Hollerith coding necessary to represent your name and Social Security number.
2. How many different characters can be represented using 12 rows?
3. Design an alternative code that could be used on a standard 80-column card.
4. Show the literal expansion of the following numbers:
   (a) 532.3_5 (b) 1642.6_8 (c) $A7C.D_{16}$
5. Convert the following binary numbers to decimal:
   (a) 101.11
   (b) 1001.1
   (c) 10111.101
   (d) 1101101.111
   (e) 1001101.1101
6. Perform the following operations in binary arithmetic:

   addition   subtraction

   (a) 110.011   (d) 1100
        111.101   − 111

   (b) 1011.101   (e) 101.100
        1110.111   −100.110

   (c) 10110.1011   (f) 1101.101
        11011.1101   −1011.110

7. Convert the following octal numbers to decimal:
   (a) 13.6
   (b) 107.4
   (c) 326.35
   (d) 1276.44
8. Convert the following hexadecimal numbers to decimal:
   (a) A.C
   (b) 1F.8
   (c) 3B9.6D
   (d) 12EA.D7

Information

9. Convert the following numbers from the base given to the base indicated, using the technique presented on page 50:
   (a) $101011101011110110101.11011101_2$ to base 16
   (b) $FEA4C.DBA_{16}$ to base 2
   (c) $10111101011101110111.101110101011_2$ to base 8
   (d) 367154.663_8 to base 2

10. Represent the following characters in EBCDIC:
    (a) 7
    (b) F
    (c) L
    (d) X

 A unit of information derives at least a part of its meaning from its relationship to other units of information. The significance of a $100,000 profit is enhanced considerably when we learn that the previous profit of the same firm was $20,000 or that the profit was made on sales of $200,000. An aggregation of individual units of information may be also meaningful. For example, we may be interested in the total number of automobile accidents at a given location or the total number of welfare recipients whose educational level exceeds the eleventh grade. Finally, we must be able to locate particular information units. To discover the relationships among information units and to locate specific information units, we must organize our data.

5 Data Organization and Storage Media

5.1 Hierarchy of Data Elements

The basic unit of external information is the character. Characters may be combined to form *fields*, or small, meaningful elements, of information. Student number, class standing, and degree program are examples of fields of information. Fields are combined into *records*, which are related by some identifying element. A particular student's record, for example, might be identified by his student number and might contain his class standing, entrance examination score, degree program, courses, and grades. All of these fields are unified into the record of an individual student. A given type of record may be either fixed- or variable-length. Variable-length records are used when the numbers of information elements vary widely from record to record. In a student record, for example, one student may have taken two courses and another student may have taken 100. Use of a fixed-length record would require that all records be long enough to contain 100 course identifications and grades, which would obviously waste space in the records of many students. The use of a variable-length record allows each record to be just long enough to contain the courses taken by the student but is achieved at the cost of additional complexity in processing the records.

Records may be grouped into *files*. A university might,

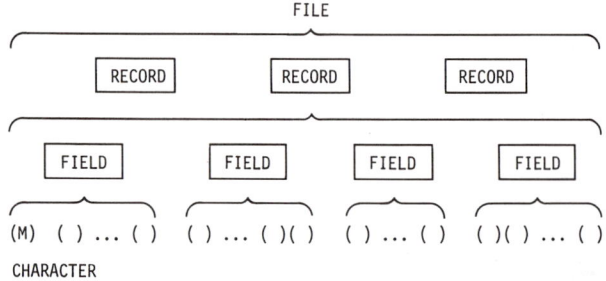

Figure 5.1 Hierarchy of external information.

for example, maintain a file of student records or a file of alumni records. A business might maintain an inventory file, customer file, file of accounts payable, and so on. The hierarchy of information is illustrated in Figure 5.1.

5.2 Sequence within Files

The sequence of records in a file is an important characteristic of the file itself. Should the file of records on wanted criminals be in ascending order by the criminal's Social Security number or in alphabetical order by the criminal's last name grouped by the type of crime committed? The choice of sequence depends essentially on the way in which the file is to be used. The device on which the file is to be stored is also important, as we shall see later in the chapter.

Sequential Organization The field used to establish sequence in a record is called the record *key*. In the sequential form of organization, records are arranged so that their keys are in ascending or descending order. This arrangement is a logical and not necessarily a physical one. When accessing each record in a sequential file, record key 1035 will follow record key 1034, but the physical location of the record containing key 1035 may be virtually anywhere relative to key 1034. One technique by which this may be accomplished is called *chaining*. Each record contains the address (physical location) of the next record in sequence, linking the records into a chain.

Sequential organization generally leads to a greater density of files in storage and a higher utilization of storage space. Records can simply be stored as close together as the characteristics of the storage device will allow. If the file processing is also sequential and a large percentage of the records in the file are affected, then sequential organization permits the most rapid access to the file's contents. For example, if all of the records are to be processed, absolutely no searching is required, and the next record to be processed is the one immediately following the record that is currently being processed.

In addition to the major key by which the file is sequenced, the file designer may provide the ability to access the file through one or more *secondary keys*. An employee master file that is normally accessed by Social Security number (the major or *primary key*) might also be accessed by skill code or occupation (secondary keys). An index to the file contains the value of the secondary key from each record and the physical address associated with that record. The index is sorted into an ascending sequence of the values of the secondary key, and the file can then be accessed in that sequence. Some physical storage devices permit the building and accessing of indexes that refer to the entire file and its placement on the storage devices. An individual record is located via the indexes, without the necessity of examining each of the records in sequence.

Random Organization In random organization, records are placed on the storage medium without regard to their position relative to other records. There is no necessary logical or physical order. Frequently, records are placed on a physical device by a randomizing technique. Physical addresses acceptable to the storage medium are calculated from the value contained in the primary key. The record is stored at the address calculated and can be retrieved by reapplying the randomizing technique to the known value of the key.

Random organization of a file may be useful when the data to be processed arrive randomly or when only a small percentage of the file is to be accessed in a given process. For example, inquiries about the balances in savings accounts would occur on a random basis without respect to the account involved. In a daily update of an inventory file, only a small percentage of the total items contained in the file might be affected. In both of these cases, the ability to go directly to the record desired avoids the reading of a number of unwanted records.

5.3 Data Base

The data base concept is that an organization's data structure should be discussed and dealt with in its entirety rather than being broken down artificially into files. This entire data structure is identified as the organization's *data base*. The data base is independent of specific application areas and suborganizations that draw on its resources. As a consequence, applications may be added or modified and organizational structure may be changed without massive reorganization of the data structure. In addition, centralizing data eliminates duplication of data elements. An element of data can be stored once and referred to by many application area systems rather than being included in a file for each system.

As the data base concept has developed, a software structure that would serve as an interface between the application systems and the data base has also been created. A data base management system maintains and controls access to the data base. It adds or deletes data elements and creates entirely new sets of elements. In addition, it accesses all the information in the data base at the request of the application system. The data base is thus protected from the consequences of user error, and the users are provided with a standard interface no matter what the nature of the data being handled.

5.4 Storage Media

Data storage devices may be divided into two categories: primary and secondary. *Primary storage* is the high-speed storage that contains programs currently in operation and the data that these programs are actually processing. This category of storage will be discussed in the next chapter. *Secondary storage* typically has a much lower speed than primary storage, but a substantially greater capacity. Secondary storage contains the input and file structures that are being processed. In some instances, output to be printed or punched is first placed on a secondary storage device and is later sent to the printer as it becomes available or is printed on another system.

Magnetic Tape Devices For many years the major secondary storage device was the magnetic tape unit (Figure 5.2). This device reads and writes on mylar or other plastic tape that has been coated with magnetizable material. Data is recorded as a pattern of magnetized spots. Figure 5.3 shows how a code is marked onto a segment of magnetic tape. The tape is usually 1/2 inch wide, up to 2400 feet long, and is wound onto reels. A tape reel which is to be read or written is placed on the tape drive (the left reel in Figure 5.4). The tape is fed around several rollers and capstans and under a read/write head, which is midway between the two tape reels. For recording, the data are converted into patterns of magnetic spots as the tape passes under the read/write head. For reading, the pattern of magnetic spots is sensed and transmitted as the tape passes under the read/write head. Data are recorded at densities up to

Figure 5.2 IBM 2401 Magnetic Tape units.

6,250 bits or characters per inch and is read from the tape drive at rates up to one and one-quarter million characters per second.

Data is written on tape in *blocks*. Several records may be combined to form a block, and the number of records

60 Chapter Five

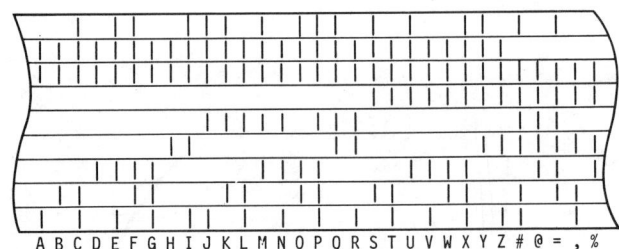

Figure 5.3 EBCDIC coding on a segment of magnetic tape.

forming a block for a given tape is described as the *blocking factor*. A space, the *inter-record gap*, is left between blocks. Normally, there are no addresses associated with positions on magnetic tape, and when a specific record is desired the tape must be searched until the record is found. This process is frequently time-consuming. Clearly, magnetic tape is not an ideal medium for random organization or random processing of data, but it is well suited for sequential organization and processing.

In some situations, magnetic tape units function as input/output devices. In a large computer system, the card reader might be too slow an input device, and a smaller computer system could be used to prepare a magnetic tape for input to the larger system.

A file of student records with each record containing the grades of one student could, for example, be recorded on magnetic tape. A file of records containing the grades made in the current quarter could be recorded on a second tape. If both files were in the same sequence of a common key such as student number, records could be read from both files and matched. Then, a new student

Figure 5.4 Honeywell Tape Drive.

Data Organization and Storage Media

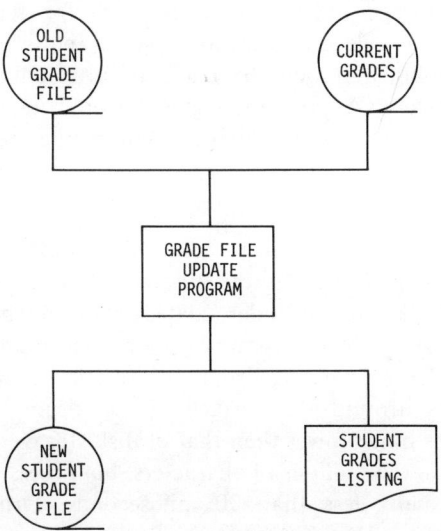

Figure 5.5 Adding current grades to a cumulative student grade file.

Figure 5.6 Honeywell Disk Storage Drive.

grade file, with current grades inserted, could be written on a third tape. This process is illustrated in Figure 5.5. At the end of the process the "old" student grade file would be retained temporarily in case reprocessing were necessary and then would be made available for use by another program.

Disk Storage Devices   Disk storage devices (Figure 5.6) are one of the category of *direct access storage devices*. The term direct access refers to the ability of the device to find and read a specific address and location without having to pass through all records in the file preceding the one being sought. The disks, which are the recording medium, are coated with a magnetizable material. They are stored in a vertical stack, rotating around a central hub, and may be either fixed or removable. Information is recorded on *tracks*, which are concentric circles on the top and bottom surfaces of each disk. The data are read by a set of read/write mechanisms attached to movable arms. Given the address of a track containing the desired record, the read/write head is advanced to that track, and the data are read during the next full revolution after the track's starting point passes. If the disks are removable, the entire set can be replaced by a new set containing different files of information. Disk-type devices can store hundreds of millions of characters of information and can access a given track in less than 100 milliseconds (thousandths of a second). Data are read from disk-type devices at rates up to 800,000 characters or bytes per second.[1]

Disk storage devices may be used for sequential or random processing. They are obviously well suited for situations in which a small percentage of the file is processed at a time, because the desired record can be accessed directly without examining intervening records. They are likewise well suited for random processing.

Disk storage devices could be used for secondary storage in a college registration system. Inquiries about class enrollments could be made over telephone lines to the system. A program segment would analyze the inquiry and then access the tracks containing the proper record.

Magnetic Drum Devices Another form of direct access storage devices is the *magnetic drum*. The drum is usually a fixed cylinder coated with magnetizable material. A set of read/write heads is fixed close to the surface of the revolving drum. Information is recorded on tracks around the surface of the drum. Storage capacity is much lower than that of disk storage devices, typically in the millions of characters, but access is much faster, usually less than 20 milliseconds. Drums are frequently used for the storage of programs and intermediate data.

Storage Hierarchy In general, in secondary storage devices there is a trade-off between storage capacity and access time. For instance, magnetic tape has a large capacity, but the average access time for a specific record is minutes. Random accessing of individual records on tape would, of course, be a misuse of the device. Effective tape processing requires that the records

---

[1] This contrasts with a rate of 1,600 characters per second for a 1,200 card-per-minute card reader.

be placed on the tape in some approximation of the order in which they will be required. The access time for disks is less but so is the capacity. Drum devices have an even lower access time and, again, an even lower capacity.

An effective use of direct access storage devices is to arrange the available devices in a hierarchy according to the volume and the frequency of need for the information to be stored. Information that is constantly required by the system can be placed on a magnetic drum, while less frequently used data is placed on a disk, and infrequently needed data is stored on a magnetic tape.

Exercises

1. A medical clinic has decided to develop a patient history computer system. There are approximately ten thousand patient records. Each record contains the following information: the patient's health insurance number, salary, Social Security number, name, address, telephone number, sex, date of birth; names, birthdates, and health of spouse, children, and parents; a complete blood type, weight and height, and medical history to the date the patient first came to the clinic (this includes diseases, surgery, and the name and address of the patient's previous physician). Each time the patient visits the clinic his complaint, the results of all tests and examinations, the diagnosis, and the treatment are added to the history. The major function of the Patient History System will be to aid the physician who is currently treating the patient. Develop an organization plan for this data. How many files are necessary? What primary key? What sequence? Would secondary keys be useful? Should the records be fixed- or variable-length? What device should this data be stored on?

2. Design a file for a university's student records. Specify the content, key, organization, and the device type on which the file should be stored.

3. Determine the price, access speed, and storage capacity for a representative model of each device discussed in this chapter.

4. The inter-record gap produced by a given tape drive is 0.6 inch, the density is 1600 bits per inch, and the tape itself is 2400 feet long. If our system builds records that are 800 characters in length and our blocking factor is 10, how may blocks can we fit on one tape, if we assume that the entire tape is available for recording? How many records? How many characters?

5. What problems might arise from the use of a single data base as opposed to multiple files?

6 High-Speed Storage and the Central Processing Unit

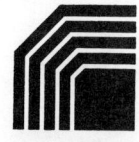

The control function is implemented by the central processing unit which, as we noted earlier, is the unifying element of the computer system. The central processing unit directs, controls, and coordinates the activities of the other devices in the computer system. The function of high-speed storage is to satisfy the immediate storage requirements of the central processing unit. Specifically, the program or programs currently being executed reside in high-speed storage together with the input data that are currently being processed and the data being prepared for output.

High-speed storage and the central processing unit are so interdependent that, for most purposes, we can consider high-speed storage to be a part of the central processing unit. If we take this approach, then the central processing unit can be broken into three subunits: high-speed storage, arithmetic and logic, and control.

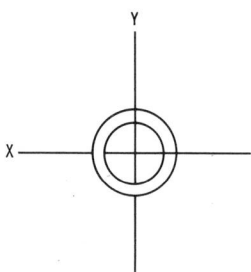

Figure 6.1 A magnetic core. The two directions of polarization are labeled *x* and *y*.

6.1 High-Speed Storage

As it is in secondary storage devices, information in high-speed storage is represented in bits. Several technologies are used for high-speed storage but *magnetic cores* are widely used. Each bit of information is represented by the direction of polarization of a single core (Figure 6.1). Information is recorded in a core by passing one-half of the current necessary to change the polarization on each wire in the target set of cores. Only cores at the intersections of wires will receive sufficient current to affect their polarity. Thousands of these cores are strung together to form *core planes* like that shown in Figure 6.2, and planes are organized into arrays.

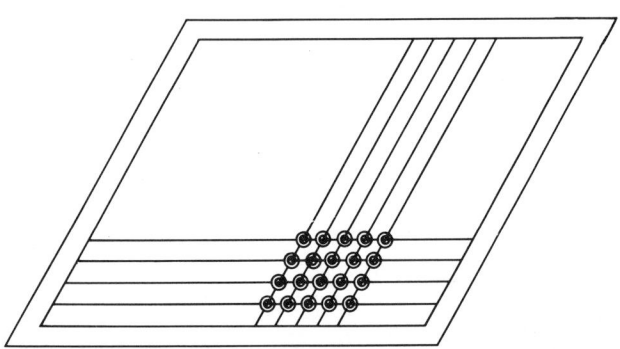

Figure 6.2 A magnetic core plane.

High-speed storage is divided into addressable units. Some number of bits can be accessed by reading or writing at a specific address. A common addressing unit is 32 bits. This unit is described as a *word* of storage. The address 1071, for example, may refer to a specific word of 32 bits, which is located at a point in storage identified as 1071. It is also common to find that the word of 32 bits is made up of 4 eight-bit bytes and that each byte can be individually addressed as well. Remember that the address of a word is not contained at that location nor does it describe the contents of the location. It merely identifies the location and is somewhat analogous to a street address in this regard.

Data may be represented within a word of storage in

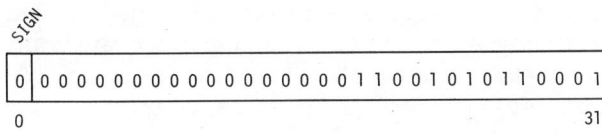

Figure 6.3 Internal representation of the number 12987 as a fixed-point binary number in a 32-bit word. (A 0 sign bit indicates that the value is positive.)

several forms. Alphanumeric data may be represented in the EBCDIC code or in an equivalent code. Numeric data may be represented in the *fixed-point system* or in the *floating-point system*. A fixed-point number is a number that is represented in the word of storage without a radix point. The number is carried as a signed integer and in most computer systems as a pure binary integer (Figure 6.3). All conventional arithmetic operations can be performed on this number but neither the hardware system nor the software system will locate the radix point in the result of the calculations. It is the programmer's responsibility to keep track of the location of the radix point through a series of computations. A floating-point number is a number that is represented in a word of storage as an exponent and a fraction. With this form of representation the hardware system keeps track of the radix point automatically during computation. Current high-speed storage devices access their contents in microseconds (millionths of a second) or, in many cases, in hundreds of nanoseconds (billionths of a second).

6.2 Central Processing Unit

The operation of a computer system is directed by *instructions* or *commands*. These commands are organized into programs, which are sequences of commands arranged to direct the performance of a specific calculation or task. Programs are brought into high-speed storage as they are needed and this loading process is directed, in turn, by other programs that have previously been loaded into high-speed storage. Nevertheless, the end result is a sequence of instructions resident in high-speed storage that direct the operation of the computer system to the achievement of some objective.

At this point we are left with several pertinent questions. Of the sequence of instructions in high-speed storage how does the computer select the one instruction that must be performed next? How is this instruction interpreted? How is it executed? In general, the functions of the control unit provide answers to these questions. The control unit:

1. selects the next instruction to be executed,
2. interprets the instruction,
3. initiates the execution of the instruction.

The function of the *arithmetic and logic unit* (*ALU*) is to execute the instructions that have been selected and interpreted by the control element. A simplified view of the interaction of all of the functional categories is presented in Figure 6.4. The program to be executed has already been loaded into high-speed storage locations 10, 11, 12, and 13. To begin execution of this program, the control unit needs one additional item of information—which instruction is to be executed first. In our diagram, the human operator of the computer system places the location number of the first instruction to be executed in the *instruction counter* of the control unit. The instruction counter is a *register*, a unit of special-purpose, temporary storage. The *address register* and the *instruction register* are similar. Having provided the starting address, the operator presses the start button and execution of the program begins.

The address contained in the instruction counter points to the next instruction to be executed (1). In this case, it causes the contents of location 10 in high-speed storage to be copied into the instruction register (2). The control unit then decodes or interprets the meaning of the instruction—in this case a card read instruction that will cause the transfer of the data on the next available card in the card reader into high-speed storage location 20. At this point the control element causes the address 20 to be placed in the address register (3) and then notifies the arithmetic and logic unit to begin execution (4). The ALU takes over at this point and orders the card reader to read the next card (5). The data on the card will be placed into high-speed storage at the address recorded in the address register—20 (6).

When this operation is completed, the ALU notifies the control element (7). The control element begins the next selection process by increasing the contents of the instruction counter by 1 (8). Thus, the instruction located in high-speed storage location 11 will be selected, interpreted, and executed next, followed by the instructions in locations 12 and 13 in that order. In general, instructions are executed in sequence, and the instruction counter simply advances by 1 following the execution of each instruction. We will see in the next chapter that this sequence can be modified with appropriate instructions. Finally, although we have illustrated the interaction of the functional categories with an example involving the card reader, or input, the interaction is basically the same with the secondary storage and the output categories.

6.3 A Brief History of Computer Development

There is an understandable tendency on the part of the uninitiated to think of the computer system as a development of the late 1950s and the 1960s. The most impressive

High-Speed Storage and the Central Processing Unit

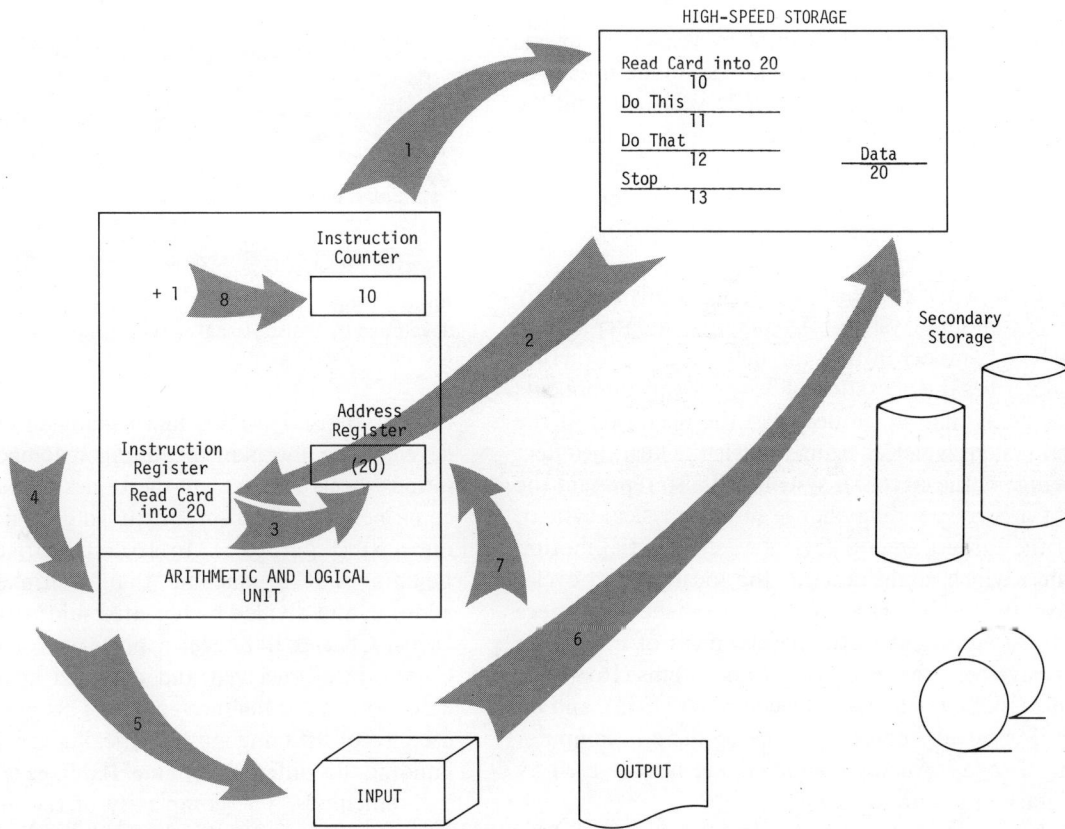

Figure 6.4 Functional interactions in a computer system.

growth and development of computer systems so far has occurred during this period, but the modern era of computer systems began more than 35 years ago and the earliest developments occurred before the Christian era.

The evolution of computer systems can be broken into four separate but concurrent lines of development—those of measuring devices, counting devices, logical devices, and punched cards.

The development of measuring devices leads ultimately to analog computer systems. An analog computer system is, in effect, a model in that the mathematical structure which describes the operation of its electrical components is the same as that which describes the operation of the physical system which is being modeled. Thus, the effect of a change in the electrical system will also represent the effect of a corresponding change in the physical system. One of the earliest analog devices was a celestial motion computer, which could describe the location and cycles of heavenly bodies. This device was made in Greece around 100 B.C. Steps in the development of measuring devices have been the invention of logarithms (1614), the slide rule (1622), the first analog computer (1915), and on to the hybrid or combined analog-digital computer systems of today. Analog computers are heavily used by the military in gunfire control.

The development of counting devices can be said to date from the appearance of the abacus in about 450 B.C.

Figure 6.5 The first mechanical adding machine, developed by Blaise Pascal in 1642. (International Business Machines Corporation.)

In 1642 Blaise Pascal, a mathematician and philosopher, developed a mechanical adding machine that used rotating wheels to represent the values of the digits and that contained a mechanism for carrying from one position to the next (Figure 6.5). In 1673 Gottfried Wilhelm von Leibniz built a machine that multiplied by repeated addition and divided by repeated subtraction. In the early 1800s, Charles Babbage, a professor of mathematics at Cambridge, conceived and designed a machine that he described as a difference engine. This machine was to be used in constructing mathematical tables. However, while building this difference engine, Babbage encountered endless difficulties. The complexity of the machine and the nature of its parts were beyond the limits of the then current technology. Many of the parts, for example, were

beyond the capabilities of the metal working industry, and Babbage had to design and build them himself. During this project, Babbage conceived of a more powerful machine, which he called an analytical engine (Figure 6.6). This device was intended to perform diverse arithmetic calculations. It was to include a "store" of one thousand fifty-digit numbers, a "mill" to process these numbers, and output engraved on copper plates. In addition, the analytical engine had a control mechanism, it operated with a stored program, and it made use of the concept of iteration in program operation. The machine was not completed during Babbage's lifetime, but the conceptual similarity between the analytical engine and the modern digital computer system is uncanny.

The third line of development—that of logical devices—begins with the syllogism. A syllogism is a formal argument consisting of a major and a minor premise and a conclusion (as in "honesty is a virtue; virtue is admired; therefore, honesty is admired"). Not only were attempts made to mechanize such deductions but syllogisms led also to the development of symbolic logic and, ultimately, to the development of logical algebra by George Boole

Figure 6.6 Charles Babbage's analytical engine, with additions, 1910. (British Crown Copyright. Science Museum, London).

Chapter Six

Figure 6.7 IBM Automatic Sequence Controlled Calculator Mark I.

(1854). More complex logic-oriented devices were invented, but this line of development joined with that of counting devices to culminate in the evolution of modern computers. Between 1937 and 1940, George Stibitz of the Bell Laboratories constructed the first electromechanical calculator. This device, called the Complex Calculator, used relays to represent information. Also in 1937, Professor Howard G. Aiken of Harvard University began developing a device which was eventually named the Automatic Sequence Controlled Calculator, Mark I

(Figure 6.7). The Mark I, built by the International Business Machines Corporation, also used relays; it was completed in 1944. One year later, the Electronic Numerical Integrator and Calculator (ENIAC) was completed. The ENIAC was built by Dr. John W. Mauchly and J. Presper Eckert at the University of Pennsylvania. Since it used vacuum tubes rather than relays to represent information it was the first all-electronic computer to be completed.

The final line of development—that of the punched card—began in the latter part of the eighteenth century with the use of punched cards to control the patterns woven by looms. In the 1890 census, punched cards and punched card equipment were used to process the census data. Hermann Hollerith, a statistician, had been commissioned to develop better methods of processing census data, and the results of his efforts were several card processing machines (Figure 6.8). Data were recorded on cards by a card punch and tabulated on a machine that had electromechanical sensing devices. By the use of Hollerith's system, the 1890 census was completed in one-third the time required for the 1880 census. Professors Mauchly and Eckert left the University of Pennsylvania and formed their own company. They built a computer called the UNIVersal Automatic Computer, or UNIVAC, the first of which was delivered to the Bureau of the Census in 1951. In 1953 IBM delivered the IBM 701,

Figure 6.8 The tabulating machine designed by Hermann Hollerith, 1890. (International Business Machines Corporation.)

and in 1956 they delivered the first IBM 705, which used magnetic core memory. The race was on. Innovations since the mid-fifties have mostly increased the speed and capacity of computers while decreasing their size and cost.

By 1957 the first transistorized, or second generation,[1] computer was available, and a major surge in the number of computers installed and on-order had begun. In 1964 the third generation of computer hardware appeared in the form of IBM's System/360. Some would argue that the IBM 370 is a fourth generation computer but this is subject to debate. In the late 1960s the number of computers installed skyrocketed, and an important trend toward very small minicomputer systems developed. These and other trends will be explored in Chapter 12.

Exercises

1. A transfer instruction is used to change the sequence of execution of instructions. Suggest a way in which this change of sequence could be effected in the central processing unit.
2. Could the program currently being executed by a central processing unit be stored on a disk drive rather than in high-speed storage?
3. What would happen if the operator placed an incorrect starting address in the instruction counter?
4. Distinguish between the concepts of a *word* and a *field* of information.
5. Describe the function of the instruction counter.
6. What rule must the programmer follow in placing the instructions that make up his program into high-speed storage?

---

[1] First generation generally denotes all computers that use vacuum tubes, second generation those using transistors, and third generation those using miniaturized solid logic technology.

7 Programming

In discussing the functional category of control in the last chapter we noted that the operation of a computer system is directed by sequences of instructions or commands contained in the high-speed storage unit. These commands are arranged into specific sequences that direct the computer system to perform a particular calculation or task. The arrangements of commands are called *programs*, and the control of the computer by internally stored programs is described as *stored program capability*. A given computer system will have a multitude of different programs associated with it. The various programs available to a computer system are stored either in the secondary storage units or in an external medium such as cards or paper tape. Thus, when a particular program is needed to perform some specific task it is called into high-speed storage from one of the subsidiary storage units or is physically brought from external storage to one of the system's input units to be read into high-speed storage.

Stored program capability is extremely significant when assessing the power and importance of a computer system. First, because the program is available internally, its sequence and, in fact, the program itself may be altered during operation. Second, because programs can be called as they are required, the computer system becomes both a general purpose machine and the equivalent of an array of different special purpose machines. For instance, when a payroll program is loaded into high-speed storage, the computer system becomes a payroll computer system. Forty minutes later when an inventory control program is loaded into high-speed storage, the system becomes an inventory computer system. The wonder of this capability is certainly not dimmed by the addition of *multiprogramming* capability—the ability of a computer system to process more than one program at a time. For example, the payroll program may be in high-speed storage, together with a program that up-dates inventory and a program that responds to inquiries about customer credit. Control is passed back and forth between these programs based on their needs and, to the outside observer, the various programs operate simultaneously. This, then, is a special purpose machine with three special purposes.

For a program to be executed on a particular computer, it must be in machine-processable form and must include only those instructions and addresses acceptable to that computer. A program satisfying these restrictions is called a *machine-language program*. The set of instructions and the instruction forms acceptable to a particular computer constitute its machine language. The program executed on a UNIVAC 1108 must be represented in UNIVAC 1108 machine language, and the program executed on an IBM System 360/40 must be represented in System 360/40 machine language. The two languages are not interchangeable. Other languages, such as FORTRAN and COBOL, are independent of computer hardware systems and may be used to write programs for a number of different systems. However, before programs written in these languages can be executed on a particular computer, they must be converted to that computer's machine language. We will examine several of these higher-level languages later in this chapter, but now let us take a look at the evolution of computer programming languages.

7.1 The Development of Programming Languages

Before the development of the stored program concept, programs were wired into the computer hardware or were executed directly from punched paper tape. In the case of ENIAC, programs were installed by engineers who wired the components in the proper combinations and sequences to perform a particular task. When the program had to be changed, it was rewired.

The use of a stored program was suggested by John von Neumann, a mathematician, who proposed the concept in a report of a 1945 study. This report, which defined a proposed machine called EDVAC (Electronic Discrete Variable Computer), stimulated the development in England of a machine called EDSAC (Electronic Delay Storage Automatic Calculator). EDSAC was the first stored-program machine to be completed.

In the early computer hardware systems, the only programming languages available were machine languages. There were and are many varieties of format in the available machine languages, but a typical instruction format would contain an operation part with one or two digits, and one, two, or three addresses. An add command, for example, might be represented by the letter G, and G 1974 might mean add the contents of high-speed storage location 1974 to a register.

Some machine languages are quite complex. An interesting example of the complexity of programming in machine language is the IBM 650. A magnetic drum was used for high-speed storage, with memory locations arranged in bands around the circumference. This led to a difficult decision in the placement of the program in high-speed storage. If the instructions were simply placed in sequence in consecutive storage locations, the computer would probably have to wait between instructions for the drum to revolve so that the next instruction could be accessed, significantly increasing the time required to execute the program. As an alternative, the programmer could calculate how long the execution of a particular instruction would take, translate this time into the distance the drum would travel during the execution, and place the next instruction at that point on the drum rather than in the next position in sequence. Although this process resulted in a faster program, it added a substantial complication to the programmer's task.

There are significant difficulties associated with machine languages. It is difficult to remember the codes for each operation. It is even more difficult to remember the actual addresses at which both instructions and data have been stored. The crowning difficulty occurs when the programmer desires to insert or delete a single instruction or piece of data in an existing program. Such an insertion or deletion is likely to cause many, if not all, of the addresses in the other instructions to be incorrect.

A first step in eliminating these difficulties was the development of *mnemonic* operation codes, codes that suggest the operation they represent. The letter G, which we mentioned earlier as the machine operation code for

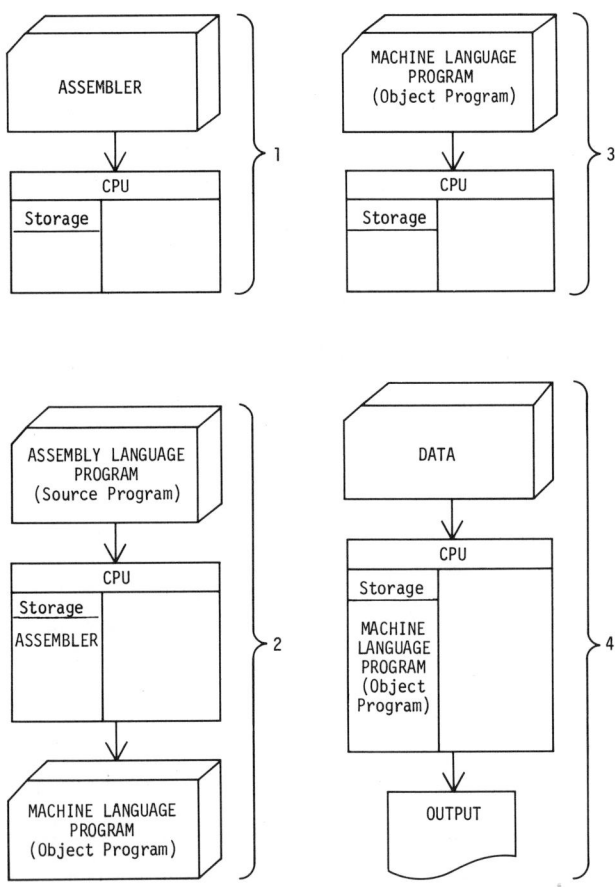

addition, might be replaced with the mnemonic code ADD. A more important development was symbolic addressing. Instead of having to refer to the actual address 1974, the programmer was given the opportunity of referring to the names LOC7 or HOURS, which are both symbolic and mnemonic. The earliest symbolic addresses were numeric.

The development of symbolic operation codes and addresses did not alter the fact that a given machine could actually execute only its own machine language. Instead, this development forced an intermediate step in the program operation process. An additional program is necessary to convert the program from symbolic notation to machine language. This program is called an *assembler*, and the symbolic language that it converts is generally called an *assembly language* program. One of the earliest assemblers was the Symbolic Assembly Program, or SAP, which was used on the IBM 704. The assembly process is illustrated in Figure 7.1.

The assembler is loaded into the high-speed storage of the computer in the first step. The assembler program is then executed with the assembly language program as input. The latter program is known as the *source* program. The mnemonic operation codes are converted to machine

Figure 7.1 The assembly process.

language codes and the symbolic addresses are converted to actual addresses, thus producing the equivalent machine language, or *object*, program. In step three the machine language program is loaded into high-speed storage, and in step four this program is executed with data as input. The process of translating from a source program to the object program is known as *compilation* and the translation program is called a *compiler*.

The subsequent development of higher-level languages includes literally dozens of distinct systems. One of the most significant of the higher-level systems is the FORmula TRANslation, or *FORTRAN*, system. FORTRAN, which was developed by IBM, was defined as early as 1954 and was implemented on the IBM 704 in 1957. FORTRAN is a *procedure-oriented* language, which simply means that the programmer must specify both the operations to be executed and the sequence in which they must be executed. In addition, the term *procedure-oriented* carries the connotation that the procedures supplied in a specific language will relate generally to a particular problem area. In FORTRAN, for example, the procedures of the language relate generally to algebra.

The major benefit to the programmer of procedure-oriented languages in general, and of FORTRAN in particular, is the severance of the one-to-one relationship between the instructions of the source program and the machine-language object program. A single executable statement in FORTRAN, may generate tens if not hundreds of machine-language commands. The FORTRAN statement W=X**2+2.*X*Y+Z means calculate a value W that is equal to $X^2 + 2XY + Z$. This statement could require three multiplies and two adds in machine language.

Although FORTRAN was not initially intended to be machine-independent—the 704 version included statements that referred to hardware features—later versions of the language became increasingly independent of specific hardware.

In 1958 an international committee of representatives of various organizations published a report that set forth the specifications for a new language. This language was the first to be designed by a group of organizations rather than by a single organization (usually a computer manufacturer). The new language was ALGOL (ALGOrithmic Language), and the original report is now known as ALGOL 58. ALGOL is directed to the same general application area as FORTRAN, and in several respects it is a much more powerful language. Three different levels of ALGOL are recognized. The reference (or defining) language is used as a guide by those who create the various compilers. The second level of ALGOL is the publication language, which is constructed for ease of printed communication; this is a major use of ALGOL in this country. Finally, ALGOL exists in various hardware representations, which consist of the reference language tailored to the character sets and peculiarities of specific hardware systems. ALGOL is more widely used in Europe than in the United States, and its use in this country is largely limited to the academic community.

Another milestone in the advance of higher-level languages was the development of the COmmon Business Oriented Language (COBOL). A procedure-oriented language, COBOL is stated in English notation and in narrative form. It was conceived in May 1959 at a meeting called by the Department of Defense to determine both the feasibility and desirability of establishing a common language for business applications. Representatives of major computer manufacturers, computer users, and the government were present. Several committees were established, and the eventual outcome was a report entitled "COBOL—A Report to the Conference on Data Systems Languages, including Initial Specifications for a Common Business Oriented Language (COBOL) for Programming Electronic Digital Computers." This report, which has since become known as COBOL, has been followed by revised editions known as COBOL-61, COBOL-61 Extended, COBOL Edition 1965, and ANSI (or American National Standard) COBOL. In addition to the benefits of procedure-oriented languages discussed earlier, the English notation and the narrative form of COBOL would be readable enough to serve as built-in documentation for the program. The following COBOL statement, for example, is self-explanatory:

IF HOURS ARE GREATER THAN 40.0
THEN GO TO CALCULATE-OVERTIME
ELSE COMPUTE GROSS = HOURS * RATE

Note the contrast between these statements and the equivalent FORTRAN statements below.

IF (HOURS − 40.0) 5,5,10
5 GROSS = HOURS * RATE
$\vdots$
10 ⌒

The last procedure-oriented language we will mention is PL/1 (Programming Language One). Initially PL/1 was a joint effort of IBM and SHARE, an organization of IBM computer users. The first compiler for PL/1 was released in 1966 for the System 360. PL/1 is intended as a more general language to serve both the scientific and business communities. In addition, it is designed to meet shortcomings of both FORTRAN and COBOL.

Besides the procedure-oriented languages described above, a separate category of higher-level, *problem-oriented* languages have become important. A problem-oriented language is directed primarily to a single application area. The nature of the language generally makes it more intelligible to users in that particular application. The notation of such languages is frequently similar to the notation used in the application. SIMSCRIPT and GPSS are languages used for simulation, COGO is used in civil engineering and RPG in the preparation of administrative reports.

This "applications" meaning of the term *problem-oriented* is not universally accepted. Some writers consider FORTRAN, COBOL, and PL/1 to be problem-oriented, and some writers categorize languages such as GPSS and COGO as *application-oriented*. A problem-oriented language may also be nonprocedural, in that the programmer is not required to specify the sequence of operations. In RPG, for example, the programmer describes inputs, outputs, and unique processing steps, but he does not have to specify the order or sequence of operations.

7.2   Problem Analysis

Programming is actually the third step in the chain of events that leads from a problem (or opportunity) to a computer solution. First, someone must have recognized the problem. Second, the processes of systems analysis and design must have occurred, during which the overall solution to the problem is designed and described in detail. This overall solution generally involves a number of different programs, and a particular programmer will be assigned to develop one or more of these programs.

The output of the systems analysis and design function is thus the major input to the programming process. Specifically, this input consists of:

1. A systems flowchart that indicates the flow of information between programs in the system and the relative positions of programs within the system.
2. Detailed layouts of all of the data structures that will be referenced by the program. These data structures include input records, required output records, documents, and files.
3. A program narrative, providing detailed information on the processing that the program must perform as well as information on the handling of data structures.

This information, which the systems analyst provides to the programmer, defines the parameters within which the programmer must construct his program. Although the parameters are normally not absolute requirements, the programmer usually must justify any change to them which he recommends.

The programming process itself consists of six distinct steps, which are illustrated in Figure 7.2. In problem analysis, the first of these steps, the programmer must consider:

82 Chapter Seven

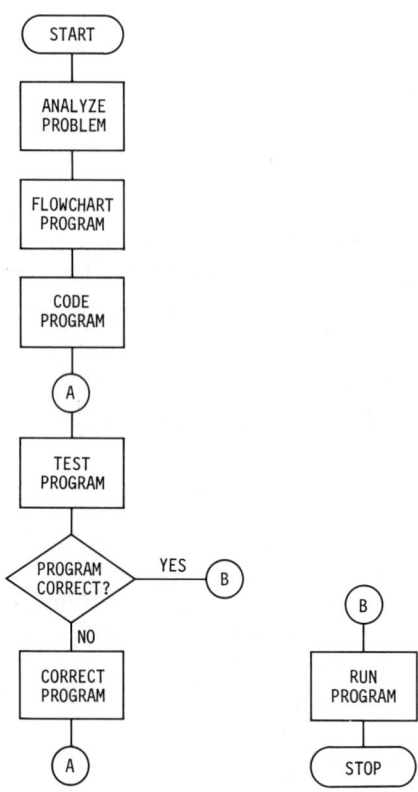

Figure 7.2 Steps in the programming process.

1. the resources available for construction of the program,
2. program design objectives and restrictions,
3. program performance requirements.

Resources The major resource available to the programmer is, of course, the computer hardware system on which his program will be implemented. The high-speed storage capacity, the input and output devices, and the secondary storage devices and their capacity are most important. In addition, the available programming languages and their features are key resources to the programmer. Programming languages vary widely in their efficient use of hardware facilities, ease of writing, time required in compilation or assembly, efficiency of object code, machine independence, and inherent documentation. Each of these features is potentially important to the construction of a program. Finally, the features and capabilities of other software available in the installation also qualify as resources, Examples of this other software are *job control languages*, which effect the flow of programs and data during execution on the hardware system, and data base management systems.

Program Design Objectives and Restrictions Design objectives—required outputs and processing steps—are a part of the parameters supplied to the programmer by the systems analyst. In addition, the programmer establishes and works toward program objectives. He may decide, for example, that simplicity of structure should be a design objective during program construction. He may feel that it is more important to make the program clear and easily understood than it is to save microseconds[1] during its execution.[2] Other objectives might include:

1. minimum storage requirements,
2. flexibility,
3. modularity—the construction of the program as a set of self-contained and independent modules,
4. minimum execution time,
5. self-containment,
6. ease of maintenance or modification.

In addition to these objectives, the programmer may be faced with design restrictions. For instance, the running time of a given program may be critical. In an airline reservation system, the response of the system to a reservation agent's request must occur within seconds, so the programmer must develop his program to operate within a specified time span. Storage limitation is a frequent restriction. Particularly in a multiprogramming environment, high-speed storage is a scarce resource. So the restriction may be that the program cannot take up more than N units of storage.

Besides the limitations unique to a specific program, each installation will have *programming standards*. Methods of documentation, data controls, testing procedures, program coding techniques, standard routines, and many other points may be specified in detail and may be required of all programs and programmers.

Program Performance Requirements Processing time and storage limitation might also be included under program performance requirements. For example, the restriction on processing time will typically be an outer limit, while an appropriate time range may be specified as a performance objective. Other performance requirements may be less objective but equally important. Examples are:

1. Program operation should require minimal operator intervention.
2. The program should be able to respond to every possible input condition.

---

[1] Microseconds (μs) are millionths of a second.

[2] In the author's opinion, the two most important program design objectives are that the program work correctly and that the program should be as simple and clear as possible. If the program is unnecessarily complex, it may be difficult, or impossible to transfer the program from one programmer to another and additional debugging effort will be required. The potential saving in program execution time is far outweighed in all but a few cases. (The exceptions occur almost exclusively in on-line systems, where response and access time are critical.)

3. The program should produce clear, concise output messages.
4. The program should perform maximum editing of input data.

Analysis With the systems chart, data structures, program narrative, resources, programming objectives, restrictions, and performance requirements given, the programmer begins the analysis which will lead to a program. He must construct a sequence of programmable events that will lead from the specified inputs to the specified outputs, while at the same time satisfying the other requirements. The events need not be described in detail at this point. It is sufficient to note the point at which a file update must be performed; it is not necessary to state exactly how the update will be performed. Typically, the programmer mentally or graphically arranges a sequence of events and then evaluates the imagined functioning of this arrangement in terms of the performance, objective, and resource specifications. If the results are unsatisfactory, or if an improvement can be made, the sequence of events is rearranged and modified and the process is repeated. This sequence is a rough algorithm.[3] It must now be broken into more detailed operations representing the operations that will actually be coded in a computer programming language.[4] A useful device in this activity is the *flowchart*, or *detailed logic chart*.

7.3 Flowcharting

A flowchart is a graphic display of the events in a process. In Figure 7.3, for example, the process of preparing for the next day's class is presented graphically. The obvious advantage of a graphic rather than narrative form is that the flow of events and their relationship are much more apparent. Regardless of your own priorities, the priority of exam over quiz over date over homework in this chart is immediately apparent. The iterative nature of exam study and the omission of new material when studying for a quiz are also readily apparent. The clarity of a flowchart leads to its more important function as a logic aid. The flowchart enables the programmer to graphically display the algorithm he is designing. This graphic display permits an easier and more effective grasp of the algorithm flow and, more important, of the errors in logic.

---

[3] Defined in footnote 1, Chapter 2.

[4] When the algorithm has been translated into a specific programming language we will call it a program.

Programming

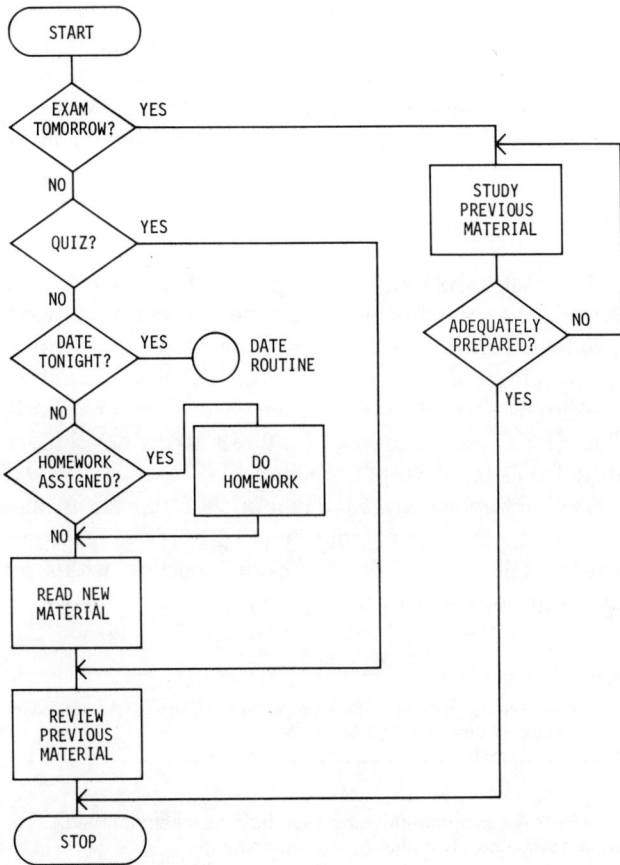

A second function of the flowchart is as documentation of the algorithm design. When a programmer must return to a program in order to check or modify an algorithm, the flowchart helps him refamiliarize himself with the algorithm logic. If a new programmer must take over an existing program, it is extremely difficult, sometimes nearly impossible, to accomplish this by examining the coded algorithm. So the flowchart, with its visual display and nonprogramming language descriptions, is an almost indispensible aid to the transfer of programs between programmers.

The use of the flowchart in program documentation has been enhanced by the development of automatic flow-charting programs. In its simplest form, automatic flowcharting takes the form of keypunching the type and descriptive contents of each block, and presenting this data as input to a program that simply arranges the blocks on a page with appropriate connectors and prints them. A significant advantage of even this basic approach is that additions and deletions to the chart can be made without extensive redrawing of the charts by the programmer. In a more advanced automatic flowcharting technique, the source program is used as input data to produce a corresponding flowchart. This, of course,

Figure 7.3 Class preparation flowchart.

86 Chapter Seven

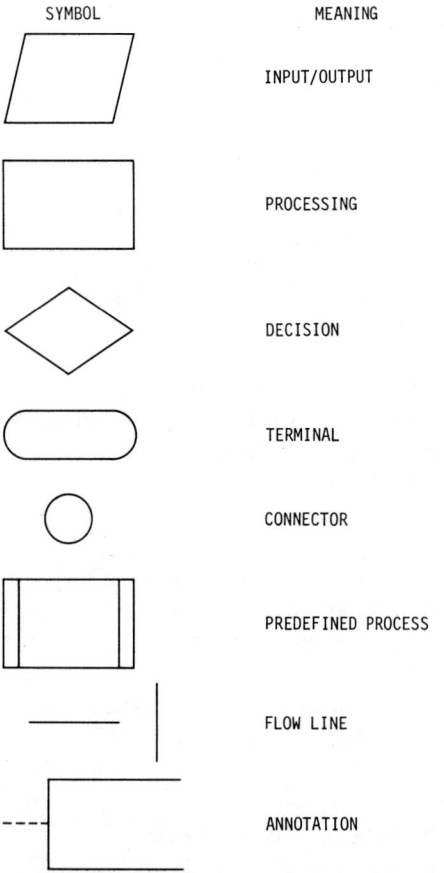

completely relieves the programmer of flowcharting chores, but it has the substantial disadvantage of presenting the descriptive content of each block in the programming language. A programmer unfamiliar with the source language would have difficulty reading the flowchart, and its communicative ability is thus greatly reduced.

Flowchart Symbols The *input/output symbol* (Figure 7.5) indicates any function of an input or output device.[5] Reading from a device to high-speed storage, writing from high-speed storage to a device, as well as specialized operations such as rewinding magnetic tape or seeking (locating a specific address) on direct access devices, are included as input/output functions.

The *processing symbol* (Figure 7.6) represents any operation other than input/output, decision, or termination. The bulk of the processing function within an algorithm is represented by this symbol.

---

[5] This includes the input and output operations of the secondary storage devices discussed in Chapter 5.

Figure 7.4 Program flowchart symbols, as recommended by the American National Standards Institute.

Programming

Figure 7.5 Input/output symbols.

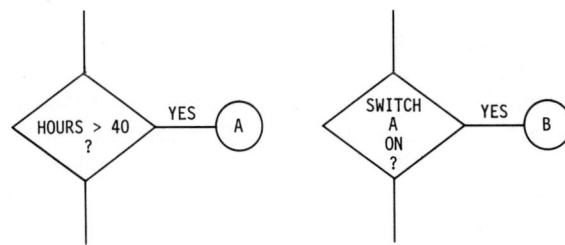

Figure 7.7 Decision symbols.

The *decision symbol* (Figure 7.7) indicates a choice between alternative paths based on the examination of a specific criterion. This criterion may be the result of a comparison of two values or the existence of some status or condition.

The *terminal symbol* (Figure 7.8) simply indicates starting and stopping points within an algorithm.

The *connector symbol* denotes entry points and exit directions within the flowchart. The use of this symbol for an exit indicates that the flow of processing terminates at this particular point of this flowchart leg but will resume at the entry point specified within the connector. The

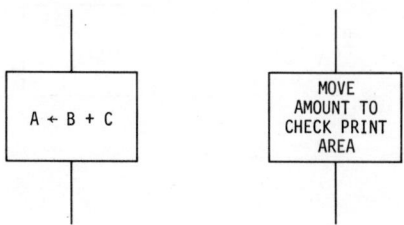

Figure 7.6 Processing symbols.

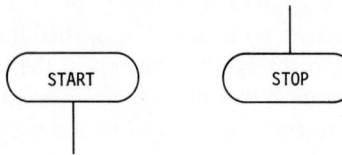

Figure 7.8 Terminal symbols.

entry point connector simply indicates a junction or a point in the flowchart at which one or more lines of flow connect. The entry connector is placed on the *flow line symbol*. In most cases, the nature of the processing within the flowchart makes the distinction between entry and exit points obvious. However, as the symbol itself does not distinguish between these functions, it may be necessary to add arrows or pointers to the chart to avoid ambiguity. In Figure 7.9 for example, it should be obvious that the connector between block two and block three is an entry point, while the connector on the "no" leg of the decision block is an exit point. This could be clarified, however, by simply adding a direction indicator at the end of the "no" leg.

The *predefined process symbol* (Figure 7.10) indicates a set of operations, not defined on this flowchart, constituting a subalgorithm.

The *annotation symbol* (Figure 7.11) provides the means for adding explanatory notes to the flowchart. The symbol may be connected to any point in the flowchart from any direction by means of a dashed line.

In addition to the symbol meanings, there is a widely accepted convention that flow moves from top to bottom and from left to right, unless arrows are used to indicate otherwise. An important question in the drawing of a flowchart concerns the amount of detail in the chart. How explicitly should individual operations in the algorithm

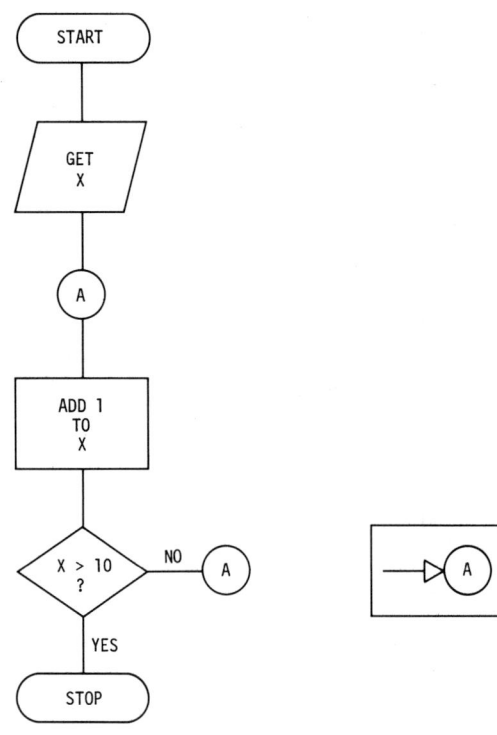

Figure 7.9 Connector symbols.

Programming

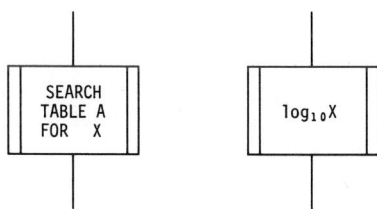

Figure 7.10 Predefined process symbols.

be shown on the chart? In answering this question it is useful to examine the possible extremes of detail. In Figure 7.12, the calculation of net pay is encompassed by a single block in one instance, while in the other instance virtually every distinct step would be shown. In the latter case, 20 or 30 or more blocks might be used. Which, then, is the better approach? The answer depends on who will be using the flowchart. The flowchart is both an aid to logic and a means of documentation, but in both cases it is a communication device. The flowchart must convey the structure and nature of the algorithm, both to its designer and to future readers. The amount of detail must insure this communication. If, for example, it can be assumed that all individuals dealing with this chart will be acquainted with the details of calculating net pay, then there is no need to elaborate the process. If not, the process must be specified in detail.

The block notation must also contribute to communication. As we noted earlier, the notation should be programming language-independent. The explanation within each block should be concise but as near to the normal terms of communication within an application area as possible. A relevant question concerning the flowchart might be: Can this flowchart be understood by someone conversant with the application area but having only a basic computer orientation?

A final convention must be noted concerning the use of the arrow as an *assignment*, or *replacement*, *operator*. In computer program operations it is frequently necessary to alter the contents of a location (to alter the value of a

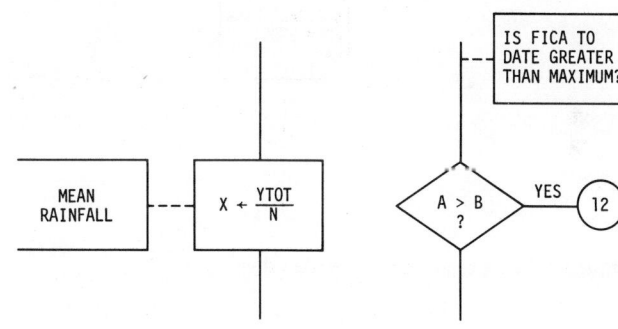

Figure 7.11 Annotation symbols.

90 Chapter Seven

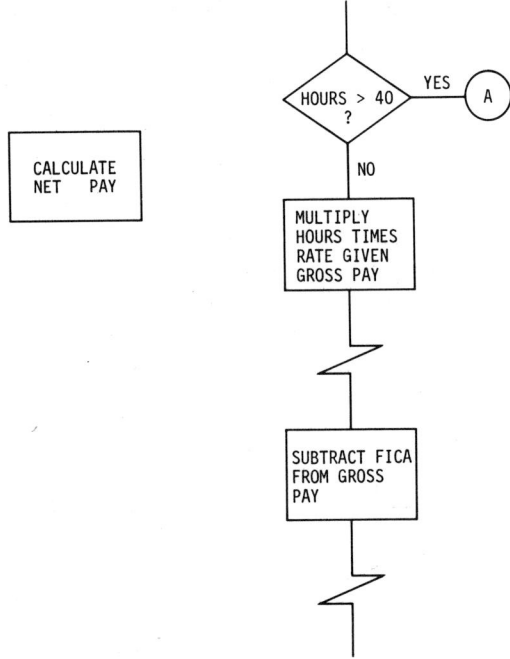

Figure 7.12 Examples of flowchart detail.

variable). This alteration may be the establishment of an initial value for this variable or a current calculated value. In either case, an arrow pointing from right to left ($\leftarrow$) is used to indicate this operation. The variable to the left of the arrow is the variable to be altered, and its current value is always destroyed and replaced by the value represented to the right of the arrow. The values to the right of the arrow are not destroyed. Thus in the statement $X \leftarrow Y + Z$, the value of Y and the value of Z are added and the sum is placed in X, destroying its previous value. The value of Y and the value of Z would remain the same. The statement $X \leftarrow 7$ would result in a value of 7 being assigned to the variable X.

A Flowcharting Example The flowchart in Figure 7.13 deals with a file in which each card contains a single student's identification and the examination score made by the student. There is an indeterminate number of cards in the file, so the algorithm must be constructed to be capable of processing a volume of cards that will vary in number with each process.

The programmer must design an algorithm that will determine the average and the highest score made on the examination. He might begin the process of algorithm design with a rough sequence of events as we suggested earlier. He might, for example, decide that the algorithm must contain the general sequence:

Programming

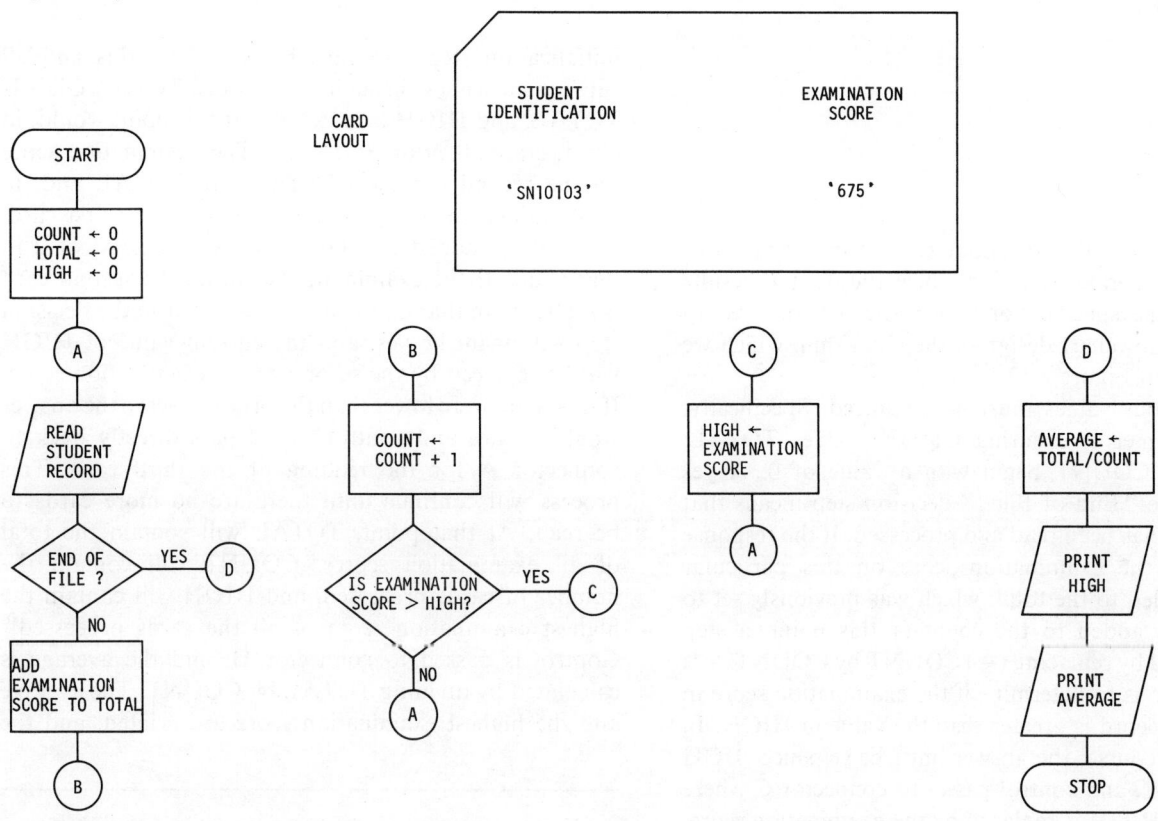

Figure 7.13 A flowchart of an algorithm for determining the average score made on an examination and the highest score made on the examination.

1. initialize
2. read
3. develop total
4. find high grade
5. find average

If, on evaluation, the programmer determines that this sequence of operations will produce the desired results and satisfy the specifications given, he will proceed to the detailed flowchart design of the algorithm, which we have shown in Figure 7.13.

First, various values must be initialized. Specifically, the programmer is ensuring that the values TOTAL, HIGH, and COUNT begin with a value of 0. A yes answer at the "End of File?" decision step means that the last card has been read and processed. If the response is negative, the examination score on this particular record is added to the total, which was previously set to zero. A 1 is added to the count at this point, a step accomplished by replacing ($\leftarrow$) COUNT by COUNT + 1. The next step is to determine if the examination score in the current record is greater than the value in HIGH. In this case, of course, the answer must be yes since HIGH contains zeros, and control passes to connector C where the value in HIGH is replaced by the examination score. At this point control returns to connector A and the process repeats with the reading of the next card. The initialization steps are thus by-passed on this and all subsequent passes through the process. To set COUNT, TOTAL, and HIGH back to zero at this point would, in effect, erase all prior processing. The examination score on the second card will be added to TOTAL and, in effect, added to the examination score of the first card. A 1 will be added to COUNT making a total of 2 in that value. If the examination score on the second card is higher than that on the first, the answer in the decision step will again be yes, and the current value of HIGH will be replaced by the second card's examination score. If this score were lower than the previous score the answer would be no, and control would pass directly back to connector A for the reading of the third card. This process will continue until there are no more cards to be read. At that point, TOTAL will contain the total of all examination scores, COUNT will contain the number of cards processed, and HIGH will contain the highest examination score of all the cards processed.[6] Control is passed to connector D, and the average is calculated by dividing TOTAL by COUNT. The average and the highest examination score are printed, and the

---

[6] If there are several equally high examination scores, the first of these will be retained in HIGH, although this makes no difference since the algorithm does not retain the identification of the students who made the highest examination scores.

process is terminated. It is not possible for the process to continue from this point. If more records had to be processed it would be necessary to completely restart the process, beginning at the START block.

Looping   Looping is a particularly important programming technique. It is the repeated, controlled execution of a sequence of operations. A loop will be terminated by the program when some predetermined condition occurs. The predetermined condition may be completion of a particular number of iterations of the loop, or it may be the occurrence of an event such as the matching of an element in a table of values.

In its most useful applications, the loop will deal with a large number of values stored in a corresponding number of locations. A loop might be constructed to add 100 values stored in 100 consecutive locations in high-speed storage. The loop will accomplish this addition with one add operation together with the other portions of the loop structure, while a routine designed to add these values without looping would require 100 add operations. This ability to use one command that deals with multiple high-speed storage locations requires specific hardware or software capabilities. A common hardware feature that provides this capability is *indexing*.

In brief, indexing uses special registers whose contents can be added to the original address of a command to form a new *effective address*. To change the address one simply changes the contents of the index register. We will note variable addresses with the use of a subscript value. A variable name followed by a subscript I, that is, (I), indicates an effective address, regardless of the hardware or software capabilities necessary to create this address.

Figure 7.14 is a flowchart of an algorithm using a loop that will add 100 consecutive values. In the second block of this diagram, the value known as TOTAL and the value known as I are initialized with values of 0 and 1, respectively. In the next block, the value of VALUE subscripted by I is added to the total. Since I is equal to 1, the first value will be added to the total. At this point we ask if I is equal to 100, for if it were, all 100 values would have been added to TOTAL and we could simply print this value and then terminate the algorithm. If the answer is no, I is then increased by one and control is returned to connector A for an additional iteration of the loop. As the reader can see, this iteration will involve the addition of the second value to the total. Subsequent iterations will cause the addition of the third through the hundredth values to the total.

The importance of the looping technique in programming is twofold. First, it conserves the programmer's time. Instead of writing 100 add operations in the last example the programmer was able to accomplish the

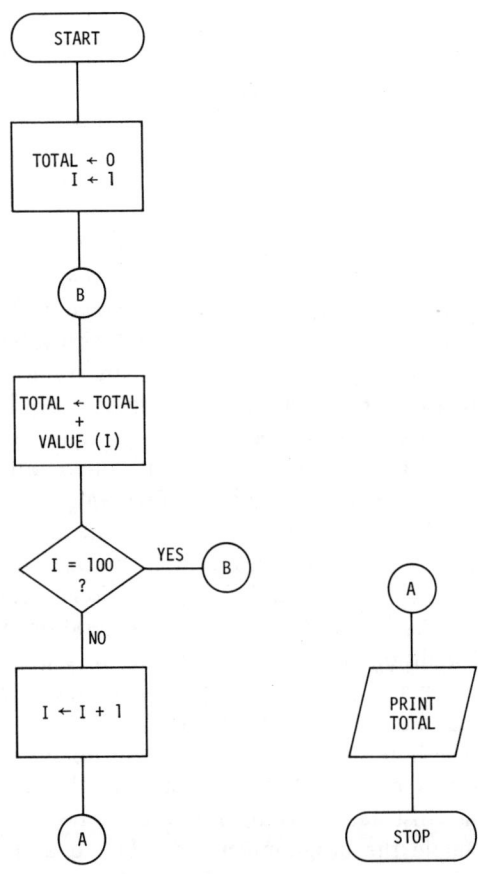

same result in three steps, although admittedly these three steps may require more than three executable commands in some programming languages. Second, the space required to store this program in high-speed storage is a fraction of the space which would be required to store the nonlooped version. Looping has a disadvantage, however, and this is the increase in algorithm execution time necessary to count iterations of the loop and test this count. Nevertheless, the balance is substantially in favor of using loops.

7.4 Machine-Level Programming Language

In our earlier discussion, we identified machine languages as languages whose instructions were subject to direct interpretation by the circuitry of the computer involved. This level of language is, in fact, the only one that can be directly interpreted by the computer. The two distinguishing features of a machine-language instruction are, first, the specification of its operation by a cryptic code rather than a more meaningful symbol

Figure 7.14 An algorithm for the addition of 100 values.

and, second, its use of actual machine high-speed storage addresses rather than symbolic addresses.

In general, the format of a machine-language instruction consists of an operation code and one or more operands. The operation code, which may be alphabetic or numeric, and which may be represented in the octal or hexadecimal number system, indicates precisely what must be done. Typically, these operations fall into the general categories of input/output, arithmetic, data transfer, logic, and control. The operand, which indicates either the object of the operation or a resource to be used in the performance of the operation, may take the form of:

1. an address in high-speed storage,[7]
2. a *literal*, which is the actual value or data to be operated on,
3. a specific unit of the hardware system.

Actual machine languages tend to be complex. To illustrate the concepts associated with machine languages without the attendant complexities of an actual machine language, we will use a language defined for an oversimplified artificial computer.

Our artificial computer contains 100 high-speed storage locations (words), with each word composed of four characters. The arithmetic and logic unit contains a four-character *accumulator*, which is a register devoted to data movement as well as addition and subtraction operations. The hardware system includes a card reader and a printer.

The instruction set or machine language, which we will call *ACL* (Artificial Computer Language),[8] is presented in Table 7.1. Rather than explaining each instruction, we will examine the entire instruction set within the context of an example problem.

The first five four-digit fields on an inventory card contain: (1) the inventory item number, (2) the quantity on hand in warehouse A, (3) the quantity on hand in warehouse B, (4) the quantity on order, and (5) the reorder point (the quantity level at which the item must be reordered). This card is illustrated in Figure 7.15. The number of individual records will vary from process to process, and thus for the purpose of writing the program the number of records in the input file must be considered indeterminate.

---

[7] On some hardware systems, the address may be that of a register rather than of a location in high-speed storage. The effect is basically the same.

[8] The basic idea for ACL is drawn from SNAIL (Student Non-Assembly Instructional Language), developed by Professor Gordon C. Howell at Georgia State University.

Figure 7.15 Example problem input card.

Table 7.1 ACL Instruction Set.

Operation Code	Operand	Description
1	aaa	Read a card and store the card data in twenty locations beginning with the address specified in the operand.
2	aaa	Load the accumulator with the contents of address specified in the operand.
3	aaa	Subtract the contents of the address specified in the operand from the accumulator.
4	aaa	Add the contents of the address specified in the operand to the accumulator.
5	aaa	Store the contents of the accumulator at the address specified in the operand.
6	aaa	Print the contents of the address specified in the operand.
7	aaa	Transfer control to the address specified in the operand.
8	aaa	If the contents of the accumulator is positive, transfer control to the address specified in the operand, otherwise control passes to the next command.
9		Stop

Our problem here is to draw a flowchart and write a program in ACL to print the inventory item number for all items in the file whose total of quantities on hand in both warehouses, plus the quantity on order, is less than or equal to the reorder point. The problem requires little analysis. Each record or card will simply be read in its turn, its values summed, and the relation of the sum to the reorder point determined. It is important to note that the indeterminate number of records in the input file, together with the restricted storage capacity, precludes the reading of all records into high-speed storage before processing. Figure 7.16 presents the flowchart for this program, and the corresponding ACL program is shown in Figure 7.17. The program is already located in high-speed storage, specifically, in locations 020 through 032. In practice, the program would have to be loaded into high-speed storage, usually by another program. Information can also be placed in memory using external switches or keyboards and, for our purposes, it will be sufficient to assume that the program was actually loaded in this fashion.

The first instruction to be executed is located in high-speed storage location 020. This instruction causes all 80 characters of information on the first card to be transferred to locations 040–059 (20 locations × 4 characters per location = 80). Thus, the item number will now be found in location 040, the quantity on hand in warehouse A (QOHA) in location 041, the quantity on hand in warehouse B (QOHB) in location 042, the quantity on order (QOO) in location 043, and the reorder point (ROP) in location 044. The remaining 15 locations (045–059) are blank, since the remaining 60 columns on the card were blank.

98 Chapter Seven

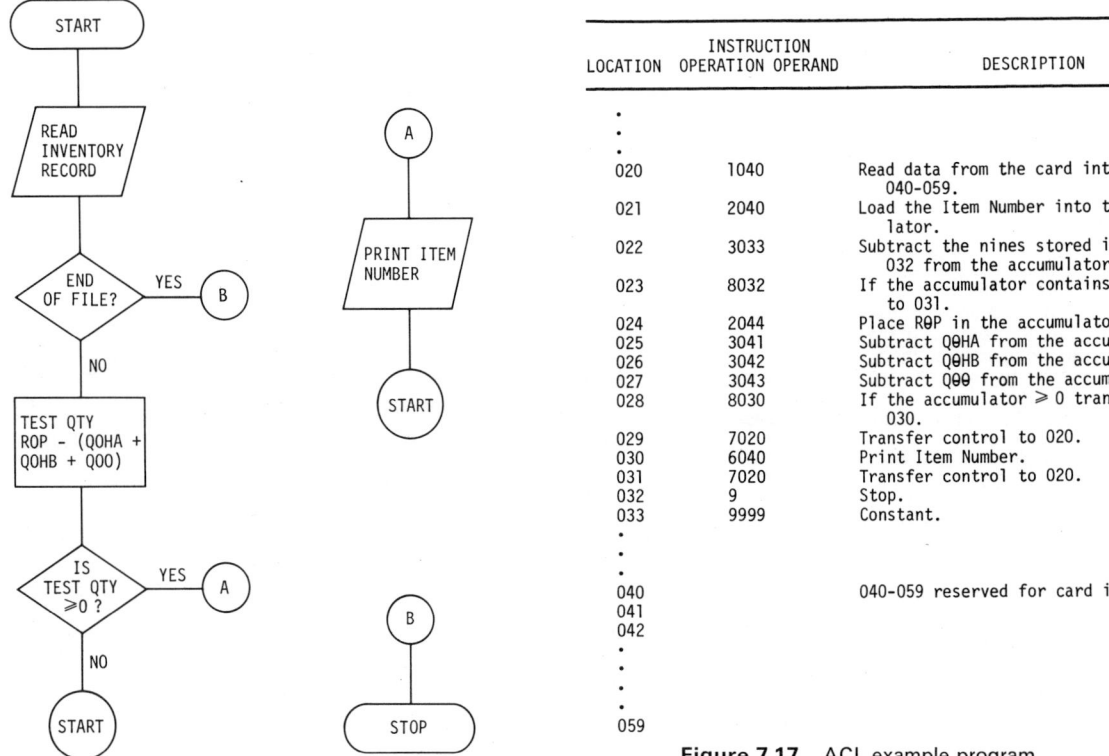

Figure 7.16 Example problem flowchart—an algorithm for checking inventory on hand and on order against reorder point.

LOCATION	INSTRUCTION OPERATION OPERAND	DESCRIPTION
⋮		
020	1040	Read data from the card into locations 040-059.
021	2040	Load the Item Number into the accumulator.
022	3033	Subtract the nines stored in location 032 from the accumulator.
023	8032	If the accumulator contains 0 transfer to 031.
024	2044	Place ROP in the accumulator.
025	3041	Subtract QOHA from the accumulator.
026	3042	Subtract QOHB from the accumulator.
027	3043	Subtract QOO from the accumulator.
028	8030	If the accumulator ≥ 0 transfer to 030.
029	7020	Transfer control to 020.
030	6040	Print Item Number.
031	7020	Transfer control to 020.
032	9	Stop.
033	9999	Constant.
⋮		
040		040-059 reserved for card input.
041		
042		
⋮		
059		

Figure 7.17 ACL example program.

The next instruction loads the accumulator with the contents of location 040, which is the item number. The next command causes a constant of 9999, which has been stored at location 033, to be subtracted from the item number. If the result is negative (9999 is greater than the item number) then control will pass through the next command to location 024. If the result is zero or positive then control will be transferred to location 032, meaning simply that the next instruction to be executed will be drawn from location 032. This type of command is described as a *conditional transfer* command. The constant 9999 is a *sentinel*. The operator will place a card with item number 9999 immediately following the last valid data card in the card deck. When this card is read, the subtraction in location 022 will produce a 0 in the accumulator and a transfer to 032. The only requirement of such a sentinel is that its value must never legitimately occur in the data.

In this artificial computer all arithmetic is performed in the accumulator, and thus the first step in any arithmetic operation must be the loading of this device. Therefore, the next instruction loads the reorder point into the accumulator. The next three instructions (in locations 025, 026, and 027) subtract QOHA, QOHB, and QOO from the accumulator, leaving the value named 'TEST QTY' in the flowchart. Location 028 contains another conditional transfer instruction. If the contents of the accumulator are greater than or equal to zero then control is transferred to location 030, where the item number is to be printed. (If after subtracting QOHA, QOHB, and QOO we still have a positive value in the accumulator, then the sum of those three values is below the reorder point and the item number must be printed.) If the value in the accumulator is negative, then the total of on-hand plus on-order must be greater than the reorder point. So, control is passed to location 029, which has an *unconditional transfer* of control to location 020, where the next card is read. The transfer is unconditional, in that each time control passes to location 029 it will subsequently pass to location 020 automatically. In location 030, the item number is printed and control passes to location 031, where there is another unconditional transfer back to location 020. When the last card has been processed, the condition for the transfer in location 023 will be met, and control will pass to location 032, where operation is halted.

Several observations must be made at this point. First, the choice of storage locations is arbitrary. As long as the instructions are placed so that control may flow from one directly into another, it makes no difference where within high-speed storage they are placed. Furthermore, the contents of locations other than those containing the program or its data are irrelevant to the program operation. We simply do not care what is contained in locations 001–019, 034–039, or 060–100 in the above example. Finally, the key point is the flow of control. When control flows from instruction to instruction there is no problem, but if through error control passes to a location in which there is no instruction, the computer will attempt to execute the contents of that location, regardless of its nature. Depending on the computer and the circumstances, this will result in a halt on an error condition, or worse.

7.5 Assembly-Level Programming Language

As we noted earlier, the two most significant features of assembly-level programming languages are the use of mnemonic operation codes and the use of symbolic addresses. The first feature makes the program more easily readable, and the second relieves the programmer of keeping track of the actual addresses within his program.

To illustrate assembly language programming, we will code the algorithm that was flowcharted in Figure 7.13 into System 360 Assembly Language. This program is shown in Figure 7.18. Deferring the discussion of input

Figure 7.18 360/assembly language example program.

Card Columns → 1	10	16
CARD	DTFCD	BLKSIZE = 80,
		DEVADDR = SYSRDER,
		DEVICE = 1442
		IORAEI = CARDIN
		RECFORM = FIXUNB
		TYPEFLE = INPUT
		EOFADDR = END
PRINTER	DTFPR	BLKSIZE = 132,
		DEVADDR = SYSLST
		DEVICE = 1443,
		IOAREAI = PRINTOUT
		RECFORM = FIXUNB
	OPEN	CARD, PRINTER
READ	GET	CARD
	PACK	EXAMP, EXAM
	AP	TOTAL, EXAMP
	AP	COUNT, ONE
	CP	EXAMP, HIGH
	BH	STHGH
	B	READ
STHGH	MVC	HIGH, EXAMP
	B	READ
END	DP	TOTAL, COUNT
	UNPK	HGH, HIGH
	UNPK	AVGE, TOTAL
	PUT	PRINTER, PRINTOUT
	CLOSE	CARD, PRINTER
	EOJ	
EXAMP	DS	PL2
TOTAL	DC	PL4'0'
COUNT	DC	PL2'0'
ONE	DC	PL1'1'
HIGH	DC	PL2'0'
CARDIN	DS	OCL80
ID	DS	CL7
EXAM	DS	CL3
PRINTOUT	DS	OCL132
	DC	CL10' '
HGH	DS	CL3
	DC	CL10' '
AVGE	DS	CL4
	DC	CL105' '

operations for the moment, we begin our discussion with the command immediately below PACK EXAMP, EXAM. (Note that values for the variables ID and EXAM will have been input during the preceding operations.)

The command AP TOTAL, EXAMP results in the addition of the contents of the area identified as EXAMP to the contents of TOTAL, which is defined by a define constant (DC) operation to be a packed field of length 4 (PL4), which initially contains zero ('0'). The next command results in the addition of a field identified as ONE, which is defined by a DC operation as a constant of one, to a field called COUNT, which is defined as a constant of length 2 initialized with zeros. Following this, the contents of EXAMP are compared to the contents of a location defined by a PL as a two-character constant known as HIGH and initialized with zeros. In the next command, the result of this comparison is tested by a branch high (BH). If the result of the comparison is the setting of a high condition code, then control is transferred to the command labeled STHGH. Otherwise control is transferred to READ, where the next record is read. At STHGH, the contents of EXAMP are copied into HIGH by the MVC or move character command, and again a branch (B) is made to READ.

Input and output operations include a wide array of different activities. The detection and handling of error conditions, file labeling, the handling of end-of-file conditions, and provision for multiple file organizations are some input and output operations. The full range of these activities confronts the programmer with a rather complex problem. To simplify the programming of these activities a program known as the input/output control system (IOCS) is provided. IOCS takes over many of the activities that would otherwise have to be programmed. To perform these activities, IOCS must have certain information concerning the files to be processed, and this is provided by file definition entries such as CARD and PRINTER in our example problem. These file definitions provide information such as the size of the block to be processed, the device on which the file resides, its address, the associated storage area address, and the address of the end of file routine. With this information provided, the programmer simply must specify GET and the name of the file that contains the next record. In our example program we begin processing with an OPEN statement, which prepares the input and output equipment (specifically the card reader and printer) for use. In the next statement we GET or read a card from the file identified and defined as CARD. The information from this card is made available in an area defined by the lines labeled CARDIN, ID, and EXAM below. The statements on these lines are known as declaratives and are used to define areas of storage. The line labeled

CARDIN is a Define Storage Declarative. It states that CARDIN refers to an area of storage containing bytes or characters (c), and the length of this area is 80 bytes (L80). The zero indicates that this field is to be redefined. This redefinition is accomplished by the two DS entries which immediately follow and define character fields of length 7 (ID) and 3 (EXAM). This redefinition permits any one of the three labels CARDIN, ID, or EXAM to be used when referring to this input record.

At end-of-file, control is transferred to END—this is specified in the DTFCD entries by the EOFADDR = END entry. The value in TOTAL is divided (DP) by the value in COUNT and the quotient is left in TOTAL. HIGH and TOTAL are unpacked and moved to the areas HGH and AVGE, which are a part of a redefinition of the 132-character area called PRINTOUT. PRINTOUT is written on the file called PRINTER, and then both the input and the output are closed, which simply terminates the use of the equipment.

7.6 A FORTRAN Problem

Figure 7.19 presents the flowchart solution to the problem of finding the mean of a set of values when one value is punched on each card and the total number of incoming cards is specified on the first card. The algorithm begins by setting two values, SUMX and CT, equal to zero. The first card to be read specifies the number of data cards that follow, and this becomes a limit to the operations of the program. In the next step, the first data card is read and the value of X is added to the value of SUMX. The value of CT is set equal to itself plus one. The next step is to determine if all of the incoming data cards have been processed—if we have reached the limit. If the count CT is not equal to the limit, control returns to the read step to continue the process. The reader should note that on each successive iteration of these blocks the incoming value of X will be added to the total, which is the sum of all the previous values of X. Likewise, the count will equal the total number of cards (X values) which have been read. When the count finally reaches the limit, the decision block allows control to pass through the block rather than returning to connector 1. The mean is calculated by dividing the sum of the X values by the count of the X values, the mean is printed, and the algorithm is terminated.

The FORTRAN program written from this flowchart is shown in Figure 7.20. The first line, 100 FORMAT (I3), is a nonexecutable command that describes the

Programming

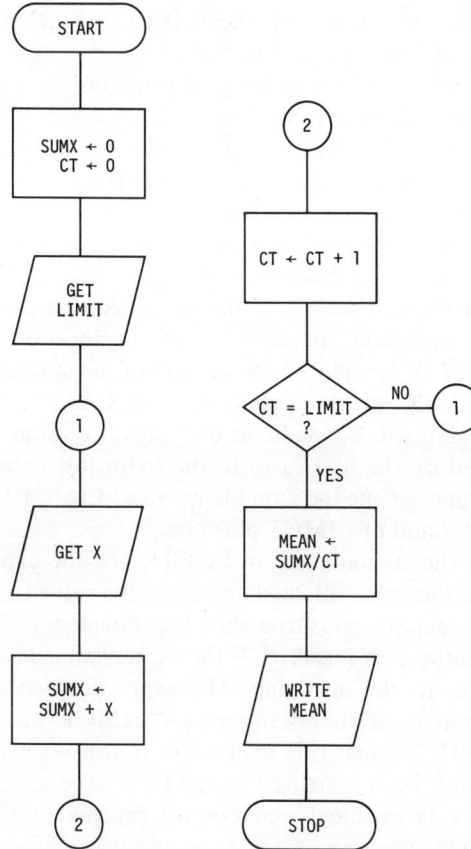

```
CARD
COLUMNS  1 2 3 4 5 6 7
             1 0 0    FORMAT (I3)
             1 0 1    FORMAT (F4.0)
             1 1 0    FORMAT (1H1, 6X, 'MEAN', 3X, F6.1)
                      SUMX = 0
                      LIMCT = 0
                      READ (5,100) LIMIT
             1        READ (5,101) X
                      SUMX = SUMX + X
                      LIMCT = LIMCT + 1
                      IF (LIMCT.NE.LIMIT) GO TO 1
                      CT = LIMCT
                      XMEAN = SUMX/CT
                      WRITE (6,110) XMEAN
                      STOP
                      END
```

Figure 7.20 FORTRAN example program.

input card to be used during the compilation of the program. In this case, 100 is a statement number identifying this particular FORMAT, while (I3) specifies that the first three positions of the record that is read according to this format will be a three-digit integer. The second FORMAT (101) provides for a four-digit number that will normally be a whole number on input but might also carry a fraction. The FORMAT identified by statement

Figure 7.19 FORTRAN example problem flowchart of an algorithm for finding the mean of a set of values when the number of values is specified by the first value read.

110 specifies that the literal 'MEAN', preceded by six spaces and followed by three, will be written followed by a six-digit number with one decimal place. The 6 in F6.1 actually indicates the total number of positions that will be occupied by the number (including the decimal point and a position reserved for a negative sign in some cases). Thus the number printed might look like *nnnn.n*. The specification of 1H in 1H1 means that a one-character Hollerith, or literal, string will immediately follow the H and should be included as is in the overall character string that is being established. The one character, in this case 1, takes the first position in the string that is being created. The string will eventually be printed, and the first character in the string, called the *carriage control character*, controls the carriage of the printer, in particular the vertical movement or spacing of the paper. A carriage control character of 1 causes the paper to advance to the top of the next page, before printing the line.

The first executable statement in the program is SUMX=0. The equal sign in FORTRAN is equivalent to the replacement operator ←, which we discussed in flowcharting, and is better read as "is set equal to" or "is replaced by." The equals operator thus indicates a necessary action rather than an equivalence. The statement gives the value known as SUMX a value of 0. The value known as LIMCT will contain 0 after execution of the next statement. Next, the value LIMIT is read from the first card. The 5 in the parentheses indicates that the READ is to be performed on the card reader rather than some other device. The 100 indicates that the record to be read will be in the format specified in FORMAT statement 100. The effect of READ (5,100) LIMIT will be to assign to the variable LIMIT the three-digit value taken from the first three columns of the first card. The statement numbered 1 reads the value X from the first four columns of subsequent cards. In the next statement the contents of the location identified as SUMX is replaced by the sum of the current contents of SUMX plus the current value of X. For the first card, this sum will be made up of 0 plus the value of X contained on the first card. In the following statement, the contents of the location identified as LIMCT is replaced by the sum of LIMCT plus one.

In the IF statement in FORTRAN, the expression in parentheses is evaluated and given the value true or false. If the expression is true, then the statement following the parentheses is executed. If the expression is false, control passes to the next line. The expression within the IF statement in the example is "LIMCT not equal to LIMIT." When this expression is true—when LIMCT has not been increased to the limit—the statement GO TO 1 is executed and control returns to the second READ statement. GO TO is an unconditional transfer by itself, but the entire IF statement functions as a conditional transfer. When LIMCT finally does become equal to LIMIT control passes to the statement CT= LIMCT. In the next statement, we want to divide the sum by the count but SUMX carries a fraction while LIMCT does not, and FORTRAN requires that the variables within an expression be consistent with regard to the presence of a fractional part. (According to the syntax of FORTRAN, a variable whose name begins with I, J, K, L, M, or N will not carry a fraction and all other variables will.) So, we take the value in LIMCT and place it in CT, thus converting it to fractional form.

The character / (stroke) specifies the divide operation in FORTRAN, so the statement XMEAN=SUMX/CT places the quotient of the division of SUMX by CT in the location XMEAN. Since XMEAN does not occur on the right side of the equal sign, there was no need to initialize XMEAN before the calculation. In the next statement the 6 inside the parentheses specifies that the printer is the unit to be written on, and the 110 indicates the FORMAT statement to be referenced. Thus WRITE (6,10) XMEAN specifies that the value XMEAN is to be printed according to the format specified in FORMAT 110. The value of XMEAN will be printed in the location specified as F6.1 and the printed line will appear at the top of a page as 'MEAN *nnnn.n*'. The program then terminates.

7.7 A COBOL Problem

Figure 7.21 shows the flowchart for an algorithm whose basic function is the calculation of gross pay. The problem is to read a file containing an indeterminate number of cards, which are punched according to the format shown in Figure 7.22, calculate gross pay, and print the results as shown in Figure 7.23. The calculation of gross pay includes paying time and one-half for all hours in excess of 40 for the pay period. In addition, only 50 lines are to be printed on each page, and the headings shown in Figure 7.23 are to be printed at the top of each page.

The first step in the algorithm is to initialize the total hours and the total gross pay at zero. In COBOL, this operation does not require a processing step but rather is a function of data definition. Nevertheless, in accordance with our policy of making our flowcharts language-independent, and for the sake of completeness, we have included it here. In the next step, the headings are printed at the top of the first page and a count of the lines of detailed information printed is set to zero.

Then, a transaction or card record is read and tested to determine if all the records in the file have previously been read (end-of-file). If end-of-file has not been reached, the hours punched in the card are compared against 40. If the hours are not greater than 40, then no overtime calculation is required and control is passed to

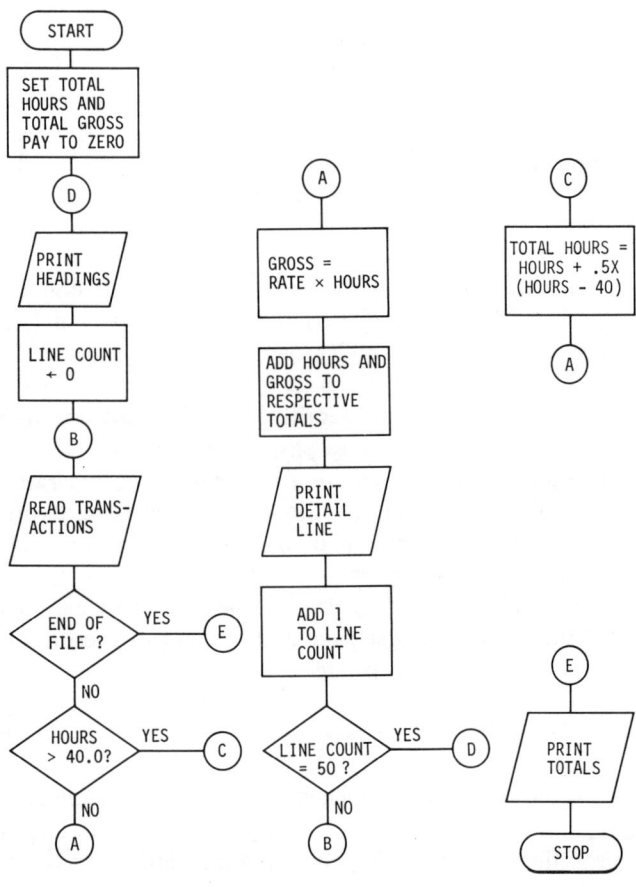

the next block, where gross is calculated to be the product of rate and hours. If the hours had been greater than 40, control would have been passed to connector C where one-half of the hours in excess of 40 would have been added to the total hours. (If an employee has worked 60 hours, and is due time and a half for the last 20 hours then we can accomplish this by adding one-half of the hours in excess of 40 to the total, thus paying the employee for 70 hours.) After the hours have been increased to allow for overtime, control returns to connector A and normal processing continues. The calculated gross pay is added to a total of gross pay and the hours for this transaction to a total of hours. The line of detailed information is printed, and 1 is added to the line count, which is then tested to see if 50 lines have been printed on this page. If so, control is passed to connector D, where headings are printed before the next card is read; if not, control is passed directly to connector B where the next card is read. When the end-of-file is reached, control passes to connector E, where the totals are printed and the flowchart terminates.

A COBOL program is broken into four basic divisions—the Identification Division, the Environment Division, the Data Division, and the Procedure Division. The

Figure 7.21 COBOL example problem flowchart.

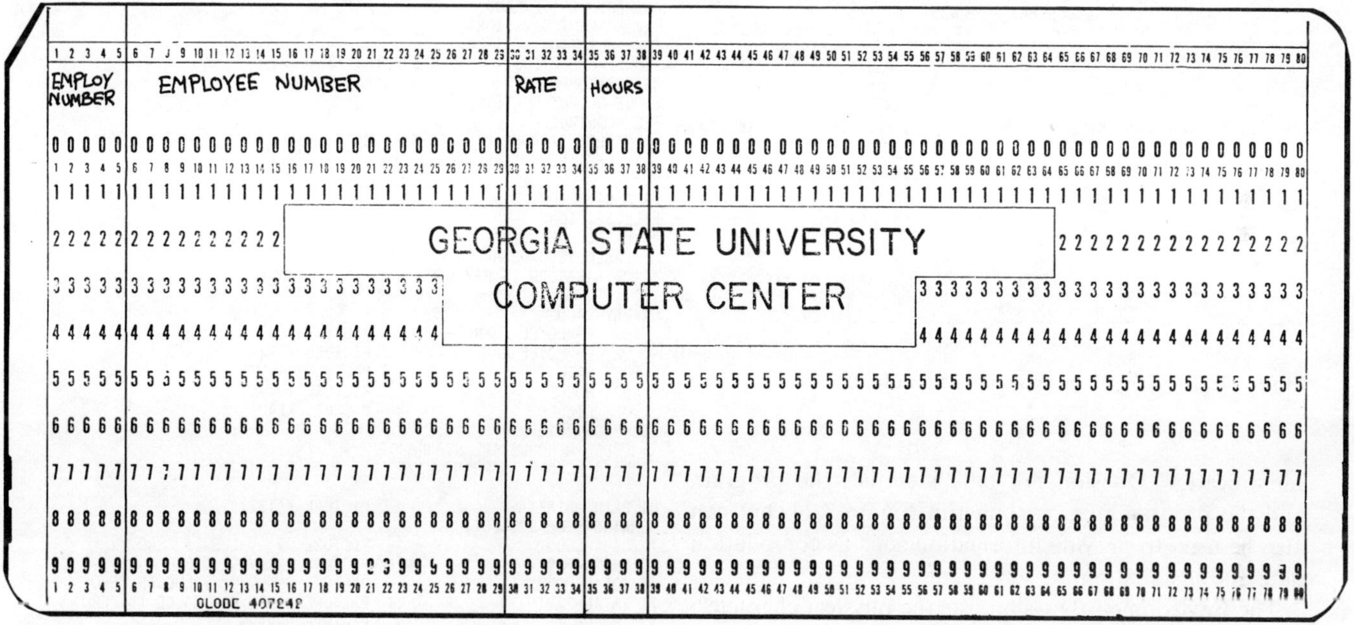

Figure 7.22 COBOL example problem input card.

```
------------------------------------
         GROSS PAY SUMMARY

     EMPLOYEE                HOURS      GROSS
NUMBER      NAME      RATE   WORKED     PAY

10711    Allen, H. S.  2.700  60.0      189.00

10799    Arnold, M. N. 1.850

10834    Bates, I. L.

10998

                TOTAL      XX,XXX.X   XXX,XXX.XX
------------------------------------
```

Figure 7.23 COBOL example problem output.

Identification Division not only identifies the program and the programmer, as shown in Figure 7.24, but can also be used to provide information such as compilation date and installation.

The Environment Division lists the physical characteristics of the computer systems to be used. The Configuration Section identifies both the system on which the program will be compiled (the source-computer) and the system on which it will be executed (the object-computer). The Input-Output Section relates the logical files to the physical devices that will deal with these files. In our example program, the file of pay cards, which is called

```
IDENTIFICATION DIVISION.
PROGRAM-ID.  'GROSS PAY'.
AUTHOR.  COTTERMAN.
ENVIRONMENT DIVISION.
CONFIGURATION SECTION.
SOURCE-COMPUTER.       RCA-SPECTRA 70-46G.
OBJECT-COMPUTER.       RCA-SPECTRA 70-46G.
INPUT-OUTPUT SECTION.
FILE-CONTROL.
    SELECT PAYROLL-FILE ASSIGN TO SYSIN.
    SELECT REPORT ASSIGN TO SYSOU.

DATA DIVISION.
FILE SECTION.
FD PAYROLL-FILE.
    LABEL RECORDS ARE STANDARD
    DATA RECORD IS PAY-CARD.

01 PAY-CARD.
    02 EMPLOYEE-NUMBER      PICTURE 9(5).
    02 EMPLOYEE-NAME        PICTURE X(24).
    02 RATE                 PICTURE 99V999.
    02 HOURS                PICTURE 99V99.
    02 FILLER               PICTURE X(42).
FD REPORT-FILE.
    LABEL RECORDS ARE STANDARD
    DATA RECORD IS PRINT-LINE.

01 PRINT-LINE               PICTURE X(132).
WORKING-STORAGE SECTION.
77 LINE-COUNT               PICTURE 99, VALUE IS ZERO.
77 GROSS-PAY                PICTURE 9999V99.
77 TOTAL-HOURS              PICTURE 9999V99, VALUE IS ZERO.
77 TOTAL-PAY                PICTURE 99999V99, VALUE IS ZERO.
77 XHOURS                   PICTURE 999V99.

01 PAGE-HEADING.
    02 FILLER               PICTURE X(33), VALUE SPACES.
    02 FILLER               PICTURE X(17), VALUE 'GROSS PAY
                                SUMMARY'.
    02 FILLER               PICTURE X(82), VALUE SPACES.

01 COLUMN-HEADING-1.
    02 FILLER               PICTURE X(17), VALUE SPACES.
    02 FILLER               PICTURE X(8), VALUE 'EMPLOYEE'.
    02 FILLER               PICTURE X(34), VALUE SPACES.
```

```
        02  FILLER                  PICTURE X(19), VALUE
                                        'HOURSbbbbbbbbbGROSS'.
        02  FILLER                  PICTURE X(54), VALUE SPACES.
    01  COLUMN-HEADING-2.
        02  FILLER                  PICTURE X(7), VALUE SPACES.
        02  FILLER                  PICTURE X(6), VALUE 'NUMBER'.
        02  FILLER                  PICTURE X(14), VALUE SPACES.
        02  FILLER                  PICTURE X(4), VALUE 'NAME'.
        02  FILLER                  PICTURE X(17), VALUE SPACES.
        02  FILLER                  PICTURE X(28), VALUE
                                        'RATEbbbbbbWORKEDbbbbbbbbbbPAY'.
        02  FILLER                  PICTURE X(46), VALUE SPACES.
    01  DETAIL.
        02  FILLER                  PICTURE X(7), VALUE SPACES.
        02  NUMBER                  PICTURE 9(5).
        02  FILLER                  PICTURE X(5), VALUE SPACES.
        02  NAME                    PICTURE X(24).
        02  FILLER                  PICTURE X(6), VALUE SPACES.
        02  RATE                    PICTURE ZZ.999.
        02  FILLER                  PICTURE X(6), VALUE SPACES.
        02  HOURS                   PICTURE ZZ.99.
        02  FILLER                  PICTURE X(6), VALUE SPACES.
        02  GROSS                   PICTURE $$$9.99.
        02  FILLER                  PICTURE X(55), VALUE SPACES.
    01  TOTAL.
        02  FILLER                  PICTURE X(41), VALUE SPACES.
        02  FILLER                  PICTURE X(5), VALUE 'TOTAL'.
        02  HOURS                   PICTURE ZZZ9.99.
        02  FILLER                  PICTURE X(5), VALUE SPACES.
        02  PAY                     PICTURE $$$$9.99.
        02  FILLER                  PICTURE X(66), VALUE SPACES.
    PROCEDURE DIVISION.
    BEGIN.
        OPEN INPUT PAYROLL-FILE.
        OPEN OUTPUT REPORT.
    PRINT-HEADINGS.
        MOVE PAGE-HEADING TO PRINT-LINE.
        WRITE PRINT-LINE AFTER ADVANCING TOP-OF-PAGE LINES.
        MOVE COLUMN-HEADING-1 TO PRINT-LINE.
        WRITE PRINT-LINE AFTER ADVANCING 2 LINES.
        MOVE COLUMN-HEADING-2 TO PRINT-LINE.
        WRITE PRINT-LINE AFTER ADVANCING 1 LINES.
        MOVE ZERO TO LINE-COUNTER.
    PROCESS.
        READ PAYROLL-FILE RECORD AT END GO TO END-OF-FILE.
        IF HOURS IS GREATER THAN 40 GO TO CALCULATE-OVERTIME.
        MOVE HOURS TO XHOURS.
    CALCULATE.
        MULTIPLY XHOURS BY RATE
            GIVING GROSS-PAY ROUNDED.  ADD HOURS TO
            TOTAL-HOURS.  ADD GROSS TO TOTAL-PAY.
        MOVE EMPLOYEE-NUMBER TO NUMBER.
        MOVE EMPLOYEE-NAME TO NAME.
        MOVE RATE IN PAY-CARD TO RATE IN DETAIL.
        MOVE HOURS IN PAY-CARD TO HOURS IN DETAIL.
        MOVE GROSS-PAY TO GROSS.
        MOVE DETAIL TO PRINT-LINE.
        WRITE DETAIL AFTER ADVANCING 1 LINES.
        ADD 1 TO LINE-COUNTER.
        IF LINE-COUNTER IS EQUAL TO 50 GO TO PRINT-HEADINGS.
        GO TO PROCESS.
    CALCULATE-OVERTIME.
        COMPUTE XHOURS = HOURS + .5 * (HOURS - 40).
        GO TO CALCULATE.
    END-OF-FILE.
        MOVE TOTAL-HOURS TO HOURS IN TOTAL.
        MOVE TOTAL PAY TO PAY.
        MOVE TOTAL TO PRINT-LINE
        WRITE TOTAL AFTER ADVANCING 2 LINES
        CLOSE PAYROLL-FILE, REPORT.
        STOP RUN.
```

Figure 7.24 COBOL example program.

PAYROLL-FILE, is assigned to the card reader identified in the system as SYSIN. The report, which we have called REPORT, is assigned to the printer named SYSOU.

In the Data Division, the files and the layout of the records contained in these files are specified in detail. In our example, certain aspects of PAYROLL-FILE and REPORT-FILE are described under FD entries. The logical record PAY-CARD is described under the level 01 entry. It is shown to contain a five-digit numeric field [9(5)], which can be identified by the label EMPLOYEE-NUMBER. A field identified by the label EMPLOYEE-NAME consists of 24 alphanumeric (X) characters. RATE is a five-digit field made up of up to two whole numbers and three decimal positions, HOURS is a four-digit field of two whole numbers and two decimals, and the remainder of the record is described as FILLER or irrelevant to this program. So 01 describes the entire card illustrated in Figure 7.22. In the File Section the 01 level entry PRINT-LINE is described simply as consisting of 132 alphanumeric characters. In the Working-Storage Section below, however, detail is provided on five different lines to be printed. The first level 01 entry, for example, describes the page-heading line. Since no variable information is required in this line, and there is no other need to refer directly to its contents, it is called FILLER. Each field is given a PICTURE clause describing it as alphanumeric with a specific length. In addition, the contents of each field is specified by a VALUE clause. In the first filler, the value is specified as SPACES meaning that, when the line is printed, the first 33 characters will be spaces. The next 17 characters are given the value 'GROSS PAY SUMMARY', the exact characters that will be printed. The next two 01 level entries are constructed in the same fashion. The 01 level entries for DETAIL and TOTAL are somewhat different in that they contain a mixture of filler and label-identified fields. This means, in effect, that some of the material to be printed will have to be supplied before a meaningful line can be printed. If rate or hours contain less than two whole numbers, the Zs in their picture clauses will suppress, or prevent, the printing of zeros. The $s in the GROSS picture clause will cause a $ to appear immediately to the left of the first significant digit. In addition to the 01 level entries, the Working-Storage Section contains several 77 level entries which are used as work areas.

The Procedure Division contains the actual processing operations to be performed by the program. The first paragraph in our example is entitled BEGIN and consists of two OPEN statements (control statements that initiate the processing of files). The second paragraph prints the heading lines for the report illustrated in Figure 7.23. First, the heading line that was built under the 01 level entry labeled PAGE-HEADING is moved to the area described by the 01 level entry PRINT-LINE. This is printed after the paper has advanced to the top of the next page (AFTER ADVANCING TOP-OF-PAGE LINES). The second and third heading lines are printed after double-spacing and single-spacing respectively. In the paragraph labeled PROCESS the first pay card is read and if the hours are greater than 40, control is transferred to the paragraph labeled CALCULATE-OVERTIME. Otherwise, the hours worked are moved to a work area entitled XHOURS, which was set up in working storage. The first statement in the CALCULATE paragraph is executed next. Hours are multiplied by rate to give gross pay, and both hours and gross pay are added to their respective totals. Employee number, name, rate, hours, and gross pay are moved to the DETAIL print area, and this layout is moved to the print area and is printed. At this point a 1 is added to a work area entitled LINE-COUNTER, and this value is tested against the constant 50. If the counter is equal to 50, 50 detail lines have been printed and control is then transferred back to the paragraph entitled PRINT-HEADINGS, where the same three heading lines are printed at the top of the next page and the counter is reset to zero. If the counter is not equal to 50, then PRINT-HEADINGS is bypassed by a transfer of control to the paragraph labeled PROCESS. If hours are greater than 40, so that control is transferred to CALCULATE-OVERTIME, XHOURS is made equal to the total of all the hours plus an additional one-half of the excess over 40 hours. When end-of-file occurs, the READ statement transfers control to the END-OF-FILE paragraph, where the totals are printed, the files are closed, and the program is terminated.

In COBOL, the programmer is forced to give considerable time and attention to the nature and organization of the data. He devotes a considerable amount of time to a detailed description of individual input and output records. This is obviously not the case in FORTRAN, where the record is described in a highly compact FORMAT statement. This distinction between the two languages is essentially a function of their target application areas. In business applications data manipulation tends to be a major part of the computing task, but in scientific applications computation is much more important than data manipulation. Largely as a result of the detailed specification of data layouts, COBOL source programs tend to contain many more source statements than do FORTRAN programs. As a consequence, programmers who have been programming in FORTRAN or other relatively concise languages find COBOL wordy and somewhat tedious to write.

Many advantages arise from the use of FORTRAN, COBOL, or any procedure-oriented language. The most obvious advantage is the economy of operations. One

FORTRAN statement may generate dozens of machine-language operations. Not only does the programmer not have to write these operations but they are, in effect, predebugged and he does not have to investigate them during the debugging process. The programmer may usually safely assume that if he has written the FORTRAN statement correctly the machine-language instructions will be error-free.

In addition, a procedure-oriented language is easier to learn and easier to write. Because the language tends more toward the problem area than toward the machine, it is more readily grasped. Furthermore, the language format is much less restrictive than that of either machine or assembly-level languages. Finally, as we noted earlier, procedure-oriented languages are relatively free of hardware detail and are thus machine-independent.

Among the disadvantages of procedure-oriented languages is an increased time required to translate the program into a form that can be executed by the hardware system. Also, in some cases, it may not be possible to take full advantage of the power and capabilities of a particular hardware system. Finally, both high-speed storage usage and operating speed are less efficient compared with programs written in machine or assembly-level language. The extent of efficiency loss depends on the nature of the compiler and hardware system, as well as on the competence of the programmer.

7.8 Debugging

As we noted in Figure 7.2, the programmer codes his program, tests it, makes any necessary corrections, and tests the program again. The testing and correction process is called *debugging*. Debugging is a major or a relatively minor part of the programming process, depending on the care with which the programmer has undertaken the previous steps.

Two general types of errors are found in the debugging process. The first is the category of *syntactical errors*, in which the programmer has violated the syntax of the programming language. Misspelling words in the language is a syntactical error, for example. Syntactical errors are usually recognized by the compiler and are brought to the programmer's attention by appropriate error messages. Typically, syntactical errors are easy to find and simple to correct.

The second category is *logical errors*. In this case, the programmer's analysis or design is faulty, and the program fails to perform as it was intended. The program may produce an incorrect paycheck, for example. This type of error may be extremely difficult to detect or solve. The best approach to logical problems is prevention. The programmer should concentrate his effort on the program analysis and program design, or flowcharting, stage. Coding should be a relatively minor part of the process. By the time coding starts, the programmer should have absolute confidence in the logic of his program.

Exercises

1. Each card in a file contains the identification number of a single student and the scores that student made on a battery of 12 tests. Design an algorithm and draw a flowchart that will find the highest average score for the 12 tests made by any student.

2. Given the situation in problem 1, design an algorithm and draw a flowchart that will find the average of the scores made by all the students for each test.

3. Design an algorithm and draw a flowchart using a loop to find the highest and lowest temperatures in an array of 200 temperature recordings.

4. A card contains the following fields:
   (a) date—month, day, and year
   (b) rainfall in inches
   (c) low temperature
   (d) high temperature
   Draw a flowchart and write a program in ACL that will print the total rainfall and the highest and lowest temperatures for the dates (cards) processed.

5. Repeat problem 4 using System 360 Assembly Language.

6. Repeat problem 4 using FORTRAN.

7. Examine the algorithm flowcharted in Figure 7.13. What changes should be made to retain and print the identification of the student making the highest examination score?

8. What changes would be required in the algorithm flowcharted in Figure 7.13 to find the lowest examination score?

9. A card contains the following information:

   Columns
   1–6 X value $nnn.nn$
   7–11 Y value $nn.nn$
   12–16 Z value $nn.nn$

   Draw a flowchart and write a FORTRAN program that will calculate the value $W = X^2 + 2X^2Y + Z^2$ for each card and will print W, X, Y, and Z only if $W \geqslant 100.0$. An X value of all nines will identify the last card.

10. Expand the program in problem 7 to print the following information:
    (a) total number of cards processed
    (b) total number of W values printed
    (c) average W value printed
    (d) average W value not printed
    (e) average of all W values

11. A card is maintained for each student containing the following information:
    (a) identification—7 digits, numeric
    (b) name—24 digits, alphabetic
    (c) major—5 digits, alphabetic
    (d) enrollment date—6 digits, numeric (month, day, and year)
    (e) credit hours—3 digits, numeric
    (f) class standing—9 digits, alphabetic

Draw a flowchart and write a COBOL program to print one line for each student who enrolled before June 1, 1973. The report should contain headings and data as shown below.

Class Standing

Student Identification	Name	Major	Enrollment Date	Credit Hours	Class Standing
1001451	ANDREWS	PSYCH	01-02-70	112	JUNIOR
1001503	ARNOLD	CHEM	03-23-71	45	FRESHMAN
1002071	CHAPMAN	POLSC	09-19-68	212	JUNIOR *

TOTAL NUMBER OF STUDENTS REPORTED 1217
AVERAGE CREDIT HOURS 107

Print an asterisk by the class standing of a student who has over 200 credit hours and who does not have a class standing of Senior.

12. Rewrite the ACL program illustrated in Figure 7.17 in 360/Assembly language, in FORTRAN, and in COBOL.

13. Rewrite the 360/Assembly language program illustrated in Figure 7.18 in ACL, in FORTRAN, and in COBOL.

14. Rewrite the FORTRAN program illustrated in Figure 7.20 in ACL, in 360/Assembly language, and in COBOL.

15. Rewrite the COBOL program illustrated in Figure 7.24 in ACL, in 360/Assembly language, and in FORTRAN.

8 The System

The term *system* can easily be misinterpreted. It has a broad definition—an interacting or interdependent group of entities that when taken together form a whole—and thus can be used to cover an entire array of situations. And the concept represented by this term is equally universal. The concept of a system is applicable in physics, aerospace engineering, politics, economics, biology, and management to name only a few subject areas. In a compounding of the problem of interpretation, it is now fashionable to develop, analyze, define, view, and conceive systems. To begin we will discuss three approaches to systems that are not directly within our area of interest, but that might be confused with the systems analysis and design process associated with computer-based information systems.

First is the developing body of knowledge known as *general system theory*.[1] Ludwig Von Bertalanffy postulated such a theory based on observations that general problems and viewpoints in the various branches of science are similar, and that many important developments occur on the borderlines between disciplines. Von Bertalanffy felt that this general system theory might become the vehicle for the unification of science. This point of view is supported by our observation in the first paragraph that the concept of a system is applicable to virtually all disciplines.

The term *systems analysis* is also used in the management process, where it refers to a comparative evaluation of the alternatives facing a decision maker. This evaluation may use such tools as management science and operations research, but the critical factor that distinguishes it from other decision-making processes is the orientation of the analyst. The systems analyst attempts to treat each problem according to the objectives of the larger system within which the problem occurs. He develops criteria for evaluating alternative decisions, and insofar as possible, provides the decision maker with quantitative estimates of the effectiveness and cost of each alternative.

Finally, the process of systems engineering is similar to that of the systems analysis that we will describe in connection with computer-based information systems. The difference lies in the nature of the system involved. Systems engineers typically design systems that have physical and human, as well as informational, elements, and the physical elements tend to be emphasized. Thus, the object of a systems engineering effort might be a petroleum refining system, a weapons system, a transportation system, or a laboratory system. A computer-based information system might well be a part of each of these systems, but its significance is clearly secondary.

The goal of a computer-based information system is, of course, to provide information. Both the raw material input and the resultant output consist of information. So, a working definition of *computer-based information system* might be—an interrelationship of men, operations, documents, and computer systems organized to process and report information. It is important to realize that the system includes both data sources and information users. The computer system, then, is a subsystem of the information system.

---

[1] See Ludwig Von Bertalanffy, "General System Theory: A New Approach to Unity of Science." *Human Biology*, 23: 4 (1951), pp. 302–361.

8.1 Systems Analysis and Design

Systems analysis and design is the evaluation and creation of computer-based information systems. Its relationship with programming is illustrated in Figure 8.1. The entire process begins with the recognition of a problem or an opportunity. The problem may be specific, such as excessive delays in registering a student, or the general idea that control could be enhanced by a more effective computer-based information system. In either case, the next step is a feasibility study, which is intended to evaluate the necessity and the economic and technological feasibility of a solution to the problem. If the project is feasible, a general outline of the proposed solution is fleshed out into a detailed design. This detailed design is literally the specification that is supplied to programming. The first three steps—problem recognition, feasibility study, and subsystem design—constitute systems analysis and design.

The remaining three steps are: programming, implementation (putting the system into operation), and review and evaluation (checking the effectiveness of the process and of the finished product). The role of the systems

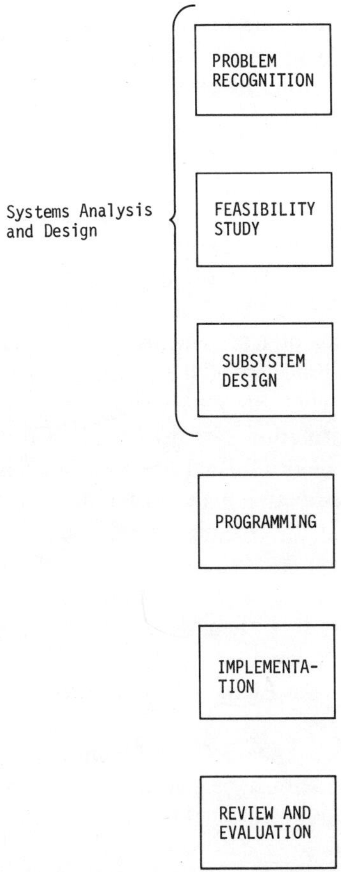

Figure 8.1 Steps in the process of developing a computer-based information system.

analyst in these last three steps varies from organization to organization. In some instances, the systems analyst has no authority over programming, implementation, or review and evaluation; in other cases, he has total responsibility for and control of these processes. In this book, we will consider the systems analyst in the latter role.

Systems analysis is an interdisciplinary and an interorganizational function. The resultant system combines elements of computer science with the elements of the application area. Process control in a refinery, for example, normally combines at least chemistry, engineering, and accounting, so the design of the process control system must deal effectively with all of those elements. Ideally, the designed information system should be functionally oriented, able to ignore formal organization boundaries. The dividing lines between the order department, production scheduling, and accounts receivable, for example, are rather arbitrary, as are the lines between the registrar's office, business office, and academic affairs in a university. But an information system need not be oriented to organizational alignment. In fact, inefficiency and duplication tend to arise as a consequence of arbitrary boundaries.

For the designed system to be functionally oriented, the systems analyst must be free to organize it without regard to formal organizational boundaries. This requires the support of a manager whose authority crosses those boundaries. So, if all new systems are being installed in accounting and related areas, the systems function should report to the controller or the treasurer. If systems are being installed throughout the organization, however, the systems analysis and design function should report to the chief executive officer of the organization. Until recently, both the data processing and systems analysis and design functions most often reported to the controller or treasurer. In recent years, the trend has been toward making the manager of the data processing function an officer of the organization, reporting directly to the chief executive officer.

The relationship between data processing and systems analysis and design varies widely. In a few instances, the manager of the systems function manages the entire data processing activity, including programming and operations. More frequently, systems analysis and design reports to a manager of data processing or separately to a higher authority.

8.2 The Systems Analyst

The qualifications of a systems analyst are unique. He is usually a college graduate (often with an advanced degree), although there are impressive exceptions to this rule. Because of the interdisciplinary and interdepartmental nature of his job, the systems analyst is aptly characterized as a generalist, so the breadth of knowledge and background implied by the possession of a college degree is an asset. A systems analyst must also have a thorough grasp of programming and programs. He must be able to organize the complete set of tasks for a given system into a series of interrelated programs, estimating the time and hardware system resource requirements for these programs, and estimating the time it will take to design, write, and debug the programs. Thus, a systems analyst should have a substantial amount of practical programming experience before attempting to design a computer-based information system. At the same time, the general characteristics and skills required of systems analysts are not the same as those required of programmers. A successful programmer will not necessarily be a successful systems analyst. Most analysts are programmers who have been promoted but some are drawn from particular application areas, and others may come from academic programs that are now being developed specifically for the training of systems analysts.

Three personal characteristics are important for systems analysts. First, the systems analyst must possess substantial human relations skills. He must be able to draw significant and accurate information from the personnel using the current system, and he must "sell" his new design to the people who will operate the new system and use its output. Second, the systems analyst must be naturally curious. Success in a system design depends in large measure on the analyst's grasp of the nature of the necessary mechanisms and relationships, and curiosity is an incentive in achieving the grasp. Finally the systems analyst must have at least a tolerance for detail. Although a critical step is the conception of the "grand" or overall design, the systems analyst must also elaborate this general design with extremely detailed pieces that not only fit together but work together to achieve the system objective.

8.3   The Feasibility Study

The feasibility study analyzes the practicality and economics of installing a new system in one or more application areas within an organization. The classic reason for a feasibility study is that the organization is considering computer-based information systems for the first time. The question to be answered is whether computer-based information systems should be designed for one or more of the organization's application areas. If it is decided that such design is an intelligent investment of the organization's resources, the general nature of the system and the specific computer hardware must be decided.

A feasibility study might also be triggered by an advance in technology. The development of significantly improved computer hardware systems might lead an organization to consider upgrading its present system. (Quite a few feasibility studies took place in the years immediately following the announcement of third generation computer hardware systems.) A significant change in the organization's environment might trigger a feasibility study, or such a study might be a periodic event. A feasibility study may be scheduled every five to seven years as a matter of organizational policy.

Staffing the Feasibility Study The size of the feasibility study team is obviously dictated by the size of the system being studied and the time available for the study. At a minimum, however, the study team should contain two people. A feasibility study is too important for an organization to depend on the judgment of a single individual. In addition, the organization cannot afford the risk that a single individual may leave and carry with him the knowledge gained during a feasibility study. The detailed background information underlying a new design is essential to its implementation, and the organization cannot afford to lose it.

Potential sources of study team personnel are the computer manufacturer, consultants, new employees, and existing staff. Although the computer manufacturer will normally have a wealth of knowledge and experience on his staff, this is a particularly poor source for the staffing of a user feasibility study. The user requires complete objectivity about hardware systems and even about whether the designed information system should be computer based at all. The manufacturer's personnel cannot be relied on to provide this kind of objectivity. If a new information system is designed, the study team members can offer a depth of knowledge concerning the organization and its operations that will be particularly beneficial. If the new system is implemented, the study team members are an obvious nucleus for the implementation staff and can easily answer questions about particular points in the new design. This availability of study team members cannot be guaranteed where manufacturer or consultant personnel are involved. More important, with either manufacturer's personnel or consultants a great deal of the knowledge that is developed will subsequently be lost to the organization. On the other hand, a user who has no existing systems analysis and design capability may be reluctant to add such skills to his staff until after the feasibility study is complete and the decision to implement the system is made. In this case, consultants are a source of temporary expertise. A common compromise is to use both consultants and existing personnel to staff the feasibility study. Systems experts are employed while an in-house staff is being developed. New employees are, of course, a source of expertise that can be retained by the organization.

Mixed skills are required of the feasibility study team. The two most important are knowledge of the organization and the particular applications areas being studied and knowledge of systems analysis and design. Besides the general communications and human relations skills, the list of potentially helpful knowledge and skills is endless. Perhaps the best rule is simply to maximize the kinds of knowledge and skills within the team.

Initiating the Study The scope of the feasibility study must be clearly defined, and this definition is management's responsibility. The feasibility study may encompass a single application area or the entire operation of the organization. The team may be free to completely redesign the information system, or they may be limited to modification of the existing system. If management considers accuracy, response time, flexibility, or any other factor a necessary objective or goal, the study team must be informed. Otherwise, they will consider and design to a wide range of goals, with no single goal having a prior importance.

The feasibility study must have the full support of the top management of the organization or of the area within the organization in which the study is taking place. The study team should have substantial authority, with its leader reporting directly to the top executive in the area.

An initial step of the feasibility study is the conceptual division of an operation into distinct segments by function—that is, by logical relationships and not arbitrary organizational structure. For an entire organization, the segments might be development and response to demand, production of finished goods, material support, and control, rather than the familiar organizational breakdown into sales, production control, scheduling, traffic, purchasing, and so on. The key advantage of the functional breakdown is that it continually helps direct the study team away from the artificial organizational orientation, leaving it free to develop a new system design unaffected by formal boundaries.

After the operation is broken into distinct segments a study plan is developed. The study plan includes specific assignments, provides for progress reports and management review, and includes a detailed and firm time schedule.

The Study After establishing goals and objectives, the study team begins to collect information about the current system and its environment. The information needed includes:

1. Industry background
2. Organization background
3. Organization plans
4. Organization policies
5. Current and projected volume of activity
6. The nature of the current system

One potentially important source of some of this information is existing documents. Previous studies may cover portions of the desired subject areas. Procedure manuals are extremely valuable sources of information concerning the current system. An intelligent first step in the feasibility study is to search out all the written material that pertains to the area being studied. The major sources of information, however, are the individuals who make up the organization being studied. In some cases, questionnaires and reports may supply this information. But most instances, personal interviews are necessary. Interviewing during the feasibility study tends to be directed to individuals who have relatively high rank in the organization.

The feasibility of an information system can be established without a full array of supporting detail. With the exception of a few key points, the analyst needs only a general operational understanding of the system. The analyst must grasp the function and relationships of the system operations, inputs, outputs, and files, but he does not need supporting detail on every operation, input, output, and file. The analyst must develop a valid conception of the system's operation and the relationship of its parts, so he constructs a conceptual model, which he uses in the assimilation and evaluation of all new information. The analyst normally begins with a rough input–process–output model and then elaborates this conception with additional information. If some information fails to fit the existing model, then the analyst must question and adjust either his model or the information. The use of such a conceptual model may help the analyst to avoid the trap of becoming a mere collector of facts. He is able to evaluate information as he receives it and redirect his line of questioning accordingly.

By interviewing employees and examining pertinent documents the analyst learns (1) the sequence of operations, (2) the function of each operation, and (3) the relationship between operations. He must select the critical and the key points in the existing system, and concentrate the majority of his data gathering efforts there.

In addition, the analyst must determine the requirements imposed on the current system. Legal requirements, policy requirements, labor contract requirements, and some less official requirements—such as those of industry practice or custom—must be explicitly recognized. Finally, the performance requirements by which the system is judged must be uncovered and stated as precisely as possible. If the system must respond to a particular input within six hours, for example, this should be stated. Performance requirements should be stated quantitatively whenever possible.

When they understand the existing system, the study team begins to develop a new overall design. In the first step of this process, design objectives are selected. In some instances, a general design concept may be chosen first. This design concept could be a feature or an approach of such importance that its incorporation in the new system design is required of the design effort. As an example, an organization with far-flung operations may have had decentralized data processing in the past with installations in each location. The design concept may be the centralization of data processing. Other potential design concepts are that the majority of a system's files should be direct access or that data collection and system inquiry should be on-line. The design concept is, of course, a direct response to the problem situation.

The development of the new system design is frequently an iterative process. The analyst conceives and roughs out a design that is consistent with the design concept and a majority of the design objectives. The operation of the rough design is then visualized to determine whether it is workable and whether it will satisfy the design objectives. To the extent that a design fails these tests, the process is repeated and a new design is evaluated. Frequently, it is decided that to implement the new design in its entirety is too risky a step. Instead, the new system will be implemented in stages that may actually be a series of new designs culminating in the desired system.

Documentation of the new system design is done in four basic parts: (1) general processing steps, (2) data structures, (3) performance requirements, and (4) an implementation plan. The key element of documentation is the operational systems chart, an example of which is shown in Figure 8.2. This chart shows the actual flow of processing from input document to output, and clearly portrays the usage of files and the relationships between the programs in the system. Data structures that include inputs and outputs as well as files are documented as shown in Figure 8.3. The data structures will contain information about content and medium (card, document, video display) only; they will not be accompanied by a complete form or report design. This greater detail can be provided in the detailed subsystem design.

The study team will specify detailed performance requirements for the new system design. Performance requirements should be quantitative if possible, and if not they should still be specific. Performance requirements may be specified in the areas of time, cost, accuracy, capacity, efficiency, acceptance, flexibility, quality, reliability, and security.

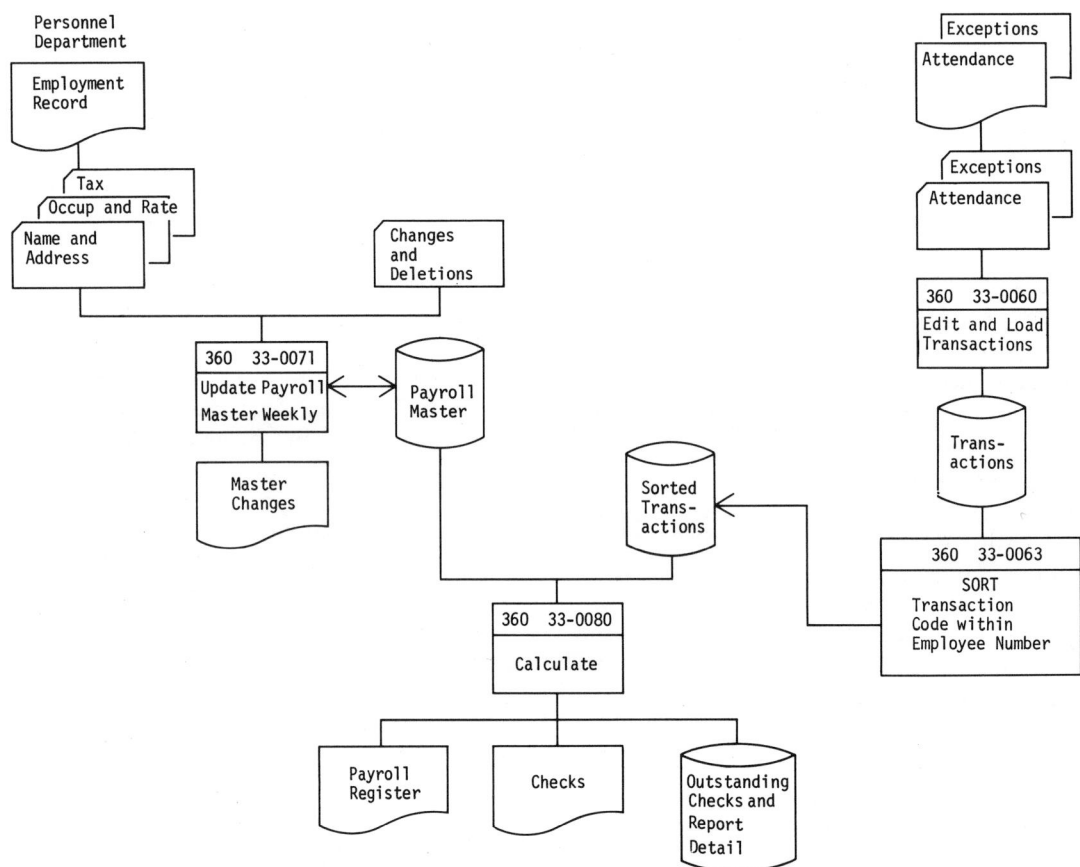

Figure 8.2 Operational systems chart for part of a hypothetical payroll system.

PROJECT	PAYROLL - 33			Page	4	of	20
SEGMENT	NA			Date		12-1-72	
ANALYST	COTTERMAN			Index		33-012	

DATA STRUCTURE	NAME					
INPUT (OUTPUT) FILE	CHECK					
MEDIUM	PAPER	VOLUME	2800/Week	COPIES (Output only)		1
SEQUENCE (File only)						
RETENTION	NA					
DESCRIPTIONS:	STUB ATTACHED TO RIGHT SIDE OF CHECK FOR SIMULTANEOUS PRINTING					

RECORD CONTENTS				
ELEMENT NUMBER	NAME/DESCRIPTION	FREQ	CHARACTER	A/N
1	EMPLOYEE NUMBER	2	5	N
2	EMPLOYEE NAME	2	30	A
3	GROSS PAY	1	7	N
4	FEDERAL TAX WITHHELD	1	7	N
5	STATE TAX WITHHELD	1	5	N
6	FICA	1	5	N
7	GROUP INSURANCE DEDUCTION	1	5	N
8	OTHER DEDUCTIONS	1	5	N
9	NET PAY	2	7	N
10	GROSS PAY YEAR-TO-DATE	1	7	N
11	FEDERAL TAX WITHHELD YEAR-TO-DATE	1	7	N
12	STATE TAX WITHHELD YEAR-TO-DATE	1	5	N
13	FICA YEAR-TO-DATE	1	5	N
14	NET PAY YEAR-TO-DATE	1	7	N

Figure 8.3 Selected data structure from a hypothetical payroll system.

The last major element of documentation is the implementation plan, the preparation of which is one of the final steps in the feasibility study. We will defer discussion of this activity until the end of this section.

Management review and approval is a necessity throughout the feasibility process, but particularly so following the development and documentation of the new general design. If the proposed design is acceptable to management, then equipment is selected to implement that design. As we noted earlier, even if the task is only to upgrade or add to an existing hardware system, equipment selection is a difficult and lengthy process. Part of the difficulty stems from the sheer complexity of the equipment, part from the great number and variety of hardware systems available, and part because of separately priced, or *unbundled*, services. Instead of charging one purchase or monthly rental price for a hardware system and its attendant services some manufacturers price each desired service separately. Software, education, systems and programming support, manuals, as well as the hardware system itself, must be purchased separately. This means that, theoretically, the study team can select the best software system, hardware system, and services necessary to implement their new system design. The opportunity, however, brings with it the difficulty of selecting among the various competing products and services. Because many of these are new and untried, the study team often takes a risk when attempting to use a new combination in implementing their system. In fact, a severe problem of the entire computer industry has been a tendency to release incomplete products and to let the customer participate in the final stages of debugging. This has caused a great deal of difficulty for many users and has produced an unhealthy attitude toward new products. It has almost become axiomatic that to pioneer in the use of a product or service is to subject oneself to certain and yet unnecessary hazards.

The documentation prepared for the new system design may be used as a part of a specification package to be submitted to suppliers for the preparation of their bids. The specification package may also include a set of restrictions to be applied to the bids. Restrictions may cover the cost of the system, the facilities such as space and raised flooring necessary to accommodate the hardware system, language compatibility, or delivery dates. The bids that have been submitted are then evaluated—that is, the claims and pertinent facts contained in the various bids are validated and compared. The study team cannot afford to accept a bid uncritically; the group must assure itself that the hardware and software systems proposed will, in fact, support the system. Finally, the study team compares the validated bids, considering both cost and performance, and selects the appropriate hardware and software systems.

Then, the study team analyzes the cost and benefits of the proposed system. Costs deriving from the implementation of a system include:

1. The cost of the computer hardware system
2. The cost of the software system
3. The aquisition of or additions to the systems and programming staff
4. Staff training
5. Site preparation
6. Physical facilities
7. Security
8. Detailed systems analysis and design
9. Program development and testing
10. User training
11. Parallel operation
12. Conversion

The magnitude of these costs can obviously be substantial, depending on the size of the system. A rough rule of thumb is that the dollar cost of the computer hardware system will be about one-third the total cost of an operating installation. Thus, the user who leases a computer hardware system costing $200,000 per year can expect total costs of more than $600,000 per year.

Benefits from the installation of a computer-based information system range from the direct and objective benefit of dollar savings because fewer clerical personnel are needed, to an indirect and subjective improvement in management control. In some cases, dollar savings alone are sufficient to justify the system. More commonly, however, the computer-based information system produces a net dollar cost rather than a saving. This is not to say that such systems are unjustified, but that dollar savings are not the key benefit. That the organization is more responsive to its clients and its environment, that results of operations are known today rather than two weeks from today, that low-level decisions can be automated and can thus be made consistently and correctly each time they are required, that the system operates with greater accuracy, and finally, that management control is improved are all intangible or subjective benefits from the installation of a computer-based information system. The system is an investment, and the return projected on this investment should be the basis for management's decision. The study team must, however, ensure that management recognizes the various intangible benefits as a legitimate part of that return.

Following determination of the costs and benefits, the study team prepares a detailed implementation plan, a step-by-step listing of the events and their time schedule. The events that must be included in such an implementation plan are:

1. The selection and training of personnel
2. Hardware system installation
3. A detailed design of each subsystem
4. Program development and testing
5. Preparation of written procedures
6. User training
7. Data structure generation
8. Parallel operation
9. Installation
10. Review and evaluation

Finally, we must note that some authors and practitioners recommend a lengthier form of feasibility study that provides essentially the same results as we have outlined above and also provides the detail necessary for subsystem design. Under this approach the study team spends substantially more time studying and documenting the current system, and the resulting documentation becomes input to the analyst who designs the subsystem. So the subsystem analyst can bypass the analysis phase of his design. The author believes that this is a misuse of the study team resources, and that it results in unnecessary duplication of effort, if not a total loss of the additional effort. First, the study team staff tends to be of a higher level of skill and credentials than the analysts who will ultimately implement their design. In fact, the study team members may supervise the subsequent efforts. Because so much of the analysis of the present system is clerical, the collection of detail should take place during system redesign with less highly qualified (and less expensive)

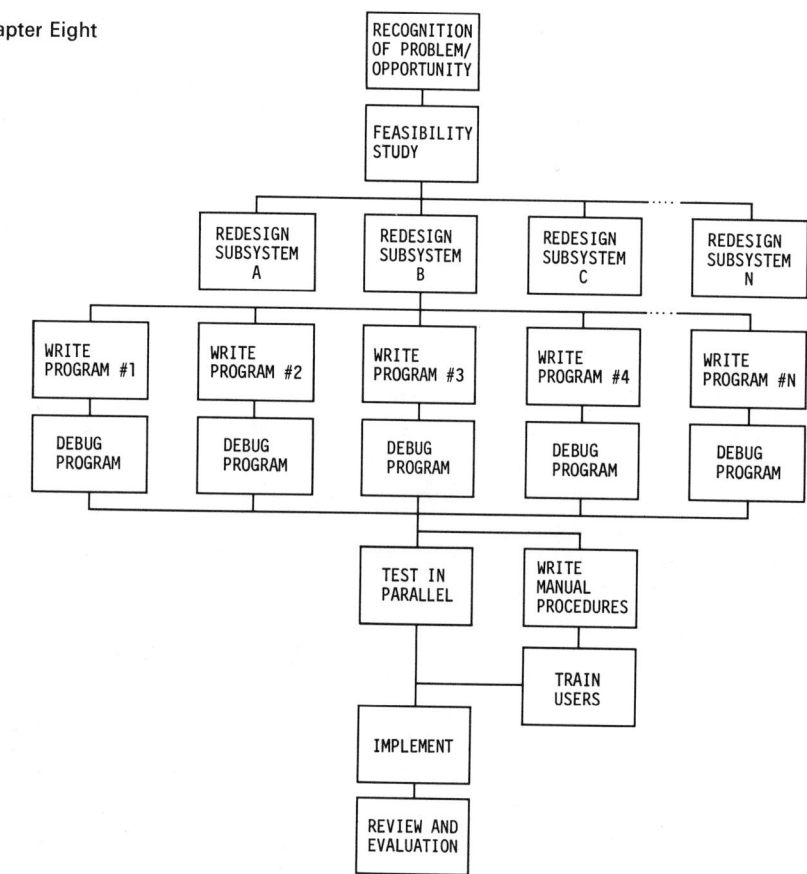

Figure 8.4 Subsystem redesign in relation to other steps in the process of developing a computer-based information system.

personnel. Second, a major benefit of analyzing the present system lies in providing the systems analyst with detailed knowledge of the area and functions that will go into his design. If the subsystem analyst does not do the detail work in the same area during the feasibility study, then he will have to duplicate previous work, regardless of the extent of the documentation. Finally, since, by definition, the result of a feasibility study could be a verdict of infeasible, undertaking a detailed analysis before this decision seems an unnecessary risk.

8.4   Systems Redesign

A systems analyst rarely has the opportunity to design a system from scratch. Typically, he works with existing systems and his design is then, in actuality, a redesign. The position of system redesign in the overall process is illustrated in Figure 8.4.

The feasibility study may have produced a general design with multiple subsystems. The systems redesign process develops a detailed design for one of the subsystems. Thus in Figure 8.4, N individual subsystems will eventually be subject to the system redesign process. The system redesign process contains five distinct steps, which are illustrated in Figure 8.5. Each step is discussed in the following pages.

System Definition   The first step in system redesign is system definition. The boundaries and content of the subsystem must be clearly defined. Much of this will already have been done during the feasibility study, although the precise location of the boundary and the supporting details will still need to be worked out. The major problem in system definition is complexity. The systems analyst is faced with a bewildering number of operations, documents, inputs, outputs, files, and endless relationships between these elements.

One way to define the boundaries of a subsystem is to include all operations that have a common goal pattern within the subsystem. Operations with different goals are excluded. Thus, all operations whose goal can be stated as "to provide the materials necessary to operate the university at the lowest possible cost" could be included in the same material input subsystem. Goal orientation depends on perspective, which depends, in turn, on the perceiver's level in the organization. Goals that seem related from the viewpoint of a university president might be conflicting in the view of the librarian or the director of athletics. The systems analyst should take the viewpoint of the highest source of authority for the system redesign effort.

A second way to define a subsystem is to combine operations that have a high degree of interaction into the same system. Operations that seldom or never interact

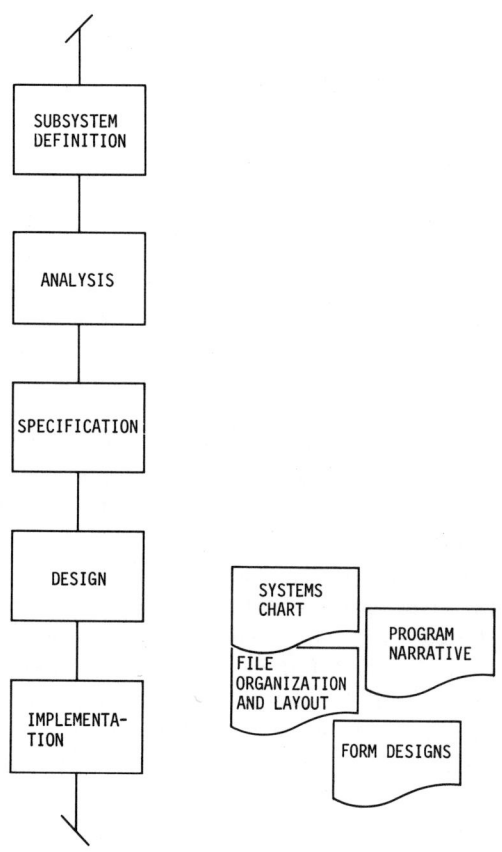

are outside the subsystem we are defining. Interaction may take several forms, ranging from a simple input/output flow to decision dependence. All of the interactions in question are assigned values on a scale according to the degree of interdependence. A point or threshold on the scale is then chosen, and all values higher than this threshold are considered to be within the system. The effect could be similar to that illustrated in Figure 8.6. When a threshold of 5 is chosen, the original large system breaks into three distinct subsystems.

System Analysis   The primary function of the analysis phase is to gather sufficient pertinent information about the existing system to provide a solid base for designing the new system. The documentation performed in this phase gives the systems designer a catalog of currently available human, machine, and information resources. Equally important, it provides the systems designer with a checklist of operations in the existing system. A significant secondary benefit of the analysis phase is the education of the systems analyst. An analyst who participates in systems redesign is rarely thoroughly familiar with both the application area and the particular organization for which the system is being designed. The analysis

---

Figure 8.5   Subsystem redesign steps.

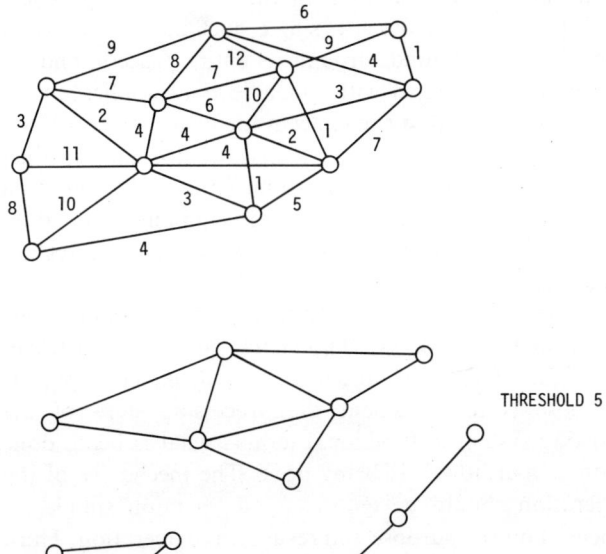

Figure 8.6 Division of a system into subsystems by establishing a threshold of 5 on some scale of interaction.

phase is an excellent opportunity to develop this familiarity. The adequacy of the final design will be, at least partially, a function of the analyst's understanding of the situation.

The objective of the analysis phase is to determine current policies, data structure, processing steps, documents, volume of transactions and other data structure elements, performance measures, costs, and environmental factors affecting the organization. Environmental factors are basically elements outside the organization that are not readily subject to control. Laws that effect the organization's operations, accepted industry practice, tradition, the state of the economy, and the collective bargaining agreement are all environmental factors. Although all essential information should be gathered during the analysis phase, one of the analyst's key abilities is to recognize what is truly essential. The information that could be gathered during the analysis phase is virtually endless, and the analyst must learn to abstract and concentrate on important elements.

As in the feasibility study, potential *information sources* include the documentation of previous studies and procedures manuals. In addition, permanent files contain a great deal of information such as record content, volumes, and exception conditions which are important to the analyst.

Again, however, the major source of information

about an existing system is the job knowledge of the people who operate and are a part of the system. This knowledge is accessed by interviewing, the major activity of the analysis phase. Unfortunately, interviewing can be rather difficult at this stage. The analyst may frequently be viewed as an outsider whose information collecting implies unknown and threatening changes. In interviewing, the process of working down through an organization is consistent with the development of a conceptual model. The earlier interviews at high levels in the organization offer an overview of the existing system and its problems, and interviews with lower-level personnel fill in necessary detail. In addition, starting at the top clearly establishes the management's perspective in the systems analyst's thinking. Although this is not necessarily the perspective that the analyst should assume, it must always be considered.

Collecting detailed information can be done in two major ways. In the station-to-station approach, a comprehensive survey is made of all operations at each work or processing station separately. All processes are covered, regardless of the fact that widely different information flows and applications may be involved. This approach follows the existing organization pattern and provides one-stop interviewing, or at least, minimizes return interviews. Its disadvantage is, of course, that information flows and applications are mixed in both the analyst's notes and in his thinking. In the alternative approach, document-flow analysis, a single document or information flow is followed through its entire process, and information associated with other flows or applications is ignored. The analyst can concentrate on a single problem, but he must hold repeated interviews, for each distinct information flow and application. Other data collection techniques include questionnaires, sampling, simulation and various statistical techniques such as regression analysis.

There are three major elements in the *documentation* of the analysis process. The *function flowchart*, illustrated in Figure 8.7, is the basic unit of documentation. Its purpose is to document the processing steps of the existing system in functional terms—what is being done rather than how it is being done. The mechanics of the operation should be ignored, and attention should be focused on the purpose and result of the operation. Thus, Figure 8.7 tells nothing about the way in which quantity, item number, and issues are recorded, but simply that they are recorded. For another example, we need not specify precisely how costs are calculated for a withdrawal, but simply that such an operation occurs.

The second major element of documentation is recording of the system's data structures—detailing the contents of inputs, outputs, and files. As Figure 8.3 indicates, the description, length, composition of characters,

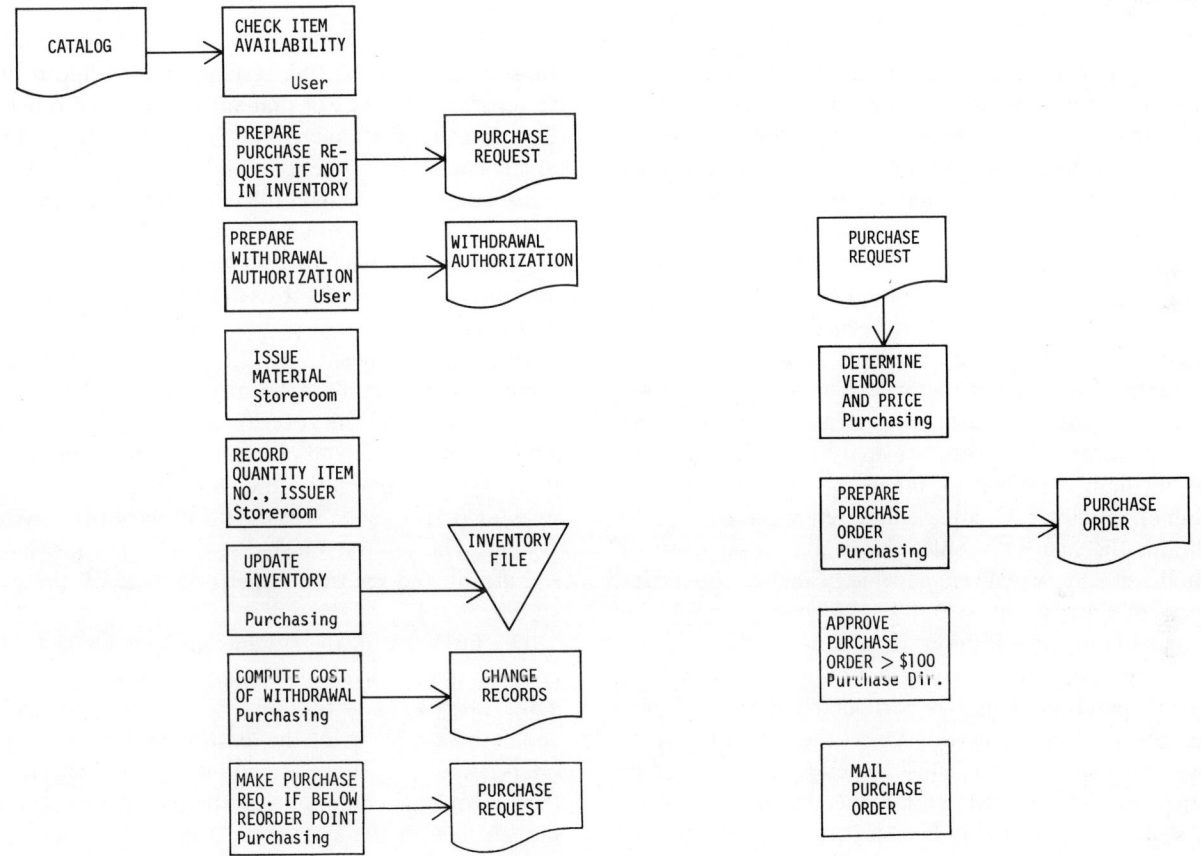

Figure 8.7 Function flowchart of a hypothetical store's inventory system.

and frequency are recorded for each field contained in the input, output, or file. For inputs and outputs, each document or record is represented by a single sheet. A single file, however, may be composed of several distinct types of records. A student file where various documents are kept in the student's file folder would constitute a multiple-record file, and so would require a separate sheet for each record. In addition to field or element description, the analyst should record the file medium —such as file folder, 80-column cards, or magnetic tape— the number of entries in the file and number of accesses per day (volume), sequence, and retention period. In the case of inputs and outputs, the analyst should again record medium, number of inputs or outputs per day (volume), number of copies, and retention period. In addition, the analyst should obtain a filled-in copy of each document whenever possible. Finally, significant aspects of the present system's performance should be documented in some fashion.

The third element of documentation defines the cost of systems operation. This is a particularly important performance measure. In a few instances the cost of the existing system is sufficient to justify the design of a new system on the basis of cost reduction alone. In either case the new system will inevitably be compared with the old on this measure. Because the analyst is dealing with a particular subsystem, one that may not even be thought of as a subsystem in the existing system, he may find it difficult to separate the costs of that subsystem from other costs. Occasionally, the analyst may be able to charge the cost of an entire department to the existing subsystem but, more commonly, he can allocate only a percentage of a department's, or even an individual's work. Costs of the existing system will also include equipment, materials, and such miscellaneous costs as training of new employees and overhead.

Other potential categories to be documented include accuracy—which might be measured by the frequency, the number, and the severity of errors—system acceptance by employees and customers, elapsed time or deadlines, system flexibility, and volume capacity. The important performance measures will vary from system to system. The analyst must discover which measures are significant and record the performances of the existing system.

The final step in the systems analysis phase of system redesign is an *analysis of the data* that have been collected. To a large extent, this analysis summarizes the weak spots and problems of the existing system. Each person interviewed may have mentioned a pet problem, but these problems could actually be merely symptoms of a hidden flaw in the system. So the analyst must be prepared to examine each stated problem critically, to determine its validity and primacy, or to place it into a pattern leading to a more basic problem. A problem stated as understaffing, for example, may really be a problem of system imbalance and inflexibility.

Many specific conditions can indicate problems in the existing system. The analyst will look for and examine points in the system where work tends to accumulate in lengthy queues, where the error rate is higher than usual, or where personnel morale seems to be a problem. In addition, he will look for duplication in data collection, processing, or reporting in the existing system, and for redundancy in reporting or file data. If identical information is collected more than once, or reported on two different reports, or maintained in separate files, the analyst will note the condition as an area of potential improvement.

System simulation is another way of analyzing data. Simulation languages such as **GPSS** and Simscript can be used to model and simulate the operations of the existing system under varying volume and workload conditions. For example, the analyst could use a **GPSS** program to simulate the operation of a registration system under the hypothetical condition of a 30 percent increase in the number of students. The results of the simulation would include information on system use, individual station loads, processing times, and queuing patterns.

Automated analysis techniques have been developed for large systems. So that the analysis phase can be completed in a reasonable period of time, uniform data collection techniques are set up, with standard formats for recording the data. From this form the data can be converted to machine-readable form and processed by a computer system. Thus, a great variety of analyses may be produced automatically for the use of the systems analyst. In addition, uniform data collection techniques frequently permit data to be collected by clerical rather than professional systems personnel.

After the system has been analyzed, the findings are presented to management. The purpose of this presentation is twofold. First, their review and approval insures that management is fully aware of the background and premises on which the subsequent design work will be based. Second, some of the information uncovered during the analysis might prove surprising to management— or some might prove to be erroneous. Then, the review by management constitutes a quality control. At the conclusion of this reviewing process management and the systems analyst will agree about the essential features of the existing system, and this concept will become the base for subsequent phases in the design.

System Specification Stated briefly, the function of system specification is to determine and document the actual requirements that must be met by the new system design. The systems analyst must determine which data structures and operations must be included in the new system. Normally, these data structures and operations will not be the same as those in the existing system, for if they are, the only design alternative is *mechanization*, or transferring to a new hardware system. Mechanization, which has been all too common in the past, is fairly accurately described as "making the same mess faster."

For the systems analyst to determine actual requirements, he must have a reasonable idea of the organization's expectations. Besides potential changes in volume, he must be aware of intended changes in organization activities. Development of new markets, more intensive development of old markets, geographical expansion, an acquisition program, plant improvement, and reorganization are events that the systems analyst must consider in his determination of system requirements. Volume figures are critically important and must be estimated for the effective life of the new system. That is, the new system must be able to handle the volumes anticipated four to eight years hence and not just the current volumes.

The systems analyst must be objective, capable of discarding operations and data structures that are not absolutely necessary to successful performance of the subsystem. Although the individuals who operate the existing system will undoubtedly have suggestions for its improvement, they normally will not have the objectivity necessary to discard some of the familiar elements of their work environment. So the analyst must be prepared to consider all suggestions, but accept only those he has carefully and objectively examined. The system analyst must also be capable of adding both operations and data structures when necessary. This is perhaps the most difficult task in the specification phase. To be able to envision a requirement which is completely ignored by the existing system requires substantial creativity. Possibly the simplest way to determine requirements is to decide what outputs are absolutely necessary and then to work in reverse through a cause-and-effect chain to the necessary input.

A major objective in the specification of requirements should be to minimize their number. Requirements are, in effect, restrictions on the system designer, and design flexibility is thus inversely proportional to both the number and tightness of the specified requirements. From another perspective, the full detail of the environment is far too complex to be dealt with directly by the systems analyst. The specification phase reduces this complexity by isolating the key factors that must be incorporated into the new system. Potential constraints on systems requirements must also be considered. Such constraints may arise from the labor contract, industry practice, customer acceptance of policy and practice, legal and audit considerations, or tradition. Whatever the source of the constraint, if it is valid it must be included and treated as a 'given' in the requirements specification process.

In documenting the requirements specification, the analyst must record:

1. Required operations
2. Required data structures
3. Required volumes
4. Performance requirements

Required operations are documented by a listing in narrative form (Figure 8.8). The narrative is a brief description of the functions that must be performed in this operation. It is extremely important that the narrative specify what must take place and when, in relation to the other operations, but not how or at which work stations. We are not even interested in whether a particular operation will be performed on a computer system, we simply want to know if it will be performed at all and, if so, what will happen. As a part of the required operation documentation, it is acceptable to name the relevant data structure elements as a cross reference. Both volume and performance requirements may also be listed, although this will be duplicated in other documentation.

OPERATION	INDEX	33-S 1
INDEX NO.	DESCRIPTION	
1.	Determine item availability.	
2.	Authorize withdrawal of material.	
3.	Request purchase of material if item is not maintained in inventory.	
4.	Update inventory to reflect withdrawal of material.	
5.	Charge the cost of material withdrawn to the user department.	
6.	Prepare purchase order for items not in inventory or with insufficient quantity in inventory.	

Figure 8.8 Required operations for a hypothetical store's inventory system.

Required data structures are documented in the same form as data structures were documented in the analysis phase. The only difference is that medium should not be specified. (Specifying that an input is to be on punched paper tape or that a file is to be on a disk is a design function.) Although the form of documentation is common between the analysis and specification phase, the content will be significantly different. Entire input, output, and file structures may be added or deleted during the specification phase, as may individual data elements within each structure.

Volume requirements can be specified in the documentation of operations and data structures, but they should also be specified on a separate volume summary sheet (as in Figure 8.9). Operations volume may be stated as the number of executions per time period, inputs and outputs as the number of instances per time period, and files as both number of entries and number of accesses per time period.

Performance requirements are stated in any appropriate form. In general, they should be stated as quantitatively as possible, and they should follow the categories discussed under the analysis phase. In rare instances, management may specify that specific resources—key individuals or equipment—be incorporated in the new system design. Where this is the case, these resources must be specified as requirements. Normally, however, resources other

VOLUME SUMMARY	INDEX	33-52
INDEX NO.	DESCRIPTION	VOLUME
1.	Withdrawal Authorizations	500/Day
2.	Purchase Requests	60/Day
3.	Purchase Orders	100/Day
4.	Inventory File	1200 Entries 1300 Accesses/Day
5.	Vendor File	800 Entries 360 Accesses/Day

Figure 8.9 Volume summary for a hypothetical store's inventory system.

than the hardware system, which was selected in the feasibility study, and the budget will not be considered requirements.

The entire specification of requirements is presented to management. These specifications are going to become the key parameters of the design process, and their accuracy and sufficiency is thus critical to the adequacy of the final designed system. Therefore, management must thoroughly examine and evaluate these specifications, and the systems analyst must be prepared to defend his conclusions. The logical integrity of the requirements must be preserved, however, and management must be thoroughly aware of the premises of the specification phase and the necessity for the recognition of absolute requirements only.

Finally, we should note a rather subtle by-product of the specification phase. Objectivity and freshness of viewpoint are essential factors in system design. To a large extent however, the analyst becomes biased by his detailed examination of what is being done now. Nevertheless, the analysis phase must be performed. The specification phase, emphasizing objectivity and the determination of absolute and logical requirements, helps to disengage the present system from design and from the new system. In theory at least, the design phase could be undertaken by a new systems analyst whose only information about the system was the specification of requirements.

System Design The design phase is the focal point of the entire system redesign process. In this phase the new design is conceived and supporting detail is elaborated to the point that the system is ready to be programmed and implemented. The designed system will be an arrangement of computer and manual steps, data structures, and documents, and the parameters of the design will be drawn from the feasibility study blueprint, the specification of requirements, and the available resources.

The new system design package being sold to management includes both costs and benefits. Although in some cases a budgetary limit may have been prespecified, more commonly the amount of resources allocated will depend on the returns from the investment. Thus, the parameter of available resources is somewhat indefinite; it both affects and is affected by the new system design. The cost of the new system must be within some reasonable limit, but within this limit the cost for an acceptable system will vary and the analyst must be prepared to justify this investment based on the benefits that it will generate.

The design process begins with the establishment of a design concept. If a system design concept was established during the feasibility study, that concept or a derivation may be used in the subsystem design. Otherwise, the analyst will develop a design concept specifically for this subsystem. Then, the analyst develops a rough outline of inputs, manual processing, computer programs, files, and outputs that is consistent with the design concept and with the parameters stated above. He evaluates the adequacy of this general subsystem design according to the performance measures established in the specifications phase. If the general design is inadequate, or if the analyst is simply not satisfied, a new alternative is developed and evaluated. The process continues until the analyst is satisfied with the evaluation.

This process is the weakest link in the entire system redesign activity. Quite simply, at present there is no way to determine whether the alternative selected is the best alternative. The analyst may be sure that alternative C meets the performance measures specified better than alternative B, but he has no way of knowing that alternative C is the optimum alternative. This failing, however, should not be a cause for lack of confidence but a subject for future investigation.

After he has chosen a general design, the analyst must develop its detail into a complete, workable, and programmable system. The guiding idea from this point on is practicality. The systems analyst must assure himself that each element of his design will work effectively and meet the performance requirements.

During detailed design the overall process is divided into specific computer programs and manual steps, and the relationships between these elements are clearly defined. Documentation takes the form of an *operational flowchart*, which was illustrated in Figure 8.2. The name "operational flowchart" stems from the detail and explicitness of the working relationships shown on the chart. In some installations, the operational flowchart is used by computer room personnel as the basic guide for operating the system under production conditions.

Another element of detailed design is the specification and layout of the data structures. For input structures, the systems analyst specifies the individual elements of information required and designs the form in which this information will be presented to the system. For output structures, the systems analyst will lay out the report format, or the form design, if necessary, besides specifying the individual data elements required. The specification and layout of file structures is more complex. As before, the data elements must be specified, but in this case the medium on which the file will be recorded, the file organization, access techniques, the possibility of blocking, and the need for file security must also be determined. Files discussing sensitive organization operations or confidential individual matters must be protected, so that they cannot be misused or destroyed. Many protection techniques are available, and this is becoming an increasingly important aspect of the systems analyst's responsibility.

Processing controls are also developed during the detailed design phase. Controls are necessary for accounting and auditing, as well as for internal verification of the system's integrity. For accounting and auditing, it is necessary to insure that all data to be processed are valid, that all valid data are processed correctly, and that the output results are accurate and complete. Internal integrity of the system requires a verification that data elements have been correctly passed between points in the system, both manual and program. Among the many control techniques available are control totals, sequence checking of input files, record counts, file labeling, validity checks, reasonableness checks, and source data listings. The development of an appropriate control structure for the system should be undertaken with the close cooperation and approval of the organization's auditors.

Minor equipment may be chosen during the design phase. Major equipment, including most of the computer hardware system, was selected during the feasibility study. Additional equipment that may be chosen now is supplementary to the existing hardware system—special features, additional storage capacity, or peripheral equipment. For example, if the design of the new system requires data capture and transmission at the source data collection equipment must be chosen.

Having developed a detailed design, the analyst must again evaluate it against the goals, objectives, and the explicit performance measures developed during the specification phase. Simulation is again a potentially valuable tool at this point. The performance of the new system design can be examined and evaluated before the system is implemented. System simulation is particularly helpful in designs that include data communication, for it enables the investigation of critical elements such as line and station loading and service time. When the systems analyst is satisfied with his evaluation of the new design he completes the documentation package with a set of program narratives, a presentation of the costs and benefits of the new system, and an implementation plan. Program narratives are detailed written descriptions of the events in each program of the new system. Program narratives are written for the programmers and are, in fact, the central element in the documentation which guides their efforts.

The implementation plan is a step-by-step list, with completion dates, of the activities necessary to begin operation of the newly designed system. These activities include the writing and testing of programs, the writing of manual procedures, the preparation of operational documentation, the training of operating personnel, user training, parallel or pilot operations, conversion of files to machine-processable form, and the actual transfer of dependence to the new system.

As with previous phases, the output of the design phase must be examined and evaluated by management. Management must be satisfied that the new design is not only correct and effective, but that the results of its implementation justify the investment. Ideally, this review by management will function as a design critique as well. This is the last point at which design changes can be made without incurring a sometimes substantial cost of modification.

Implementation The conduct of the implementation process itself is outside of the scope of this chapter, and in fact, is not essential to the purpose of the book. We will simply note two points: that the process can and should be managed in the same fashion as any other technical project and that the systems analyst is the logical person to control implementation. There has been a tendency to view systems analysis and programming as unique activities, not really subject to normal measures of management and control. This is simply not true, however; systems analysis and programming projects can be estimated, scheduled, and controlled as effectively as any other project.

Review and Evaluation This final step in the system redesign process is not directed at the modification or improvement of the newly installed system. The review and evaluation phase, which normally occurs several months after the new system has been installed, is a vehicle for improving the system redesign process itself. The goals, objectives, and performance measures that were established early in the system redesign process have now been realized to some degree. The review and evaluation will determine to what extent the new system design has failed to achieve these measures and, most important, to pinpoint the cause of this failure. Were the initial expectations unrealistic? Was the design faulty? Was the implementation process properly controlled? The system redesign process is a complex one, with a substantial measure of art as well as science. The review and evaluation phase provides valuable feedback for improving the entire process.

Exercises

1. Develop a job description for the position of systems analyst in a manufacturing concern. Be as specific as possible in describing the educational background, work experience, and personality characteristics required.
2. Develop a plan—including time schedule and personnel assignments—for a feasibility study of the need for computer systems in an organization with which you are familiar.
3. Present an argument in favor of the use of consultants only in the conduct of a feasibility study.
4. Present an argument in favor of using computer manufacturer personnel on the feasibility study team.

5. Develop a plan—including time schedule and personnel assignments—for the redesign of a system with which you are familiar.
6. Divide the operations of your university into functional activities.
7. How do the activities of the design phase of system redesign differ from the design activity that took place during the feasibility study?
8. Draw a function flowchart for the registration process at your school.
9. Develop specification phase outputs for the registration system at your school.
10. Specify a design concept that would be appropriate for (a) a university, (b) a bank with multiple branches, (c) a state health department, and (d) a hospital.

9 Computer System Applications

There are thousands of ways that computer systems are used today. These range from the simple printing of mailing lists to the complex systems used in the various space programs. This vast array of applications can be categorized by mode of processing. The two basic modes of processing are *batch* and *on-line*, terms that refer to the manner in which programs and data are presented to the system.

In batch processing, the data to be processed is accumulated until complete and then submitted to the computer system together with the processing program. The processing takes place, and the output is returned to the user. Input data is again accumulated, and the process is repeated according to a predetermined schedule. This is obviously an efficient use of the computer system, for the program is loaded once and then allowed to process a large volume of data. The computer system can service only a small number of programs at a time, however, and during this time it is unable to respond to the needs of other users. Furthermore, the *turn-around time* (the time from the submission of the job to the receipt of the output) tends to be lengthy. Twenty-four hour turn-around is likely to be the rule rather than the exception. There is little need for instantaneous response in most data processing, and so batch processing is the predominant mode of operation.

In on-line operation, data is received from devices that are directly connected to the computer system, and the data is processed when it is received. The key element is not that the devices are directly connected to the computer system, nor that data is input at the terminals irregularly, but that processing takes place immediately and that the output is immediately available to the user. (For instance, data can be entered randomly into a device that is directly connected to the computer system and the computer system, instead of processing this data immediately, will simply stack it on a storage device for batch processing later). On-line operation is thus keyed to situations in which an immediate response is important.

9.1 Development of Applications

It is significant that the first major developments of computer systems occurred during World War II. The first large-scale electronic computer, ENIAC, was built for the Ballistic Research Laboratories of the U.S. Army Ordinance Corps to be used in the calculation of trajectories and firing tables. Several types of analog devices were built and used in gunfire control.

An equally obvious need for computer systems was apparent in scientific computation. Many of the early computer systems were built by and for universities. Perhaps, the very obviousness of military and scientific computation acted as a block to the development of additional application areas. Computer systems were considered scientific tools, which tended to obscure visions of their use in nonscientific areas.

In the early 1950s the first electronic digital computer was installed in a business organization. This marked the beginning of the boom in applications. Accounting departments began the use of computer systems, and payroll was often the first application they attempted. This has always struck us as something of a mystery since payroll is frequently complicated, and always unforgiving. People who claim a total lack of arithmetic ability sometimes have a surprising ability to calculate their pay and to be vocal about discrepancies. On the other hand, payroll is probably the best defined procedure in any organization, and it generally accounts for substantial amounts of clerical resources. The former characteristic tends to reduce risk, and the latter raises the return on the investment in the new system. Accounts receivable, accounts payable, and general ledger are other early examples of accounting-oriented business systems. Later, more sophisticated business applications included inventory control and production control.

As communication capability was added to computer systems the development of on-line applications began, again with the military SAGE (Semi Automatic Ground Environment), a massive air defense system, which was developed in the 1950s. It included direct radar input to the system as well as on-line interaction with the system's operators.

On-line operation is also characteristic of industrial process control systems and in more recent years has come to include an entire subcategory of *real-time* applications. Real time is probably best described as a characteristic of system responsiveness. If the response of a system to a stimulus is fast enough to alter the nature of that stimulus, then the system has responded in real-time. In the interception of unknown aircraft, for example, information on the course and speed of both the target and the interceptor are received and processed; then the course of the interceptor is corrected so that it will contact the target. The computer system does not simply monitor and report the process, it alters the process by creating a response in real time. More recently, real-time systems have been developed in business. Airline reservation systems are a prominent example. In addition, real-time control of production, inventory, and other operations of business is now a reality.

9.2   A Batch Application

Figure 9.1 illustrates the order-entry system currently being used at Atlantic Steel Company in Atlanta, Georgia. The triggering input to this system is an order from a customer or a field salesman, which is received by telephone or mail. From this incoming information, a transmittal sheet is prepared containing the customer's name and order number, routing, descriptions and quantities of the products ordered, and the order entry and shipping dates. The transmittal sheet is taken to a device that accepts both keyed information and special, prepunched cards and produces both punched paper tape and printed output. The operator of this machine uses the customer name and product descriptions to pull cards such as the one illustrated in Figure 9.2 from their respective files. The customer card is prepunched with information, including the ship-to address, routing and billing address, and identification codes; the product card is prepunched with data describing the item and with codes. These cards, together with any special instructions and quantities entered via the keyboard, produce the formal order documents that contain all available order information. At the same time, a paper tape is punched with the order number, the customer number, and the code numbers of the products ordered. Copies of the order are routed to the required departments and files, and the paper tape is sent to the data processing department at the end of the day.

The information on the paper tape is added to an order file on disk and is printed on an "audit" listing for reference purposes. New orders on the order file are accepted as input to an order scheduling program. This program updates the finished goods inventory and produces stock lists for use by the sales department and the production scheduling department.

Shipment of the order triggers the invoicing process. A paper tape that includes order number, line number, quantity or weight shipped, and unit price is generated after shipment. It is processed against the open order file, thereby completing the items for invoicing. The customer number and product numbers are used as keys to the customer and product files, where descriptive and support information are obtained. Finally, the program produces an invoice, an entry in the sales history file, and an entry in the accounts receivable file.

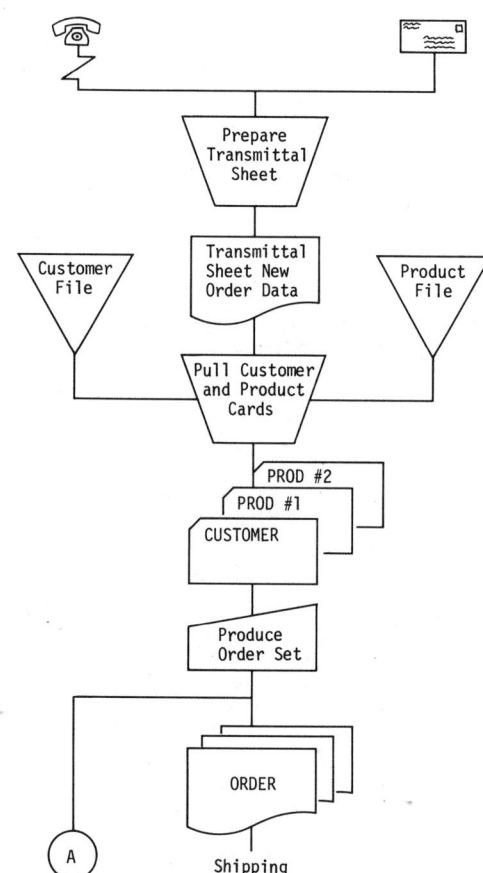

Figure 9.1 Atlantic Steel Company order-entry system.

Computer System Applications

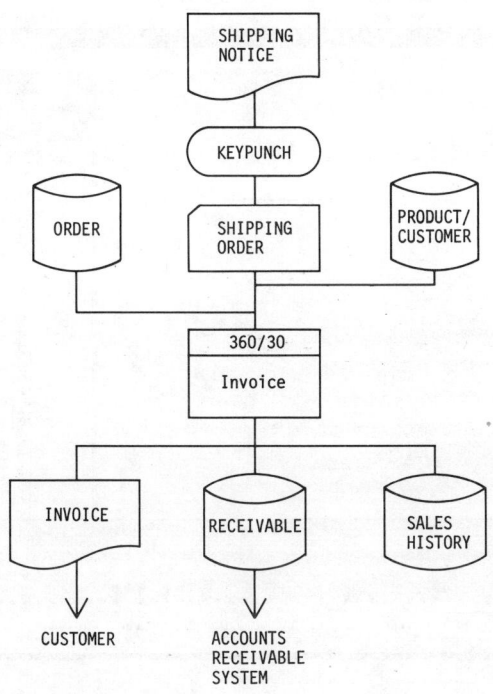
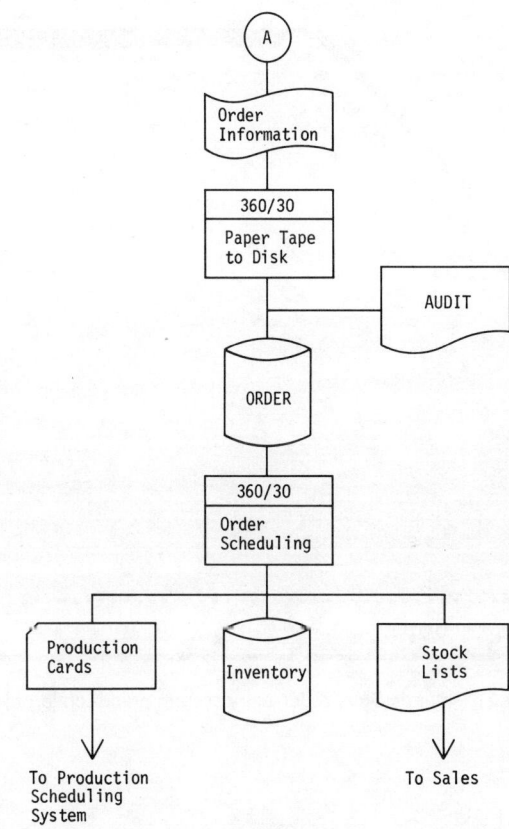

Figure 9.2 Atlantic Steel order-entry system prepunched product card.

9.3 An On-Line Application

Figure 9.3 shows a cathode-ray tube device in the Flight Control Center at Delta Air Lines. All en route flights are divided among the flight superintendents who are served by these devices. Each flight superintendent monitors the progress of 15 to 20 flights via the CRT device, which is on-line to the central flight control computer system.

Figure 9.4 illustrates the overall relationships of the flight control system. The basic input to the system is the flight schedule, which is produced by a batch system called the air information system and is recorded on magnetic tape. The schedules are transferred from magnetic tape to disk for use by the flight control system. Equipment performance factors—such as fuel consumption for specific aircraft under varying operating conditions—being relatively static are also maintained on disk files. Acceptable alternative cities are entered by the flight superintendent and finally, approximately one hour before flight time, weather and route information are entered by meteorologists. All of this information is entered via CRT terminals.

Delta's operating philosophy is such that the majority of responsibility remains with the human operators of the system—especially the meteorologists. Instead of

Figure 9.3 A cathode-ray tube device in flight control at Delta Air Lines in Atlanta, Georgia.

entering raw weather information and permitting the system to perform all calculations, the meteorologist translates actual weather conditions into adjustment factors that are used directly in the calculations performed by the system. For example, the meteorologist

152 Chapter Nine

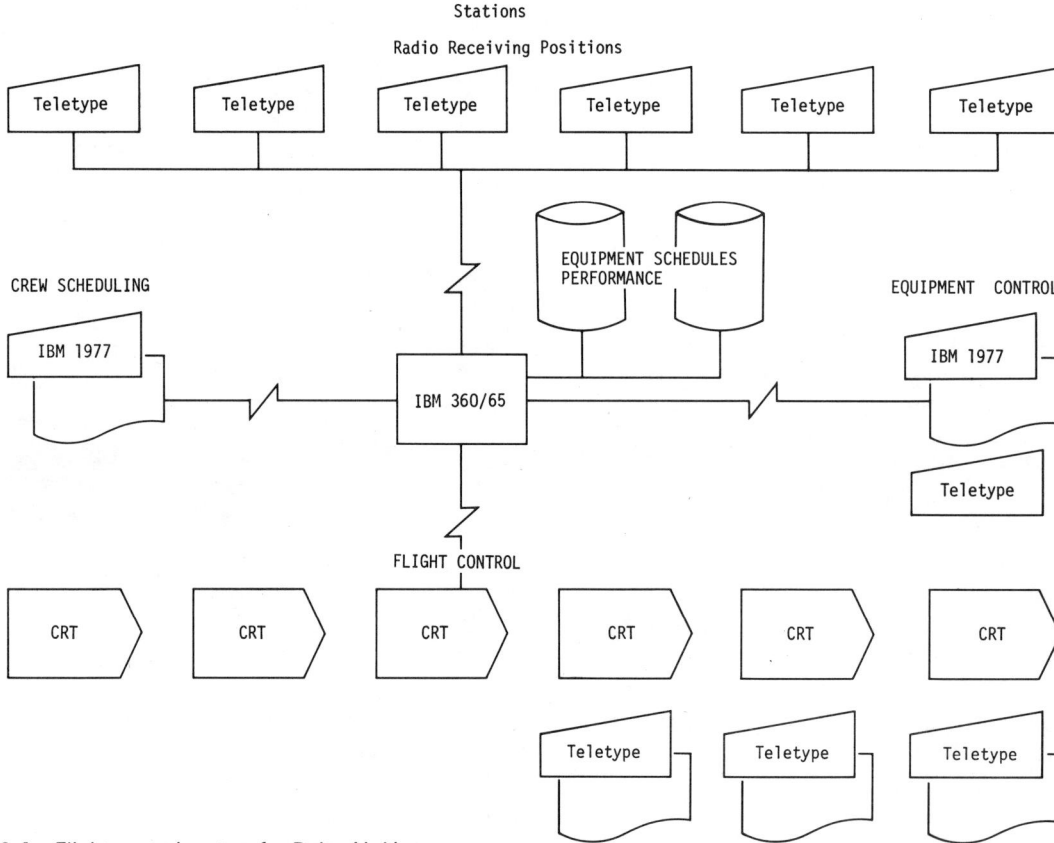

Figure 9.4 Flight control system for Delta Air Lines.

supplies a factor of $+n$ or $-n$ knots for the adjustment of the aircraft's speed rather than raw data on wind speed.

On request, the flight control system produces a flight plan. The flight plan authorizes a plane to depart and includes the flight number, aircraft number, aircraft type, route, mileage, time of departure and arrival, air speed, fuel consumption statistics, and remarks.

During the flight, each station reports in and out times. The departure station reports the time the aircraft left the loading gate. Intermediate stations report the times the aircraft arrived at and left the gate, and the destination station reports the time the aircraft arrived at the gate. All delays of over 15 minutes are also reported. All of these messages are transmitted by teletype to a message-switching computer system, which automatically routes the necessary messages into the flight control system. In addition, actual or estimated off-the-ground times are reported.

This en route progress information is used to update an automatically produced display on the flight superintendent's CRT. The flight number, aircraft number, destination city, estimated time of arrival, and remarks are displayed for each en route flight being monitored by the flight superintendent at that position. The flight superintendent may also call for the display of all messages and flight releases for a given flight.

9.4 Medical Applications

Grady Memorial Hospital in Atlanta, Georgia, has a system used in the active care of maternity patients. The system is operated by the Obstetrics-Hematology Clinic of the federally funded Maternal and Infant Care Project. As an expectant mother is accepted for treatment, information—including her name, date of birth, number of full-term infants, number of premature infants, and date of last menstrual period—is recorded and punched into cards for entry to the system. The new patient is added to the Obstetrics-Hematology master file, which is recorded on magnetic tape. The system is illustrated in Figure 9.5.

Each time the patient is examined in the clinic, the results of laboratory tests and the physicians remarks are punched into cards that update the Obstetrics-Hematology master. Specifically, the Obstetrics-Hematology Clinic detail card and the blood pressure, weight, and urine analysis cards contain laboratory results, while as many remarks cards as necessary are used to record the physician's comments.

As the systems chart indicates, the update program also produces a magnetic tape containing report transactions. The report transaction tape becomes input to the print program which produces the Delivered Report, the Undelivered Report, and the Patient Name Report.

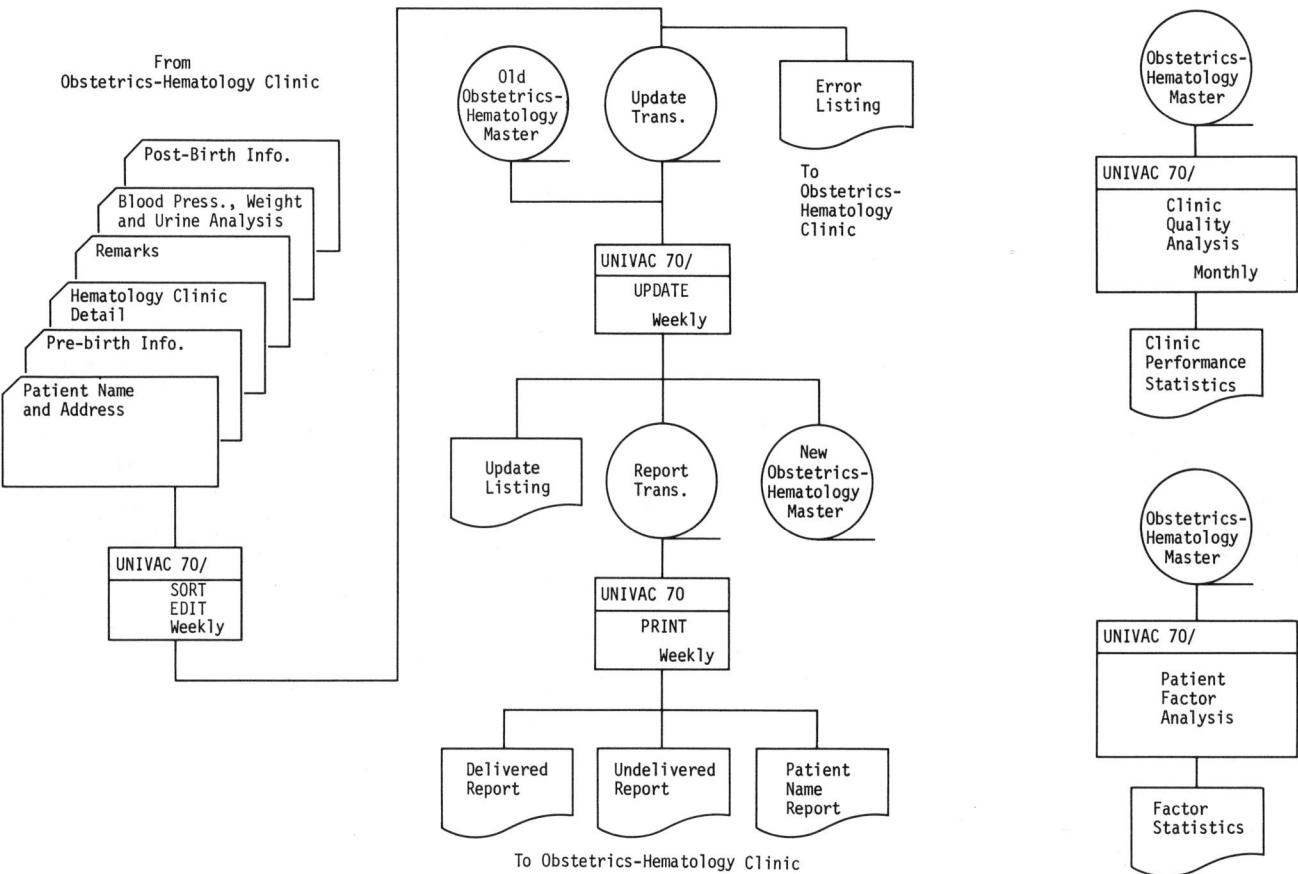

Figure 9.5 Obstetrics-Hematology Clinic system at Grady Memorial Hospital, Atlanta, Georgia.

The latter report is, in effect, a census of active patients in the clinic which lists them by name with their medical record number, lab number, birth date and estimated date of confinement.

The Undelivered Report (Figure 9.6) is printed two hours before the clinic opens and is available to the physician who is treating the patient that day. The physician thus is able to review the entire course of treatment as well as the progress of the patient's physical status. Abnormal conditions such as Rh-negative, high or low blood pressure, and level of serum iron are enclosed in asterisks or parentheses for easier visual identification. All Undelivered Reports are checked for abnormal conditions, so that patients not scheduled to attend the current clinic may be contacted and brought in if necessary.

The Delivered Report (Figure 9.7) is the last Undelivered Report updated with post-birth information. This document becomes a part of the patient's permanent medical record.

Two hundred seventy variables such as previous children, postpartum hemorrhaging, iron deficiency, folic acid deficiency, and type of delivery (for example, caesarean section) are tracked by the system. Statistics based on these variables are used first to evaluate the quality of medical care offered by the clinic. A major statistic is the perinatal mortality rate, the number of stillborn plus the number of infant deaths within the first 28 days following birth per thousand births. The number of caesarean sections, number of transfusions, method of delivery other than caesarean section, and the type of anasthesia administered are also listed. These statistics can be compared with corresponding statistics from other medical facilities and, as data is accumulated within the system, the clinic will be able to evaluate itself against past performance.

The statistics being accumulated within this system are also used in research. Currently for example, a matrix tabulation of the variables associated with each delivery is prepared. Each variable appears as both a row and a column entry and the conjunctions of variables for each delivery are tallied in the appropriate matrix element. A delivery marked by iron deficiency and postpartum hemorrhage, for example, would be tallied twice, at the intersection of the iron deficiency row and postpartum hemorrhage column and the postpartum hemorrhage row and iron deficiency column. Relationships between variables are indicated by the value at the intersection. It was found, for example, that in 1971 in this clinic 30 percent of all premature infants were from mothers who were anemic at the time of delivery. The system currently has the capability of listing the names and medical record numbers of patients by selected variables; in the future, this will be extended

```
HMR060-1           GRADY MEMORIAL HOSPITAL           PAGE   1        HMR060-1           GRADY MEMORIAL HOSPITAL           PAGE   2

M&I HEMATOLOGY CLINIC    UNDELIVERED REPORT    PROCESS DATE 10/30/72  M&I HEMATOLOGY CLINIC    UNDELIVERED REPORT    PROCESS DATE 10/30/72
                                                                                              ANTEPARTUM COURSE          ( CONTINUED )
                                FIRST CLINIC VIST            08/28/72  -----------------------------------------------------------------
0487977    LAB # 01127          EST. DATE OF CONFINEMENT 10/14/72        DATE    WKD    REMARKS :  ADMITTED TO 1200A WITH UTI
DATE OF BIRTH  10/06/52         LAST MENSTRUAL PERIOD    01/07/72       08/28/72 333
AGE 20                          DELIVERY DATE
FULL TERM INFANTS        0      DELIVERY WEEKS                           DATE    WKD    REMARKS :  BP = 100/060      URINE SUG 0 ALB 0
PREMATURE INFANTS        0      BLOOD TYPE      0 RH POSITIVE           08/28/72 333
ABORTION                 0      HB ELECTROPHORESIS            AA        -----------------------------------------------------------------
LIVING CHILDREN          0      SEROLOGY NEGATIVE                        DATE    WKD    REMARKS :  DISCHARGED FROM 1200A
                                                                        08/31/72 336
              A N T E P A R T U M   C O U R S E                         -----------------------------------------------------------------
-----------------------------------------------------------              DATE    WKD                                        FE    TIBC
   DATE    WKD     REMARKS :  PROBLEM LISTING AS FOLLOWS ---            09/07/72 346
  12/12/71 000                                                                                                               80   (519)
-----------------------------------------------------------               WBC   HCT     RBC    RETIC    PLAT  MCV   LDH
   DATE    WKD     REMARKS :  01 INTRAUTERINE PREGNANCY                  (12000) 31   (3.44) ( 4.4)    PAN    91  ( 672)
  12/13/71 000                                                          -----------------------------------------------------------------
-----------------------------------------------------------              DATE    WKD    REMARKS :  INDIRECT COOMBS -- NEGATIVE
   DATE    WKD     REMARKS :  02 PICA                                   09/07/72 346
  12/14/71 000                                                          -----------------------------------------------------------------
-----------------------------------------------------------              DATE    WKD    REMARKS :  CHECK TYPE & RH ON THIS PATIENT
   DATE    WKD     REMARKS :  03 UTI, RESOLVED                          09/07/72 346
  12/15/71 000                                                          -----------------------------------------------------------------
-----------------------------------------------------------              DATE    WKD    REMARKS :  BP = 110/070    WGT = 137.0
   DATE    WKD     REMARKS :  04 ANEMIA                                 09/07/72 346                               URINE SUG 0 ALB 0
  12/16/71 000                                                          -----------------------------------------------------------------
-----------------------------------------------------------              DATE    WKD    REMARKS :  PAGOPHAGIA
   DATE    WKD     REMARKS :  BP = 116/072                              09/07/72 346
  05/28/72 202                                                          -----------------------------------------------------------------
-----------------------------------------------------------              DATE    WKD    REMARKS :  BP = 110/070    WGT = 138.0
   DATE    WKD     REMARKS :  BP = 132/068      URINE SUG 0 ALB 0       09/14/72 356                               URINE SUG 0 ALB 0
  08/10/72 306
-----------------------------------------------------------

   DATE    WKD
  08/28/72 333

   WBC    HCT            RETIC

   9680   (29)          ( 2.2)
```

Figure 9.6 Obstetrics-Hematology Clinic Undelivered Report, Grady Memorial Hospital, Atlanta, Georgia.

```
HMR060-2            GRADY MEMORIAL HOSPITAL           PAGE  1      HMR060-2            GRADY MEMORIAL HOSPITAL           PAGE  2
M&I HEMATOLOGY CLINIC   DELIVERED REPORT   PROCESS DATE 10/30/72   M&I HEMATOLOGY CLINIC   DELIVERED REPORT   PROCESS DATE 10/30/72
                                                                                        ANTEPARTUM COURSE        ( CONTINUED )
                                 FIRST CLINIC VISIT     07/12/72
0510983   LAB # 01095            EST. DATE OF CONFINEMENT 12/07/72    DATE   WKD    REMARKS :  APPT. MADE FOR DYSPLASIA CLINIC
DATE OF BIRTH  09/27/54          LAST MENSTRUAL PERIOD  03/01/72   08/24/72  251
AGE 18                           DELIVERY DATE          10/22/72
FULL TERM INFANTS   0            DELIVERY WEEKS         33            DATE   WKD    REMARKS :  GENETIC COUNSELING
PREMATURE INFANTS   0            BLOOD TYPE  O RH POSITIVE         08/24/72  251
ABORTION            0            HB ELECTROPHORESIS *** AS ***
LIVING CHILDREN     0            SEROLOGY NEGATIVE                    DATE   WKD    REMARKS :  BP = 110/060   WGT = 152.0
                                                                  08/24/72  251                          URINE  SUG 0    ALB 0
INFANT WEIGHT  2770              METHOD        SPONT.
APGAR          10                OUTCOME       WELL                   DATE   WKD    URINE C&S: *** CONTAMINATION ***
                                                                  09/28/72  301
ANESTHESIA     LOCAL OR BLOCK    BLOOD LOSS    401 - 450 CC
INFECTION      PP UTI            TRANSFUSION   NONE                   DATE   WKD    REMARKS :  BP = 090/060   WGT = 162.5
STERILIZATION  NO                                                 09/28/72  301                          URINE  SUG 0    ALB 0

       D I A G N O S E S   A N D   C O M P L I C A T I O N S          DATE   WKD    REMARKS :  BP = 120/080   WGT = 166.5
                                                                  10/12/72  321                          URINE  SUG 0    ALB 0
       LOWER URINARY TRACT INFECTION    DYSPLASIA
       HETEROZYGOUS G6PD DEFICIENCY     RUBELLA SCREEN POSITIVE       DATE   WKD
                                                                  10/22/72  334
           A N T E P A R T U M   C O U R S E
                                                                      HCT
  DATE   WKD    CYTOLOGY :  *** DYSPLASIA ***
08/08/72 226                                                          37
                                                                  - - - - - - - - - - -  D E L I V E R Y  - - - - - - - - - - - - -
          HCT

          38

  DATE   WKD    REMARKS :  RUBELLA SCREEN POSITIVE -- PREV INFECT
00/00/72 226

  DATE   WKD    REMARKS :  BP = 100/060   WGT = 147.0
08/08/72 226                               URINE  SUG 0    ALB 0

  DATE   WKD                              FE   TIBC    METH
08/24/72 251                                           RED
                                         103  (426)   (32.0%)

                                   LDH
                                  (458)
```

Figure 9.7 Obstetrics-Hematology Clinic Delivered Report, Grady Memorial Hospital, Atlanta, Georgia.

to all variables. The researcher may thus examine the history of each delivery associated with the variables he is studying.

Computer system monitoring of critically ill patients and computer control of some treatment processes are being implemented in many hospitals.[1] Sensing devices are attached to the patient, and information is automatically gathered on such factors as heart rate, arterial pressure, venous pressure, work done by the heart, temperature, and urine output. In addition, an on-line blood chemistry unit is being developed. Information is gathered on a schedule that varies with the factor. Temperature, for example, is monitored at fifteen-minute intervals. The incoming information is displayed at the patient's bedside, is analyzed, and is recorded if significant. Significant variations in the monitored factors result in an alert to the staff. In addition, the physician or the nurse can enter information by keyboard. Drugs administered, procedures performed, and miscellaneous patient information can be entered in this fashion. The physician may call for and review the patient's entire file from the keyboard. The information is displayed on a CRT device.

The control aspect of this system includes fluid and medication administration, respiration assistance, and cardiac pacemakers. For example, the computer controls the rate of fluid administration by adjusting pump speed. The nurse requests a rate of fluid administration, the computer checks the rate for reasonableness and sets the pump speed for a more accurate flow than is provided by the current drops per minute method.

Computer systems have also been developed that automatically record a patient's medical history in an interactive process, diagnose heart disease from x-ray images, store and retrieve patient information, and determine drug dosage.

9.5 A Football Application

Figure 9.8 is a chart for the system used by the Atlanta Falcons Football Club, Inc. Every Monday morning during the football season the Falcons receive the films of four to seven games played by their next opponent. These films are carefully reviewed and analyzed by the coaching staff. A by-product of this process is a key-punch-ready game analysis. The following information is recorded on every play run by their next opponent:

---

[1] David H. Stewart, David H. Erback, and Herbert Shubin, "A Computer System for Real-Time Monitoring and Management of the Critically Ill," in *AFIPS Conference Proceedings* 33 : 1 (Fall Joint Computer Conference) (Washington, D.C.: Thompson Book Co., 1968). pp. 797–807.

Computer System Applications

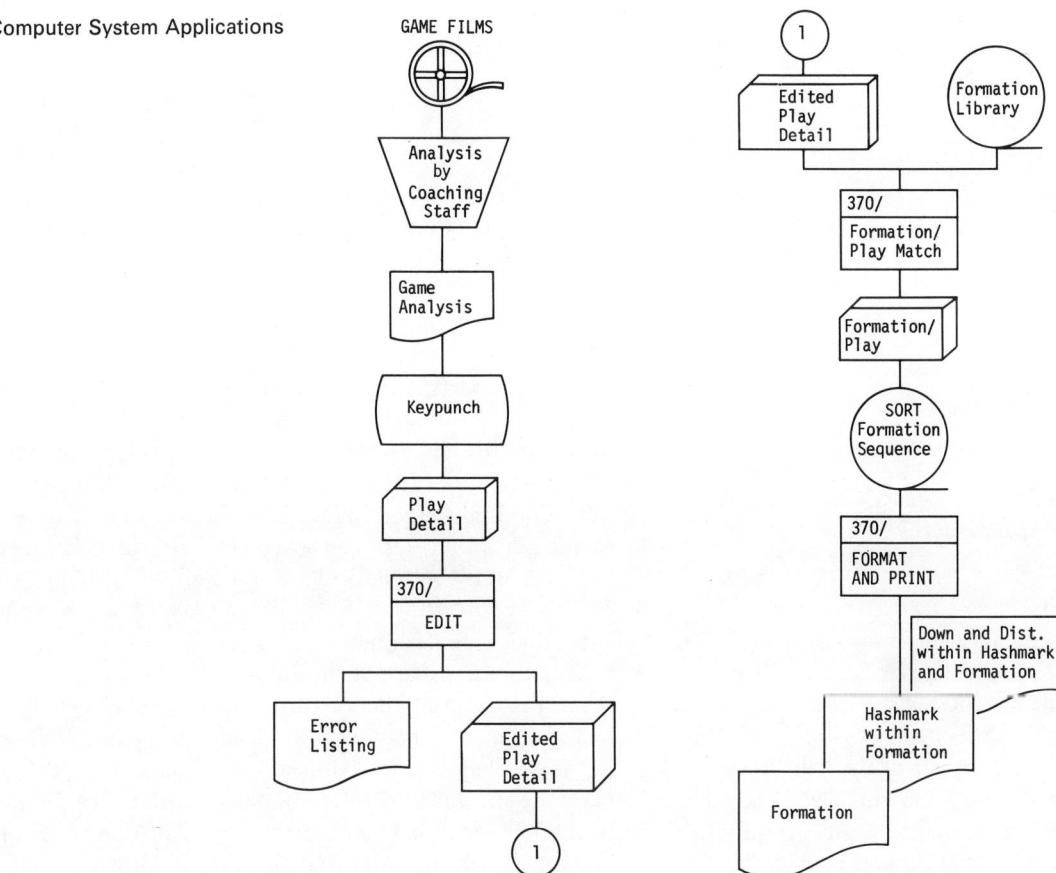

Figure 9.8 The Atlanta Falcons Football Club, Inc., scouting system showing offensive analysis.

1. formation
2. down
3. distance to a first down
4. hash mark
5. yard line
6. gain or loss on the play
7. points scored

Running Play
8. back carrying
9. hole number
10. player number of back carrying
11. type of play

Passing Play
12. pattern run by each receiver
13. player number of intended receiver
14. complete or not
15. type of play

There are 60 to 90 plays in each game, so 500 to 600 plays are recorded and keypunched one-to-a-card in analyzing each opponent. These play detail cards are input to an edit program which checks for omissions, reasonableness, and correct format of the data.

The edited play cards are then matched against a formation library, which is on magnetic tape, to produce a combined card deck of formation and play cards. The formation library contains the position of each player for over 1,000 offensive formations. Each player's position is determined in terms of a standard 132 column (print position) 66 row (lines) output form. The center, for example, may be located 44 down and 64 across. When new formations are encountered they are recorded by the coaching staff and the formation library is updated.

The combined formation/play card deck is sorted into sequence by formation and is input to a program that formats and prints the data. An example of the output of this print run is illustrated in Figure 9.9. Three different reports may be printed. Play detail may be shown by formation, hash mark within formation, or down and distance within hash mark within formation. The example is organized by hash mark within formation. The Red Left (RL) formation is shown, with details of the plays that were run when the ball was positioned at the middle hash mark. Preceding and following pages of this report show the detail of plays run from the short and wide hash marks, also.

This figure is part of an analysis of the Los Angeles Rams made during the 1971 football season. The analysis included games between the Rams and the Browns, Patriots, Chargers, Fortyniners, and Saints. The passing plays are shown at the top of the sheet, with pass attempts to the left (or right) being printed on that side. The top line on the left indicates that the pass attempt was made to player number 50. The play type is coded as N and the receivers identified as X, Y, and Z ran the patterns

```
                            ATLANTA FALCONS
                          OFFENSIVE FORMATION              RAMS                       122
                                  RL                        VS    BROWNS
                            MIDDLE HASH MARK                      PATRIOTS
                                                                  CHARGERS
                                                                  49ERS
                                                                  SAINTS

  50 N        Z-OUTUP  Y-HK    X-OUT    -      -    13 -       50 P     X-UP   Y-CROSS Z-IN   -    -   84 -
  50 N        Z-SLANT  Y-SHAL  X-UP     -      -       - 9     50 P     X-OUT  Y-LOOKI Z-OUT  -    -   48 -
  50 O7SPRT   Z-OUTSD  Y-CORN  A-CKFLT  X-IN   -    13 -
  74 SD       Z-OUT    Y-HK    X-OUT    A-CIR  -    13 -
  50 SD       Z-CORN   Y-DRAG  X-UP     -      -    13 -
  50 B        P-CKSEA  Y-STOP  Z-OUT    X-HK   -    34 - 4
  73 B        B-HK     Y-CROSS Z-UP     X-POST -    34 -
  78 B        Y-HK     Z-OUT   B-CIR    X-HK   A-FLT 80 -
  50 ABCKFLT  Z-SPOST  Y-LKI   X-SPOST  -      -    13 -

                            9 ATTEMPTS  - 13 YARDS              2 ATTEMPTS  &  0 YARDS



                                        XXXX                           XXXX
                                        X B X                          X A X
                                        X   X                          X   X
                                        XXXX                           XXXX


   XXXX
   X Z X
   X   X                                        XXXX
   XXXX                                         X QB X
                                                X    X
                                                XXXX

                 XXXX     XXXX    XXXX    XXXXXX    XXXX    XXXX                  XXXX
                 X Y X    X   X   X   X   X    X    X   X   X   X                 X X X
                 X   X    X   X   X   X   X    X    X   X   X   X                 X   X
                 XXXX     XXXX    XXXX    XXXXXX    XXXX    XXXX                  XXXX
              9 HOLE    7 HOLE   5 HOLE   1 HOLE   0 HOLE  4 HOLE  6 HOLE   8 HOLE

              27 PBO    45 DIVE                   44 NTRAP           48 BOB
              BRO 30 & 7  49E 33 & 4              BRO 35 & 3         PAT 35 & 8

              27 PBO    25 LEADRAW                                   28 FLIP
              SAI 34 & 0  BRO 25 & 20                                49E 25 & 6

              2 ATT & 7  2 ATT & 24               1 ATT & 3          2 ATT & 14
```

Figure 9.9   Offensive formation analysis from the Atlanta Falcons Football Club, Inc.

indicated. The pass was for 13 yards but was incomplete.

The running plays are listed at the bottom of the sheet under the hole at which the running play was attempted. Under the 5 hole, for example, two attempts are shown, with a total of 24 yards gained. The first attempt was by the number 4 back against the 5 hole and the play is described as DIVE. The play was run against the Fortyniners (49E), the runner was player number 33, and it gained four yards. The second attempt was against the Browns, and it gained 20 yards. Transparencies are made of the output so that the results can be projected for presentation to the team. With this output the coaches and team are able to evaluate the likelihood of a run or a pass from a given hash mark when the opponent comes out in a particular formation. Further, the likelihood that a particular player will be the chosen receiver or runner can also be evaluated. With the third report option, these evaluations can also be keyed to the down and whether the distance to the first down is short or long.

Finally, a set of statistical reports is run without reference to formation. One report, a history of plays in sequence by down and distance, is used to answer questions such as "What do they like to run when it is third and long?" A second report is sorted by side of field and yard marker, while a third is a history of plays that were run when the team was within their opponent's ten-yard line.

9.6 Time-Sharing

Time-sharing is the concurrent use of a computer system by many users. In a typical arrangement, many devices such as teletypewriters are connected via telephone lines or cables to a central computer. Each user can dial the computer system, initiate whatever task he wishes, and receive the results of this processing. The computer system can execute only one command at a time, but by jumping rapidly from user to user (multiprogramming) it is able to give the illusion of simultaneity. Each user feels that he has the entire resources of the computer system constantly at his command even though he may be sharing the system with many others.

The major reason for time-sharing is clearly economic. On the simplest level, many users share the costs as well as the capabilities of highly expensive computer system resources. At a more technical level, more users are competing for the use of the system, so idle time is less likely to occur. A varied program mix tends to balance the demands placed on all facilities, so that specific equipment resources do not become overloaded. For instance, the amount of time that the central processing unit spends waiting for input operations to be completed is drastically reduced. Instead of waiting, the CPU turns to the processing of another user's program. Time-sharing is, however, more expensive per unit of processing performed than batch processing is. The sharing process itself requires computer system resources that are, in effect, an overhead cost of time-sharing.

Both general-purpose and special-purpose time-sharing systems exist. Special-purpose systems are restricted as to the type of processing or the type of problem they accept. Some time-sharing systems, for example, do not allow file manipulation, while others are dedicated to specific applications such as computer-assisted instruction (CAI), stock market quotations, or stock feed mix calculations. In a general-purpose system, the user has access to the full power of the computer system without specific limitations.

Personal Data Services General-purpose time-sharing has developed into what might more accurately be described as personal data services. The time-sharing user, more than any other computer user, molds the capabilities of the computer system to fit his own specific needs. He creates files that contain only the specific data items which interest him, and he writes programs to answer only the questions he wants answered. In some instances the total of the services used amounts to a personal information system.

This concept is certain to be developed further in coming years. It is not difficult to conceive of terminals in many, if not most, homes connected to one or more central computer systems and supporting a personal information system for the householder. Such a personal information system might include a household accounting and budgetary system, files of names and addresses, frequently used telephone numbers, and access to centralized files of information on a variety of subjects.

The Computer Utility An extension of the idea of time-sharing leads to the concept of the computer, or information, utility. In general, a computer utility would provide information services through an economic arrangement similar to that employed by utilities such as the telephone and power companies. Local or regional information centers would provide for the normal needs of their users, but these centers would also be connected in grids, or networks, so that overload conditions could be shifted between centers. Such a system might also contain special-purpose centers available to all users via their local centers. One center, for example, might process medical diagnoses exclusively. A physician desiring such an analysis would simply dial his local information center and submit the symptoms directly into the system. The local system would analyze the request, automatically forward the message to the special-purpose center, and accept the results from that center when processing was concluded. The physician would not necessarily know or care where his request was processed but would select the services he requires from a catalog containing a list and description of services and approximate processing times. Billing might simply be based on time used.

Utilities such as we are describing could evolve out of current systems. Existing time-sharing operations might link together to provide mutual back-up and balancing capability. As the number of time-sharing operations grows, this computer utility concept may provide a stable and sufficient market for the more specialized information services.

Government regulation is almost a certainty in such a system. Economically, competition could probably be tolerated and would, in fact, be advantageous on the local basis, but a special-purpose center would probably require protection and regulation. The investment in software and system development would be substantial and, depending on the degree of specialization, one or only a few centers would be needed in each specialty. Multiple centers would probably be regional in their coverage. The special-purpose centers might thus be monopolies, requiring regulation for the protection of public interest. Regulation might also be required because of the personal and sensitive nature of some of the information entrusted to the system.

9.7 Business Integration

The "checkless–cashless society" is coming closer to being realized. The vast and increasing use of credit cards is an important first step. The development of one universally accepted meta-card will be a major second step. Banks have been processing payrolls for individual companies for years, and some have already begun to use automatic debiting and crediting of accounts or fund transfer systems. The checkless society is just one aspect of a larger phenomenon, which I have chosen to call "business integration."

A great deal of overlapping and unnecessary work takes place at the interfaces between business organizations. An organization desiring to purchase an item, for example, generates a purchase order, often out of a computer-based purchasing system, and sends this document to the selected vendor. The vendor converts this input into a form that is acceptable to his own order-entry system. The new form may be an entirely new document, or it may be converted to machine-readable form. The vendor then processes the order, ships the item ordered, and prepares an invoice for mailing to the purchaser. The purchaser converts the invoice for processing in his payables system in order to produce a check, which then proceeds on a rather tortuous processing path of its own. The procedure outlined above is filled with duplication—in particular, the repeated conversions to machine-readable form and back again and also the recording and rerecording of information. This inefficiency is typical of many interorganizational transactions.

Business integration, then, takes the form of designing computer systems that will form the interface between organizations. Possibly the simplest form of computer interface might be the placement of terminals in the purchasing offices of a vendor's best customers so that orders may be entered directly into the vendor's computer system. A more universal approach involves the development of message switching centers which would allow direct communication between computer systems. If the purchaser, the vendor, and the bank were all linked by a switching center, all of the transactions described above, including the transfer of funds, could be accomplished automatically with the transmission of standard format messages between computer systems. Achieving the necessary standardization is the major obstacle to such a scheme. Participants in the network would have to agree on a standard terminology, standard codes, and standard formats for all transactions. Each participant would then modify his own systems to accept the standard formats and codes.

Systems such as that described above are not really a new idea. In part, the concept is similar to that of payment systems that have worked in Europe for many years. The major unique feature of the proposed system is that it includes business transactions and relationships not directly concerned with the transfer of funds. Although such a system does not now exist, it seems a likely step in the evolution of computer-based information systems.

9.8 Data Banks

The term *data bank* is generally used to denote a mass of information covering a specific area which constitutes a resource in and of itself. Although a data bank may consist of a number of files, the two have important differences. All the items of information included in a file are dictated by the processing to be performed on that file, but the items of information included in a data bank are dictated by their potential usefulness to users of the bank. A file cannot be built until processing requirements are known. It is common to design a data bank, and begin the collection and recording process as soon as the need has been determined, long before processing is considered.

Data banks have been proposed and built in many diverse areas. The National Crime Information Center

(NCIC), maintained by the Federal Bureau of Investigation in Washington, D.C., is a data bank containing information on stolen items and wanted persons, specifically:

1. stolen, missing, or recovered guns
2. stolen articles
3. wanted persons
4. stolen or wanted vehicles and stolen license plates
5. stolen, embezzled, or missing securities

Under this system terminals are located in police departments, sheriff's offices, state police facilities and federal law enforcement agencies across the country. The terminal operator first enters a code, which indicates whether he is entering information or making an inquiry, and then identifies his agency. The remainder of his message depends on the nature of the entry or inquiry and the file involved. To inquire against the wanted person file, for example, the operator must enter the person's name and date of birth or some other numerical identification such as Social Security number. If that person is located in the file, the operator is given information such as height, weight, hair color, the offense for which the individual is wanted, the date of the arrest warrant, the identity of the agency holding the warrant, and that agency's case number.

Several local governments have developed "social" data banks. Information about welfare, health, law enforcement, and all community services is being accumulated on a continuing basis. The data collected will have obvious value in the planning of community services and allocation of resources. In addition, it is likely to be valuable in the analysis of community problems. Is there, for example, a detectable relationship between health conditions or welfare enrollment and crime patterns? Such a relationship may reveal new approaches to social problems. With a sufficient mass of data community planners may gain new insights and understanding of underlying social processes.

One class of data bank contains catalog-type information on the literature of a specific subject area and thus provides the basis for a literature retrieval system. Existing systems include a data base, which contains indexes or abstracts for actual documents, and a searching technique for locating these documents. Systems have been envisioned that would assist the user in locating the specific documents which are applicable to his interests, and would also present the entire documents instantaneously for his inspection. The user might have the option of requesting hard copy reproductions of the information. This instantaneous retrieval of entire documents seems to be a long way from reality in view of today's technology. The vast amounts of material, even in very specialized areas, make storage capacity alone an overwhelming problem. On the other hand, current research into techniques such as the use of lasers in recording information could well result in a breakthrough in the years ahead.

Exercises

1. Should payroll be processed in batch mode or on-line? Why?
2. Should a system that assigns police units to calls be batch or on-line? Why?
3. Develop an argument to support either batch or on-line processing of student programs in a university environment.
4. Evaluate the Delta Air Lines policy of leaving the majority of responsibility with the human operators of the system. Why is this policy of any value? What arguments can you see to justify taking all human beings out of the operation of the system?
5. Design an alternative to the Atlantic Steel Company order-entry system described in Section 9.2.
6. What advantages would a computer-based patient medical history have over a manual system? Disadvantages?
7. What likelihood would you attach to the eventual development of computer information utilities? Why?
8. Your bank has recently written you a letter offering you an automatic bill paying service. Your employer will deposit your check with the bank, and the majority of your bills will be paid either by transactions between accounts at the bank or by drawing checks. The bank will notify you of the remaining balance. Draft a letter refusing the service and giving your reasons.
9. Draft the letter from the bank which was described in question 8. Be sure that you have answered all of the objections that you cited in your letter.
10. Design a social data bank for your community. What information will it contain and what keys will be used? What are the uses of your system?
11. Report on the state of the art in computer applications in your area of interest. What future developments do you anticipate?
12. Prepare a detailed report on a computer application with which you are familiar.
13. The use of computers during a game is currently a violation of the rules of the National Football League. If this were not the case, what sort of system would you recommend to the coaching staff of an NFL team?

10 Economic Impact

The major reason for the installation of most, if not all, electronic computers is economic. Although a few installations may have been justified as an improvement in the human condition, the vast majority of computer users must be persuaded by a decrease in costs or an increase in profits. The connection does not have to be direct, but the computer must at least facilitate a capability, such as management control, that will produce decreased cost or increased profit. It is not surprising, then, that the economic impact of electronic computers tends to be the most obvious. The controversy surrounding the nature of this economic impact may be surprising, though. Some predict drastic and dangerous economic changes, while others anticipate a gradual and relatively painless assimilation of this new technology into our economic life.

In this chapter, we examine the economic arguments concerning employment, organization, management, competition, and economic control. We must be particularly careful about accepting predictions, however, because in most cases we have very little experience and concrete evidence on which to base our assessment. The unbelievably large number of variables to consider makes accurate prediction extremely difficult. It is a good idea to accept predictions in this area as indicators of direction only—not as likely events.

Before discussing individual impact areas, we need to agree on the meaning of the terms *automation* and *cybernation*. The meaning of *automation*, which in the 1940s involved the use of specific mechanical devices[1] in physical operations, has become generalized to cover the performance by machines of any previously manual operation. *Mechanization* is a synonymous term. *Cybernation* is a combination of *automation* and *cybernetics* (the science of communication and control). Cybernation is a subset of automation that refers to the presence of automatic control, particularly control by a computer system. In this chapter, we will be most concerned with the impact of cybernation and with the automation, or mechanization, of clerical and administrative activities. Some arguments, however, will deal with automation in the larger sense.

---

[1] Particularly automatic transfer and positioning devices that move work in process between successive machines or work stations.

10.1 Employment

The most alarming and, as a consequence, the most emotional arguments about economic impact have dealt with the area of employment. The computer has the obvious potential for displacing human beings. Many computer systems are at least partially justified by the savings in clerical and other labor costs. In addition to its displacement capability, computer application implies a change in job structure. It is reasonable to expect that the jobs in a system that includes a computer will differ substantially from the jobs in a system without a computer.

Quantitative Impact   Because computer systems are so often justified as labor-savers, one might expect their quantitative impact on employment to be readily apparent. However, determination of an aggregate impact has been obscured by major economic factors, the most important of which is economic growth. Even within individual organizations, there is evidence to support both the impact and the no-impact arguments. An investigator may simply choose his position and then select his supporting cases. So, at this point the quantitative impact of computer systems on employment is still unresolved.

In the late 1950s and early 1960s, pessimism was the most common position. Observers were confronted with labor-saving applications of computer systems. These early applications (such as payroll and accounts receivable) were rather elementary, but it seemed plausible that, as computer applications became more complex and more widespread, they would cause greater and greater labor displacement. Given the relatively high unemployment rate (more than 5.5 percent) and a rapid increase in productivity per man-hour, many pessimistic descriptions of social change were given. Predictions were made of unemployment so widespread as to make the depression of the thirties seem "a pleasant joke," of potentially unlimited production by systems of machines with little or no help from human beings, of the eventual production of all goods and services by 10 percent of the population.[2]

This view led to justifiable concern over the implications of massive displacement. The mechanism of displacement seemed to lead at the same time to unprecedented levels of prosperity, enabling society to support its unemployed. So, the problem became how the displaced would use their newfound leisure and also maintain a sense of their own worth. At the very minimum, a sweeping change of ethics would be required, and the work-to-eat linkage would have to be broken.

At the same time, another group of observers took the same unemployment and output per man-hour statistics together with a selection of specific cases and concluded that there was really no cause for alarm. The National Commission on Technology, Automation, and Economic Progress[3] concluded that the idea of a technological revolution with gainful employment rendered obsolete simply was not supported by the evidence. The commission was not entirely optimistic, however, and called for various measures to counteract an increasing unemployment problem.

An important factor in both the optimistic and pessimistic arguments about economic impact is the amount of time that the predictions cover. Although some of the pessimists were talking about the month after next, many were talking about twenty and even fifty years into the future. The commission, by way of contrast, was considering the next ten years. A difference of ten years can easily turn substantial agreement into conflict over projections.

---

[2] To put this last prediction in perspective, one must realize that approximately 38 percent of the population produced all of the goods and services in 1967. This is calculated from the table "Labor Force, Employment, and Earnings—Population and Labor Force," in U.S. Department of Commerce, *Business Statistics*, 16th Biennial Edition (Washington, D.C.: U.S. Government Printing Office, 1967), p. 65.

---

[3] National Commision on Technology, Automation, and Economic Progress, *Technology and the American Economy* (Washington, D.C.: U.S. Government Printing Office, 1966).

The optimists relied heavily on economic theory to support their argument. They noted that an improvement in productivity should also reduce costs and, hence, prices in a competitive market. The lowered price would cause an increase in the quantity demanded, a corresponding increase in production, and the reemployment of those who were displaced by the initial improvement in productivity. In addition, lower costs should increase profits, which would stimulate investment in capital goods. Then, employment in the industry that produces the capital goods also increases. A necessary supplementary argument holds that, as machines become more productive, both labor and capital prices will adjust to precisely that point which will clear the market of both factors.

Some pessimists responded that an economic theory based on the idea of scarcity was no longer valid in an era of virtually unlimited productive capacity. Pessimists who accepted the theory that the economy would eventually adjust asserted that it could take decades, with much human suffering in the interim. Not so, said the optimists. A firm that is automating is likely to be expanding. Not only is an expanding firm more inclined to invest because of its rosier future, but it is also likely to be experiencing the strains for which automation or cybernation are often a solution. As a consequence, there is no real displacement, because a stable amount of labor will be able to keep pace with increased production demands.

Productivity itself has been a source of continuing disagreement. Looking specifically at 1961, 1962, and 1963, the pessimists observed an average increase in productivity per man-hour of more than 3.5 percent[4] and attributed this to the increased efficiency of machine systems. With this growth in productivity added to the annual growth of the work force, the economy simply could not provide sufficient jobs. The optimists countered by choosing a longer time period. Between 1947 and 1965 productivity rose at a trend rate of about 3.2 percent a year. When agriculture is excluded, the rate drops to 2 percent before the war and 2.5 percent after. This growth in productivity was considered substantial but not revolutionary. In the late 1960s, the increase in output per man-hour declined significantly, and a number of popular articles were written to point out the ill-foundedness of the earlier fears. In late 1970 output per man-hour jumped back into the 4 percent range and, at least temporarily, both optimists and pessimists found silence to be the best response.

Although case studies are available to lend weight to either side of the argument, one industry study seems

---

[4] Bureau of the Census, "Output per Man-hour for the Private Economy—Indexes and Year-to-Year Change: 1947 to 1965." *Statistical Abstract of the United States* (Washington, D.C.: U.S. Government Printing Office, 1966).

particularly interesting. A 1970 report prepared by the Bureau of Labor Statistics[5] concluded that in the area of computer process control the impact on plant employment has been slight. This information is significant because computer process control has replaced more manual functions than most other computer applications. Yet, the same study also points out that one reason for the small displacement of labor was the fact that operating crews in the highly instrumented control rooms were generally at a minimum before introduction of the computer. Also, labor had been such a small part of the process cost in most cases that reduction of manpower was simply not an objective.

In a summary view, unemployment is a function of a number of distinct factors including demand, growth in the labor force, and productivity. Until the late 1960s demand overwhelmed all of the other factors. The growth of the U.S. population, the Vietnam war, and our efforts in space all created a demand that absorbed the increase in the labor force and buried the increased productivity caused by technological change.

We must also note that output per man-hour is a shaky peg for any argument to hang on. When economic activity reaches a peak and resources are being used to their fullest, less efficient resources are drawn into production and productivity increases become smaller. When demand and output decline, production processes are pared into more efficient shape, making excess capacity available. Then, any subsequent increase in demand is accompanied by a sharp increase in productivity. The only real significance in productivity figures lies in their trend over relatively long periods. Perhaps, by 1980 these figures will be able to provide some real evidence.

Although aggregate displacement is difficult if not impossible to measure, it is unreasonable to argue that none has occurred. To argue that attrition has absorbed the surplus labor does not alter the fact of impact. If someone is not hired to replace a leaving employee, the impact is the same as that of a firing, except that it is not directed at a specific individual. The question is whether real displacement is large enough to become a problem eventually. Here we have no real answer. Perhaps we must simply wait for a truly severe economic adjustment to occur. If at that time a previously hidden displacement emerges as an intolerable unemployment rate, we will have strong reason to consider the pessimistic thesis seriously.

Qualitative Impact The qualitative impact of computer systems includes those changes in the form and structure of employment induced by the use of computers.

---

[5] Bureau of Labor Statistics, *Outlook for Computer Process Control*, U.S. Department of Labor Bulletin #1658 (Washington, D.C.: U.S. Government Printing Office, 1970).

The most widely discussed of these possible changes concerns whether jobs impacted by computer systems tend to be upgraded or downgraded in skill content. Other possible changes concern the individual's autonomy and the degree of his personal interaction in the organization.

Before we consider these aspects of qualitative impact, however, we must examine the problem of impact perspective. There are at least three distinct questions that we might ask about the qualitative impact of computer systems on employment. We might be interested in the precise changes that will occur in a specific job or job category. Or we might be concerned with the overall effect on the entire job structure of a specific firm. Finally, we may be asking about the occupation structure of an industry or of the entire economy.

In the first instance, our approach is clear-cut. We examine the content and nature of a specific job before the computer impact and after. This in itself may be tricky, for we must wait long enough to have allowed the majority of changes to take place. The changes that occur in the structure of a job may not be planned or documented in job descriptions or formal procedures but rather may be the result of an evolutionary adjustment to the new work environment created by the computer system. In either event, after isolating the difference in structure we must then deduct any changes known to have resulted from stimuli other than the computer system. The net difference in structure is then considered to be a qualitative effect of computer application on that job.

For an entire firm, an industry, or the economy we are less concerned with the change in structure of specific jobs. We are concerned instead with shifts in the patterns of employment. Certainly, changes in the structure and content of specific job categories are important and must be noted. Of even greater importance, however, is the relative number of jobs among job categories within the entire occupational framework. Are there now fewer jobs at the laborer level and more at the technician level than there were before the computer system was installed? Or, in the case of the economy, does increasing use of computers explain at least part of the decrease in the number of jobs at the unskilled level and the increase in the number of jobs at the skilled levels? Jobs and even occupations are continually created, combined, and destroyed, with the net result far from easy to determine. Nevertheless, the qualitative impact of computer systems on employment must be examined from each of these perspectives if the view is to be accurate.

The degree of change in *job structure* brought about by the installation of computer systems depends primarily on the extent to which the process in which the job is imbedded has been rationalized. *Rationalization* here means the logical organization of tasks toward the achievement of specific objectives. The use of computers tends to force rationalization for several reasons. First, the study and analysis that precede the development of the computer system will uncover illogical and poorly organized operations. A computer system tends to be intolerant of ambiguity and illogic, forcing systems analysts and programmers to be persistent in isolating and correcting these difficulties. Second, because of the cost and, particularly, the tedium of developing the details of a computer system the operations of the system tend to be relatively uncluttered and directly goal-oriented. This frequently has the effect of orienting the associated noncomputer operations in the same fashion. The rationalization of a process does not require computerization as a trigger. It is entirely possible, even desirable, that rationalization be undertaken on its own merits. In many computer applications, a large measure of the system savings and improvement resulted from the underlying rationalization rather than from the direct effect of implementing the system. Thus, the less rationalization that has preceded implementation of the computer system, the greater will be the change in the job structure.

Some writers have seen that individual autonomy is lost as a consequence of computer system implementation. Jobs are more structured and the appropriate responses to most situations are spelled out, often in formal procedures manuals. The number of decisions the employee must make has been reduced. He has less control over his job, so the job becomes less interesting and less challenging. This is not a unanimous opinion, of course. Others argue that the implementation of a computer system does not alter the existing structure but adds a new dimension to most jobs. This position, which usually results from the individual job perspective, notes that most jobs impacted by computer systems retain their essential elements and their autonomy, and receive the added responsibility of dealing with the computer system. The jobs thus become more interesting and more challenging. This, as we noted earlier, may be a difference in perspective, not a true difference of opinion. If, for example, we note in a given study that of ten jobs impacted by the computer system eight retained their basic structure and autonomy and two were radically changed, we might conclude that there was little qualitative impact on the job structure. If, however, we learned that within three years following the installation of the computer system 47 percent of all the employees worked in the two highly impacted jobs, compared to 19 percent before computer installation, we would conclude that the qualitative impact was substantial. (In fact, no real evidence of this type is available for either side of the individual autonomy question.) It is certainly possible to find examples that substantiate both arguments, but until we can shift our perspective to the higher level nothing will have been proven.

Personal interaction in computer-impacted environments has also been a subject of discussion. Some argue that the computer reduces the need for interpersonal communication by substituting communication with the computer system itself. On the other hand, with the tighter relationships and more rapid responses induced by computer systems, it can be plausibly argued that individuals are more closely knit because of their more pervasive and immediate impact on one another. Thomas L. Whisler[6] has investigated personal interaction in a survey of 15 computer-impacted life insurance companies. He found, first, that computer systems did increase the percentage of time that clerks work alone, and that there was a pronounced drop in communication among clerks. He also found that both supervisors and managers worked alone less than before. Second, Whisler found that at both the clerical and supervisory levels there was a greater decline in the level of interpersonal communication and a greater increase in the amount of time spent working alone in companies that had been using computers for a longer time. At the managerial level, increased interpersonal communication accompanied the longer computer use. Whisler concluded that although in the short run interpersonal communication increases in order to effect the introduction of the computer system with new working patterns and information flows, in the longer run a much reduced level of communication will result in a "quiet organization."

Computer systems have changed the *skill requirements* of the jobs on which they have had an impact. Although some argue that this change has generally decreased skill requirements, the majority of writers point to a reduction in the number of low-level, routine jobs and an increase in the number of higher-skilled occupations. Here again, we encounter the problem of perspective. If we look at the individual job and the individual worker we are likely to find that the worker himself views the change as a downgrading of his skills. Whisler notes[7]:

> The way a change in skill level is viewed by a job incumbent will, of course, depend on his individual experience. If he finds, for example, that the skills he worked for years to develop are suddenly unnecessary, he will have difficulty viewing the change as anything other than a downgrading of skills. If he leaves his job, however, his replacement may well be an individual who is earning more money than ever before, and, knowing that the job is associated with the new

---

[6] Thomas L. Whisler, *Information Technology and Organizational Change* (Belmont, Calif.: Brooks/Cole Publishing Co., 1970), pp. 76–80.

[7] *Information Technology*, p. 84.

technology, will likely feel the technology tends to upgrade skills.

If, in addition, we examine the numbers employed in various occupational categories we may find a decrease in the number of clerks and an increase in the number of people employed in technical jobs such as keypunch operator, computer operator, programmer, and systems analyst. Several studies have found that average skill level has increased because the number of jobs at the bottom of the occupational structure has been reduced, while the number of jobs at higher skill levels has increased.

At this point an observation must be made. It is entirely possible for the skill requirement of a job to increase while, at the same time, the job becomes less interesting. Compare the job of keypunch operator to virtually any job that involves dealing with people. It is extremely difficult to say that keypunching is an interesting job, yet the skill required of a keypunch operator is frequently greater than that of the corresponding people-related job. To give another illustration, a computer operator must be familiar with the external operations of a number of different types of expensive equipment. This involves the mastery of dozens of distinct procedures in equipment operation. Equally important is a thorough familiarity with the operating procedures of many different information systems. In addition, the operator must be generally knowledgeable about the internal operation of the computer system, so that he can assist the system in its handling of exceptional situations and error conditions. Clearly this skill requirement is much greater than that of most clerical jobs, but mostly the operator spends his time in relatively uninteresting machine-tending—a slavish response to the needs of the system. An even better example is found in process control applications. Here, many of the remaining noncomputer jobs are maintenance jobs that consist mainly of standing by until something goes wrong. Ninety-five percent boredom, but when something does go wrong, extremely high levels of skill and knowledge are called into play. So we must be careful to distinguish between true skill requirement and factors that simply influence interest. The interest, challenge, and pleasantness of a job are important, but they are a separate issue.

Collective Bargaining   Union concern with automation and cybernation is directed primarily to three points. First, the unions are obviously concerned about and anxious to protect their members from displacement. Second, automation is a definite threat to the effectiveness of strike as a labor weapon. Third, automation has been the cause of jurisdictional disputes between unions.

With respect to labor displacement, the unions have been relatively ineffective in providing any real protection for the worker. Contract provisions have been negotiated that provide for advance notice of layoffs, early retirement, severance pay, retraining, and shorter hours. These provisions attempt to absorb labor displacement and ease the condition of the displaced worker. Negotiation of work rules that would prevent displacement has been generally unsuccessful over the long run.

As automation is introduced and production or service can be maintained with less labor, unions find it more difficult to significantly impair output by striking. Supervisory, or other nonunion, personnel are often able to maintain a substantial portion of production, in some cases almost full production. This is especially true in continuous process industries, where automation has progressed further.

Where automation has eliminated entire skills, the union must concern itself with the continuance of its jurisdiction. For instance, with the introduction of jet aircraft there was a decrease in the total demand for pilots. The Airline Pilots Association countered this trend by insisting that a pilot be used as a flight engineer. A.L.P.A. eventually won this fight, and the Flight Engineers International Association has ceased to exist. Jurisdictional problems have also occurred among labor unions in the printing trades and in ground transportation.

In some cases the unions have sought merely to protect themselves and their remaining members, rather than those who have already been displaced or those entering the work force. These unions have, in effect, negotiated for a cut of the "take" and then quit fighting. This strategy has been "successful" where it was used.

10.2   Organization

The formal organization chart shows only one element of a firm's organizational structure, the lines of formal authority and hence the decision-making or action-inducing path. It does not necessarily show functional responsibilities, the location of control, communication paths, or more generally, the flow of information within the organization. These other elements may be clearly specified and formal, or they may be very informal, undocumented, and even temporary. When organizational structure is viewed in this larger sense, the impact of computer systems is more readily apparent.

The organizational structure of a firm is the means by which the firm adapts itself to the exigencies of its entire environment, including its technological resources. The communication structure, a large portion of the informal organization, and at least a part of the formal organization structure are formed around the organization's ability to assimilate and use the large volume of information that is available and necessary for both planning and control. This same problem is, of course, a major target in the installation of a computer system, and the consequence is a substantial impact on organizational structure. Because communication structure and informal organization are difficult to identify, we will consider organizational impact in terms of lateral, vertical, and general changes.

Lateral Changes in Organizational Structure Formal organization structures in many, if not most, firms are noticeably rigid, compartmentalized, and lacking functional orientation. Whether or not this condition results from inefficiencies and difficulties of information handling, as we argued above, the fact remains that artificial boundaries often separate activities that are closely related in function and goal orientation. In manufacturing, for example, the stores inventory of spare parts, and the operating and maintenance supply (storeroom) are, in reality, an extension of the purchasing operation. These units have a common function (providing materials for the operating division) and identical goals (keeping the cost of materials to a minimum and preventing out-of-stock conditions), yet frequently they are entirely separate.

The implementation of computer systems seems to be leading toward an increase in functional integration. There are three separate but related explanations for this. First, the increase in the lateral flow of information fostered by the computer system makes coordination between activities less of a problem. In our example, the installation of a computer system might make stores inventory an integral part of the total inventory operations of the organization, for which purchasing is responsible. The system could also generate purchase orders automatically when stock needs to be replenished. The necessity for coordination would thus be eliminated. Second, with improved information available to management, a wider range of related activities might be managed together. This will be discussed further in the section on vertical changes. Finally, the interface between activities is frequently the scene of much duplication and overlap of both data structures and operations. As a consequence, these boundaries are a fertile area for systems improvement, and they tend to receive a fair share of the systems analyst's attention.

The best documented lateral change is a shift of functions to the data processing department. Except for those very few entirely new computer applications, most systems are performing tasks that were performed elsewhere in the organization. Although routine operations are most often transferred, some will be significant if not key elements. It is not uncommon to find the entire function of an organizational unit transferred to the computer system and the unit itself disbanded. This shifting of functions to data processing is reflected in its own organizational status. Where data processing was once a small service organization within the treasury function of most organizations, it is now frequently a separate department reporting directly to the chief executive officer. In some cases, the data processing department has taken operational responsibility along with the processing task, and at least one writer has suggested that all operations might eventually be shifted to data processing, with other departments turned into planning agencies.

In a more general view, some writers see a large-scale shift in power from line to staff organizations. As more and better information becomes available and more sophisticated analytical techniques are developed, staff groups seem to be making more decisions that directly impinge on the internal operations of operating departments. Although the decisions being transferred today are the more technical ones such as inventory reorder points, preventive maintenance scheduling, and credit terms, an extension of this trend to less technical decisions could result in very sharp changes in organizational structure. One may envision an organization in which all operating decisions are made by an "Analysis-Decision" group staffed by highly trained analysts and technicians and heavily supported with computer systems, while the actual operations are carried out by an action group, cybernated or not, with no decision responsibilities.

Vertical Changes in Organizational Structure Does the increasing use of computers within an organization tend to shift decision making and control upward or downward in the hierarchy of management? This question is the central element in the argument over the effect of computer systems on the trend toward decentralization. Persuasive arguments are available for both sides of both questions, with little real evidence available so far. We will review the opposing arguments.

The application of computer systems will have one of three basic effects on the level of decision making. First, the level of decision making might be raised. With complete and current information available, the manager will be in a position to make decisions that had previously been made at a lower level. The lower level is presumed to be in closer touch with the situation and thus (before the computer system) privy to a certain amount of unrecorded information. This argument, of course, ignores the factor of available time in determining the level at which a decision is to be made. Does the manager delegate his authority because he has insufficient information or because he lacks the time to consider the decision properly? A second possible effect of computer application might be a lowering of the level of responsibility for decision making. A stronger chain, a longer leash is the thinking here. With better, more timely information available, the manager can afford to delegate more authority because he is able to monitor the situation. If anything does go wrong the manager will know in sufficient time to reassert control and take corrective action. The last possible effect is no effect. The level of decision making may be a function of elements other than the nature and timeliness of information and may be totally unaffected by events that alter these factors. The level of decision making may simply depend on management philosophy, for example.

The centralization versus decentralization of authority discussion is merely an extension of the discussion about the level of decision making. One new element is distance. The units subject to the authority in question may be remote from the potentially centralized point. With data communications available, however, distance may be a relatively insignificant consideration. Another element that arises when we consider authority rather than simple decision making is the type of information that computer systems can supply. Some writers argue persuasively that top wielders of authority require subjective information to use their authority effectively. The top executive in an organization is more concerned with leadership, morale, labor relations, and, in general, subjective information than he is with the number-oriented objective information his computer produces. Thus, increasing the flow of objective information to the executive will not necessarily permit him to consolidate and centralize authority.

General Changes Possibly the most important general organizational effect of introducing computer systems is the rationalization of both operations and structure that we discussed earlier. Partly in preparation for the installation of the computer system, and partly in efforts to adjust to and live with the system, a more rational organization and operation will frequently result.

A second general effect of the installation of computer systems is an increased formalization of procedures. A computer system depends heavily on the accuracy of the information supplied to it as input. Equally important is a user who thoroughly understands the significance of system output and knows what to do with it. Realizing both of these necessities is extremely difficult without well-documented manual procedures. Thus, in many cases a concomitant of computer installation is the substitution of formal procedures for vague, loosely organized, and continuously innovated operations.

Finally, the degree of standardization tends to increase after a computer system is installed. Policies, operating procedures, forms, and other aspects of an organization's operations are standardized, partly in an attempt to decrease the variety and complexity of the overall system for the sake of system and procedures design. More generally, however, standardization is merely an additional step in the rationalization process.

10.3 Management

A great deal has been written about the impact of computer systems on management. Although this impact is being felt by all levels of management, its intensity varies substantially by level.

Top management is, and will undoubtedly continue to be, the level least affected by the installation of computer systems. The formulation of organization goals and objectives, establishment of policy, development of strategy, planning, motivation of people, and leadership are a major portion of the job of executives in the higher echelons. These activities rarely ever become routine—the very need for their performance implies novelty or a unique situation in the environment or the organization. Furthermore, the information that supports these activities tends to be subjective and nonquantitative. Is the manager of plant A reliable? Is the union membership in the mood for a strike? What effect will the current monetary and fiscal policy have on the company's capital investment program? Computer information systems at present, and in the foreseeable future, can be of little help in answering such questions. Possibly the most that we should hope for is that computer systems will be able to supply information and analyses which will reduce the uncertainty typically surrounding executive decisions.

At the other extreme, the front-line manager, the foreman or the supervisor, is relatively immune to a substantial impact from computer systems. Although he may be relieved of virtually all of his information collection and reporting duties, this will simply free him to concentrate attention on his major functions, communication and leadership. Certainly, to the extent that processes are cybernated the ranks of front-line management may be thinned, but where the job exists the function should remain unchanged by computer system impact.

Almost by default it seems, the heaviest impact of computer system installation falls on middle management. The exact nature of this impact is the subject of substantial disagreement, largely because so many jobs fit into the category described as middle management. These jobs range from high authority, almost top executive positions on one end to almost front-line supervision on the other. More importantly, these jobs range from rigidly structured and programmed ones to those which are nonpatterned and nonprogrammable. We must agree that middle-management jobs that are heavily patterned and deal largely with routine decisions will be extremely vulnerable to elimination with the installation of computer systems. Middle-management positions that function as information collection and condensation points for higher levels of management are likewise vulnerable. For those positions with a mixture of responsibilities, however, the middle manager will be able to devote more time to the really important aspects of his responsibility, such as planning and the motivation of his subordinates. It is difficult to agree with the position of some observers, who feel that the job content of middle management will become more routine and less creative as a consequence of the impact of computer systems. If anything, the elimination of highly patterned positions should make middle management, in general, a more interesting and challenging job assignment. This elimination of routine responsibilities would also seem to lessen the differences between middle and top management. The responsibilities remaining in middle-management positions would seem to be precisely those that characterize top management. This is in direct contradiction to the arguments of some, who feel that the installation of computer systems will draw the line between middle and top management more clearly and will make middle management an unsuitable training ground for top executives.

One final prediction is at least worth noting. If the thesis that we are entering an era of unprecedented productive capacity and prosperity is accepted, then it may follow that the institutions of business and industry, dealing with scarcity, will occupy a much less central role in the social structure. Such a shift may result in a redefinition of the position and the general role of management in our society. Already, a trend seems to be developing among young people away from business-oriented careers.

10.4 Competition

There are several reasons for believing that the nature of competition in the U.S. economy may be affected by the continuing development of computer systems. There is, for instance, little question that management with computer systems is going to be much more effective than management without them. Regardless of the impact on the manager or his job the computer will enable the manager to make decisions based on analysis rather than hunch or intuition. *Enable* is probably too weak a term. The day is probably near when a decision based on anything but thorough and sound analysis will be unacceptable in most organizations. At the same time management will be faced with a lengthened time perspective. With most of the day-to-day routine decisions taken over by the computer system, managers will become more concerned with planning, the anticipation of problem situations, preventive maintenance, and the design and modification of their operational systems. In general, the manager in the age of the computer will be a more finely honed competitive weapon.

Competition itself is likely to be more precisely adjusted. An organization will be able to evaluate the exact degree of opportunity and risk through simulation based on more sophisticated methods of market analysis and forecasting. Economic advantage through a competitor's blunder or inefficiency will be hard to come by. This carries an interesting implication. It has been said that small business still exists because it exploits the inefficiencies of big business. If this is true, and if computer systems tend to squeeze out the inefficiencies in their organizations, what will happen to the small business? A reinforcing point here is that continuing computerization is contributing to the increasing concentration of business. The installation of computer information systems is, as we noted earlier, an expensive process. This expense may also act as a barrier to smaller firms, although the advent of the minicomputer may lower the barrier somewhat. The advent of a computer utility would also counteract the negative effect on small firms.

10.5 Economic Control

Computer systems have the potential for significant impact on economic control activities. Possibly the most obvious impact lies in development and reliance on econometric models, which are of academic interest only without computer systems. These mathematical models, which often consist of dozens of equations, model various aspects of the economy and, in several cases, the entire economy. Through these models economic values for the economy can be predicted based on specific sets of variables, including policy prescriptions. As these models are refined, and experience is gained in their use, they are certain to influence economic policy and hence economic control.

More effective maintenance and use of information through computer systems could also influence economic control. Within the federal government is an incredible storehouse of information. Unfortunately, this information is splintered, difficult to access, and very ineffectively used. More effective maintenance and use of this information will unquestionably be a significant influence on economic control.

Finally, the computer is a potential answer to the awesome complexity of our economic system and the role which the federal government must play within that system. In reality, it is difficult to imagine how the government might hope to deal with such complexity without the aid of computer systems.

Exercises

1. What are the current figures for unemployment and productivity per man-hour? How do these figures affect the quantitative employment impact arguments presented in Section 10.1?

Economic Impact

2. Examine an organization in which computers have been installed for several years. Build an inventory of positions in the computer-affected areas of the organization. How many of these jobs are oriented heavily to the computer system? Try to determine what jobs, if any, have disappeared because the computer system was installed or if the number employed in any position has changed significantly.

3. Develop an argument supporting the position that authority will become more centralized as a consequence of the installation of computer systems.

4. Develop an argument supporting the position that authority will become more decentralized as a consequence of the installation of computer systems.

5. Define the functions and activities of lower, middle, and upper management. Analyze the impact of computer systems on each level of management, given your definition.

6. To what extent are computer systems a necessity to a business organization today?

11 Social Impact

This chapter discusses the impact of computer systems on the social environment. The economic environment is one subset of social relationships, of course, but the respective impacts are so distinct that economics has been discussed separately. Even with this separation, however, some of the significant economic impact—in particular, the possibility of enforced leisure—has implications in noneconomic areas of the social environment. So, this as well as other secondary effects of economic impact, will be discussed in the appropriate sections of this chapter.

The electronic computer is clearly a major development in human history. Although many social impacts have already been felt and others foreseen, the deepest significance of this invention may still be transparent to us and may become observable only with the passage of time. So this chapter is at best a view of the current and potential social impact of computer systems as seen from the relatively shaky vantage point of the 1970s.

11.1 General Effects

An obvious feature of modern times in post-industrial America is the increase in "giantism" in organizations of all sorts. The trend toward concentration in business was mentioned in the last chapter. Companies with billions of dollars in sales and assets, universities with tens of thousands of students, state governments with billion-dollar budgets, and certainly the federal government, are all examples of this increase in size. Many factors are responsible for this trend, and the development of computer systems is not necessarily the most significant of these factors. We can state with assurance, however, that the huge organizations we are discussing would be difficult if not impossible to achieve and manage without computer systems. The telephone system is one of the clearer instances. A telephone system of the size we have today without the benefit of computers would require immense manpower resources. Even if these resources were made available to the system, the management task would be a nightmare. It is difficult to imagine General Motors or New York City functioning without the assistance of computer systems, much less the agencies of the federal government. The computer system is at least an enabling factor in the development of large organizations. The same thing can be said about the role of the computer in the increasing rate of change that characterizes our society. Computer systems allow us to continue functioning at rates of change that could not be dealt with or controlled manually. Computer systems have also had a somewhat more subtle impact on man's continuing effort to define a unique place for himself in the universe.[1] In this effort man has had to adjust to the ideas of Copernicus, who showed that contrary to general opinion the earth was not the center of the universe, and of Darwin, who damaged man's concept of his uniqueness among other forms of life. Now the computer system raises the possibility that man may not even be unique within the realm of objects. Just as there is no clear distinction between earth and other worlds, and between man and other animals, there may be no clear distinction between man and other machines. Even if this latter possibility should prove to be true, there is little doubt that man in some way will be able to redefine his uniqueness. The crisis lies in the transition, in the changing of man's concept of himself.

The implementation of computer systems frequently has a substantial direct impact on the individuals who are associated with the systems. As we noted in the preceding

---

[1] The ideas in this paragraph are drawn in part from Bruce Mazlish, "The Fourth Discontinuity," in Melvin Kranzberg and William H. Davenport, eds., *Technology and Culture* (New York: Shocken Books. 1972), pp. 216–232.

chapter, eliminating people from a process is a major potential benefit of the implementation of computer systems. From a systems point of view, the human being is a black box whose several admirable strengths are, in most cases, far outweighed by some monumental weaknesses. The human being is the source of such a variety of errors that the system designer finds it difficult, or impossible, to build sufficient responses into his system. Man's unpredictability introduces a large random element into the system. So, when faced with the choice, a system designer will usually choose to exclude people in favor of machines. In addition the people who are not eliminated from the system must frequently adapt to the computer. The individual must adjust his performance, his expectations, and in some instances his tastes to successfully implement a computer system. This adaptation is obviously a 'social cost' of the use of computers, and the cost is rather high. Fears of dehumanization and impersonalization feed on this experience, which happens again and again. To the extent that a value structure is built into the computer system it reflects, at worst, the values of the system designer or programmer and, at best, the values of society when the design became set. In either event the particular value structure is frozen and inflexible. As society changes and the concepts of ethics, morality, justice, and value adjust accordingly, the system remains unmoved, requiring greater and greater adaptation on the part of those who must deal with it. Modification of the system is too expensive a process to be undertaken frequently, and thus human adaptation is a permanent accompaniment of computerization.

Artificial intelligence, which was treated with almost universal contempt only a few years ago, has evolved into a much more respected threat to mankind. Some researchers now feel that in time man will have created a level of intelligence equal to or greater than his own. If these anticipations are accurate, the reasonable question of man's ability to exert control arises. Can man retain his role of master if his devices are intellectually superior?

11.2   The Individual

The major response of individuals to computer systems is fear. A rational economic fear is the loss of livelihood, but in addition the computer itself is feared. This fear manifests itself in popular fiction, in editorials and commentary in the communications media, and in ordinary conversation. Although no statistical evidence is available to support this statement, fear seems to be the most common characteristic in the laymen's view of computer systems.

Fear of computers seems to take two distinct forms:

an anthropomorphic fear and a fear of a dehumanization of life-quality. The anthropomorphic fear is characterized by a view of the computer as a general threat posed by great potential power mated with the human quality of will, and perhaps an element of malevolence for good measure. The collaboration of an East computer with a West computer for the domination of the world, and a computer demanding the subservience of astronauts are fictional renderings of this feeling which, although sometimes humorous, tend to accurately caricature the more ominous extreme of the popular concept. The "arrogance" of many existing computer systems does little to allay these fears. DO NOT FOLD, SPINDLE, OR MUTILATE: THIS AMOUNT MUST BE PAID IMMEDIATELY or THIS STUB MUST BE RETURNED do little to give credibility to the idea that computer systems are designed to serve human beings and not be served by them.

This fear of computers appears to be transitional. Computer personnel, such as programmers, show virtually no evidence of such a fear, leading to the reasonable thought that familiarity will allay the anthropomorphic fear of computers. If so, this fear will be eliminated as a general phenomenon as more generations arrive with a lifelong exposure to computers, together perhaps, with computer use during the education process. On the other hand, if anticipations in the area of artificial intelligence prove to be accurate, the anthropomorphic fear of computers may well be provided with a foundation and substance.

The fear of dehumanization of life-quality seems to be subdividable into (1) a fear that individual identity will be lost and (2) a fear that the environment within which one must function will become impersonal. The loss of individual identity seems to be inherent in the increasing use of numbers for identification. We are all familiar with the proliferation of account, license, and other identification numbers. In addition, a more ominous note has been struck by the suggestion that national identification numbers be issued to all citizens. West Germany has considered such a plan and the U.S. armed services use the social security number as a general identification.

Although identification numbers may well be a cause of apprehension, the problem is a rather superficial one. Such a number is simply a code that represents an individual more efficiently than his name. It is a convenience and not an essential aspect of computer systems. A name is itself a code and the conversion between the alphabetic name and numeric code is relatively simple. If the use of number codes were truly a problem, the means to solve this problem are already available and relatively inexpensive at that. The proliferation of numbers is a problem, however. The ominous sounding proposal of a single identification number would in fact represent an improvement both in systems and in their usability by human beings.

 There is little question that our society today is more impersonal than ever before. The common situations of everyday life—supermarkets replacing the corner grocer, cashiers instead of sales clerks in department stores, the impersonality of television, massive universities—are sufficient illustrations of this point. We have deliberately omitted instances of computer-originated impersonalization until now, so that the fact that a computer prints your bills and paycheck, or gives you a telephone number, can be viewed in an appropriate perspective. Mass treatment is necessitated by the sheer number of people, and the computer is a concomitant of mass treatment rather than an underlying cause. In many instances a computer function has replaced personal services, but for the most part these instances are relatively insignificant. In fact, an argument has been made that computers tend to allow more personalization, not less. The essence of this argument is that, in a crowded society, computers handle the routine, allowing human beings the time to personally handle exceptions. In a given transaction, the greater number of people who neither need nor desire personal attention receive none, and manpower is freed to provide greater attention for the exceptional cases.

 The computer is not a blameless part of today's society. To a very large extent, computer systems enable other characteristics of society. It would be difficult if not impossible to deal with the masses of people, and the transactions they create, without the assistance of computer systems. Nor would we be able to deal with the rate of change and the sheer complexity of the world today without the capabilities of the computer. So "blame" is an inappropriate word to use; it is likely that computer systems keep society one step ahead of collapse and disaster.

 The increasing pervasiveness and significance of the computer in society leads to a potentially important impact on the individual. Since the average person has virtually no understanding and, in fact, some fear of the computer, a major part of the functioning of his world is incomprehensible to him. It is difficult to predict what effect this might have on the individual and his role in society, but the possibilities are rather broad. How does an individual relate to a society that he does not understand? What is the value of an individual's opinion if he cannot evaluate the alternatives? As computers become more pervasive, the individual may conceivably lose the connection between his actions and the effects which impinge on his existence. As a brief example visualize a computer-based system that evaluates current market demand, reduces production of a given product, and results in the termination of a shift of workers, including individual A. A computer-based national employment service scans its files and determines that there are no openings for which A is qualified. A's record is then passed to a system that selects the appropriate assistance plan and automatically enrolls A. Perhaps the example is overdrawn, but much less computerization would have served to sever the cause and effect link as far as A is concerned.

To the extent that computer systems reduce employment or the length of the work week, leisure and its use will become a socially significant factor. Although it may be regarded by some as an unqualified blessing, leisure in the quantity that we are discussing would clearly bring some problems with it. First, leisure is a rather euphemistic term for what would be initially seen as forced unemployment. If employment is substantially reduced by the use of computers and if, as usual, we fail to deal with the situation until it becomes a problem, then unemployment will be extremely painful for selected groups. Although some specialized skills might feel the impact, the groups most effected would be the relatively unskilled and low-income. Even as leisure spreads to more and more segments of society a stigma will still be attached. Work is somehow moral in our society, and it defines the major part of one's status. So in an era of abundance and leisure, forced or not, the beneficiary of this leisure would lose status and self-esteem. In addition, to a large extent the work environment both defines and regulates behavior. Because a person has a particular job, say office manager, society requires a certain role and standard of behavior from him. Some of the behavior standards are enforced with sanctions by the organization. It is difficult to estimate the cumulative effect if a majority of the population lost such behavior regulation.

The American people, in general, are poorly equipped to use leisure time. As a consequence of the growth in population and resultant overcrowding, leisure time is increasing at a time that per capita space and recreational facilities are decreasing. Because of the work ethic, the ability to play is very poorly developed in most people, and playing has a highly developed guilt mechanism attached. Thus, if increased leisure is a real possibility, several changes must be made. First, the morality of work will have to be replaced by a morality of living and self-development. A first step would be the severing of the work-to-eat linkage. If employment is limited to a few, work need not be prerequisite to a decent standard of living. Second, if individuals are to seek self-fulfillment, they must be equipped with different skills. Recreational skills, an orientation toward cultural activities, and self-development capabilities are some of these skills. Increased leisure would certainly cause some problems, but it could also be the stimulus for an unprecedented elevation of the human status. Visualize the potential of people freed from the bondage of labor, oriented to self-development, and striving to improve themselves as human beings!

11.3 Politics

Computers have been used effectively in political campaigns. More than one candidate for Congress has carefully surveyed his constituency and used a computer analysis of the results to guide him in his campaign. From a brief survey, it appears that computer applications that deal with voter information are rather primitive at the moment. But voter information is a very promising area of application, and it is reasonable to expect substantial progress in its development. Some writers have equated the voter information process to market research, with the candidate as the product and the voter as the consumer. In both cases the goal is the prediction and possibly manipulation of consumer behavior.

The development of a computerized profile of the electorate is probably the simplest voter information application. With as fine a detail as desired, groups within the electorate can be described and categorized by their politically significant characteristics and views. Given this information a candidate can precisely adjust his efforts and the issues that he emphasizes for maximum effectiveness with specific groups. The candidate could also, of course, simply match his platform as closely as possible to the profiles uncovered. In a more prosaic use of such profiles, one candidate on a rainy election day put volunteers to work driving to the polls voters whom the computer had identified as favoring him.

Historical analysis has been used extensively in connection with political campaigns. The national television networks use this analysis to project election results. Although these projections have occasionally been embarrassingly wrong, for the most part and especially in recent years, they have been amazingly accurate.

Voting simulation has been proposed as a politically significant application of computers. With an accurate profile of the electorate it would be possible to estimate the success of political positions and platforms.

The danger is that all of these applications tend to tempt the politician into following rather than leading. Instead of a process of evaluation of the issue, debate, and leadership, politicians might choose slavish and unimaginative following of current public opinion. This is certain to stifle the generation and implementation of new ideas. Majority public opinion is a notably uncreative medium.

A second danger is that with sufficient information available to the party in power and not to the other parties, the party in office could maintain its control indefinitely by a fine tuning of its efforts to the thinking of the majority. By itself this threat lacks immediacy; techniques are simply not advanced enough to make the threat of party monopoly over voter information a currently realistic one. On the other hand, a monopoly provided by a government information system does provide cause for concern.

An ultimate step in the area of voter information, which can be described as the automatic expression of opinion, has been proposed in several forms. In one form, this idea is simply an advanced form of public opinion sampling, or profiling, of the electorate to be used by the politicians as they see fit. In another form, the "instant referendum," voters would directly express their will, via terminals and communications facilities, to a central information system. This process is techologically feasible today. Issues could be presented to the voter on television, and he could then express his preference via a small special-purpose terminal and his telephone, or the telephone by itself. To the extent that corrective feedback from the public to government is being blocked by the massiveness of our society or by whatever cause, instant referenda would result in more responsive government and more effective expression of the public will. The process does, however, introduce the danger of overcorrection because of the direct linkage. Political representation, while an imperfect expression of the will of the electorate, is at the same time a moderating influence and a source of delay for debate and reconsideration.

The possibility of increased leisure is a source of concern in the political process as well as in other social areas. Will increased leisure lead to general apathy and political indifference or to activism? If citizens are apathetic, we may be faced with increasing centralization of authority and, ultimately, a governing elite. But if citizens devote some of their increased leisure time and energy to consideration and action on political issues, we might expect an informed and action-oriented electorate.

Except for the predictable point that the computer and automation are important in the economic competition between East and West, the impact of the computer on international affairs is not significant. In the future, however, we may expect the use of computer-based information systems to contribute to a more direct and more effective implementation of foreign policies by the respective governments. As with business organizations, both centralization and decentralization could follow from the use of computers. Ambassadors and other resident foreign service personnel might be allowed greater autonomy because their performance could be more immediately and more completely monitored. On the other hand, the availability of complete and current information and analyses to the central operation might allow decisions to be made more effectively at that point. In either event, the availability of better information is likely to result in better decisions and a more effective implementation of foreign policy. If nothing else, it will remove some of the noise from the flow of information between nations. At least, immediate intentions will be more accurately interpreted.

If we speculate further it is possible to visualize much more important impacts on international relations. If all nations were to develop high quality international information systems, operating from accurate and extensive data bases, the chances of miscalculation would be reduced. World powers would be less likely to select and pursue policies that threatened world security. An effective data base would also allow the use of simulation as a tool in foreign policy. The ability to simulate national policies and actions offers obvious advantages over experimentation. Finally, it is at least conceivable that a common, easily accessible international data base might become a foundation for international cooperation. There is, for example, no reason why health should not be viewed on an international basis and be an object of concern for all nations. The current international division of health efforts is an excellent example of suboptimization. The creation of an international data base containing worldwide information on disease, mortality, and nutrition might provide a reasonable beginning point for supra-national efforts. At a minimum such a data base would be a valuable information source for research.

One final political note involves the possible creation of a national information system. In many ways information is a source of power, and a critical question exists concerning who will have access to and who will control this power source. If a national information system is controlled by a governmental agency, can we reasonably expect the release of information critical of agency, executive, or party policy? Control of information may be as critical a question as that of control of the military, to our way of government.

11.4 Education

For education, the most widespread impact of computer systems has been in the curriculum. Computer-oriented courses and programs have been added to many curricula, and the computer has become an integral part of such disciplines as engineering, chemistry, physics, business, and mathematics. The content of many courses has changed, because students no longer need to spend time in tedious calculation of classroom and homework assignments. Now they can devote more time to problem formulation and to greater depth or breadth of coverage in course topics. An instructor can assign more realistic case problems, since the complexity introduced by reality is offset by an increased computational capacity. So the mechanical portions of the problem-solving process are downgraded shifting the emphasis from rote solution techniques to the much more important and conceptually difficult areas of problem definition and problem analysis.

Computer-assisted instruction (CAI) has not yet made a significant impact on education. It has for the most part remained a subject for research and testing, with little widespread application. It seems safe to predict, however, that as hardware and software costs decline, CAI will become much more important. Indeed, it may be instrumental in the break away from the archaic and stultifying classroom environment of most education today. Computer-assisted instruction offers consistent presentation of material, prepared by master teachers, yet tailored to meet the needs and abilities of the individual student. A computer-maintained record of the abilities and progress of each student can be used to guide the instructional software in selecting the precise material and technique necessary for each student. The student will thus be able to progress at the pace that is optimum for him. Contrary to popular thought, computer-assisted instruction need not be relegated to instruction that is characterized by repetition and drill. (In fact, if such instruction represented the extent of its capabilities, the system would simply not be worth the expense and effort of building it.) The real value of computer-assisted instruction is in the learning of conceptual material, which depends heavily on the student's reaction to individual problems and insights. Such material is often taught poorly in the classroom environment. With a properly designed CAI system, however, a high degree of interaction can be achieved between the student and the system, with the result being very personalized instruction.

An example is found in the teaching of computer and programming concepts such as the role and implications of the operating cycle. The simple write-on-blackboard, erase, and rewrite procedure takes so much time that the continuity and flow of events is broken and the implications are obscured. With CAI using a cathode-ray tube device, this flow of events can be controlled by the student and will proceed at the optimum speed for him. The student could repeat the cycle as many times as necessary. In addition, the student could be allowed to vary the conditions, changing the instructions, the data, or both, either as directed by the system or on his own initiative. The effectiveness of this approach, has been proven in practice by many programmers at the consoles of a variety of computers.

11.5 Privacy

The invasion of personal privacy has received more attention than any other potential social impact of the computer. To a large extent, the invasion of personal privacy results from overcrowding in our society. Non-computer elements of this invasion, particularly electronic eavesdropping (including wire tapping), personal investigations, psychological testing, and most recently, surveillance, have all been called major threats to privacy.

The role of the computer system differs from those of the threats mentioned above. The operation of a computer system is not intentionally directed at a particular individual as, for example, is wire tapping or surveillance. The computer system generally does not originate information about individuals, but accumulates existing information. In fact, the computer contributes more to an invasion of anonymity than an invasion of privacy. This is not to downgrade the threat, for anonymity—besides offering the psychological benefits of a sense of uniqueness and the ability to hide—contributes to the protection of privacy. In part, a person maintains his privacy because he is an unidentifiable part of the mass.

The current dispersal and inaccessibility of information about individuals contributes to their anonymity. The average individual in our society creates a lengthy and detailed trail of records as he goes through life. Both triumphs and failures are recorded somewhere. The danger of computer systems is, first, that revealing information might become more accessible and, second, that it might become more concentrated. With computer systems, records that might otherwise have been stored in sealed boxes in a basement may be accessible through terminals. Many groups have computer systems that contain information on individuals—there are private systems operated by credit bureaus, banks, and other business organizations and public systems operated by police departments, welfare agencies, and other arms of state and local government. The danger of concentration stems from the possibility that one or more of these groups might decide that combining their data bases would be more efficient, more valuable, or both. In addition, greater ease of access and increased concentration make illegal or unauthorized access more economically feasible.

The effect on the individual should not be underrated. In one study, more than 80 percent of a group of employers indicated that they would not consider employing a man who had been arrested for assault, even though he was later acquitted. Many feel that the accumulation of personal information is a denial of the constitutional provision against self-incrimination. Some writers, however, have overstated the threat. One suggests that with the coming of banking utilities and the checkless–cashless society, a listing of credit purchases would provide a record of the individual's every movement. This and similar arguments seem to depend on a rather unrealistic view of technological capability and economic feasibility. Imagine the magnitude of the task of tracing an individual's movement through the millions of transactions generated in even a single day. It is difficult to believe that this approach would be superior in any way to human observation.

Some writers feel that there are threats to the individual and his privacy inherent in the mere use of computer systems. It has been argued that facts, even if otherwise known, are more damaging to the individual when interpreted by a computer system, because the system is unable to make allowances. To the computer an arrest is an arrest, while to a human being an arrest for participation in a civil rights demonstration would be qualitatively distinguishable from other arrests. There are two fallacies to this argument. First, the output of the computer system is used by people, and these people can still make allowances. Second, allowances can be built into the system. In the example above, we would not record only the fact of arrest but the type of offense and the disposition of the case. Our system could operate so that any computer-made decisions that were adverse to the individual's interests would automatically receive a human review.

Another threat is that the collection and reporting of objective information will cause us to evaluate an individual by measures that are readily adaptable to computers rather than by more subjective values. But this has occurred to some extent without computers. It is much easier to measure financial worth than it is to measure loyalty, honesty, and other more subjective measures of character. As a consequence, men are frequently evaluated on their financial worth and credit performance. A "solid citizen" is sometimes a man who pays his bills and has managed to avoid being caught at anything else recently.

The National Data Center In 1965 a committee of the Social Science Research Council issued a report recommending, in part, that the federal government establish a Federal Data Center.[2] This data center, which was to be under the Bureau of the Budget, was to have the authority to obtain computer tapes and other machine-readable data produced by all federal agencies. The major motivation for this report was economic research.

Research in the social sciences depends heavily on an adequate collection of data. So much data is needed that no organization but the federal government has the resources to do it. Use of the federal statistical system, however, poses several problems. First, information is

---

[2] Social Science Research Council, *Report of the Committee on the Preservation and Use of Economic Data to the Social Science Research Council*, April 1965. The full text of this report is contained in Appendix 1 of the reference cited in footnote 4.

highly decentralized within the federal system. It is very difficult for potential users to find out merely what information is available on a given subject area. Once the information source is known it is difficult, in many cases, to gain access to it. One must know the particular individual in an agency to contact in order to gain access to a particular item of data. In one case the author received authoritative denials that an agency maintained data on a particular topic when, in fact, the agency printed a quarterly report containing this data. Because the handling of data is a secondary function of most agencies, requests for data pose a problem and often result in a disruption of normal operations. Finally, the data needed are not always in a form that researchers can use. The absence of supporting information on data tapes, incomplete data series, and incomplete editing of data are some barriers to usability.

The committee's report was a response to this situation. The Federal Data Center would possess substantial computer capability and would furnish basic information as well as respond to special requests on a reimbursable basis. In addition, the center would be responsible for the completeness of its collection and the dissemination of information about the content and nature of its collection. The Bureau of the Budget then hired a consultant to study the feasibility and advantages of a statistical data center. The consultant's report addressed many related topics and also recommended a form of national data center.[3]

In 1966 congressional hearings were begun on the subject of a federal centralized data facility, by the Special Subcommittee on Invasion of Privacy. Their report,[4] which was approved by the full Committee on Government Operations, stated that the Bureau of the Budget was making inadequate plans for the protection of privacy, and that no further work should be done until privacy protection could be guaranteed. The report also stated that the recommendations of the committee were applicable to any system, public or private, which permitted retrieval of data on individuals, thus raising the possibility of Federal control.

The critical issue, when discussing systems of this type, seems to be whether such systems are statistically oriented or intelligence-oriented. If a system is intelligence-oriented—designed to provide specific information on particular individuals or individual organizations—then no matter how well it is protected, either legally or

---

[3] Edgar S. Dunn, Jr., *Statistical Evaluation Report No. 6, Review of Proposal for a National Data Center* (Washington, D.C.: Bureau of the Budget, 1965). The full text of this report is contained in Appendix 2 of the reference cited in footnote 4.

[4] U.S. Congress, House Committee on Government Operations, *The Computer and Invasion of Privacy: Hearings before a Subcommittee of the Committee on Government Operations*, 89th Congress, 2d session (Washington, D.C.: U.S. Government Printing Office, 1966).

technically, it carries the potential for misuse. Misuse may be either legal or illegal. Legal misuse would consist of any use of the system by the government which infringed on the basic rights of its citizens. To the extent that a right to privacy can be developed from interpretation of the Constitution or from common law, the mere development of dossiers on individuals may be an invasion of privacy and, hence, a legal misuse of a system by the government. The concentration of information in an intelligence system increases the temptation to illegally misuse the information. The cost of collecting dispersed information on an individual is normally far higher than its value and misuse is thus discouraged. Concentrating the information tends to reduce the cost per unit of information misused.

In a statistically oriented system, where data is organized by type of information rather than by reporting unit, there is little direct threat to the individual. By careful selection of questions and with a restricted number of items in a data set, an investigator might be able to deduce information about an individual from an otherwise statistically oriented system. However, a system can be protected from this type of threat in several ways. The real danger lies in the possibility that such a system might be converted to dossiers. To update the data base with new or corrective data, there must be some way of relating existing data to the original reporting unit. As long as this linkage exists, the possibility of reorganizing data by reporting unit (by individual) is a cause for concern. Although it could be argued that present centralized systems are limited in the range of their information content (for example, medical, criminal), a counter-argument notes that the large centralized data bases are inherently prone to expansion. Furthermore, the content of the National Data Center as it is currently conceived is not limited. Paul Baran, a witness at the hearings, suggested that the problem is not a centralized data bank but rather the possibility that separate limited data systems could eventually be tied into a network composing a centralized data bank. Mr. Baran described the situation as potentially analogous to the growth of the railroad and telegraph systems.

Protection of Privacy Information is an essential element of progress. We cannot afford to block the development of information systems because they have the potential of invading personal privacy. We must, however, develop effective legal and technical safeguards. There are several potential constitutional bases for the legal protection of privacy, including protection from self-incrimination and the right to confront one's accusers. Whatever the foundation, the following points should be covered by law at a minimum. Those who handle personal data should be legally accountable, and there should be definite procedures for compensating those who have been injured by careless use or misuse of this information. Each individual must be allowed to know what information is recorded about him, so the individual must have the right to examine the contents of his own file. He should also be notified of every change in his file. The individual should have the right to appeal that information in his file be changed and, finally, he should be aware of all accesses to his file. Many of these protections are already the law.

Data in machine-readable form possesses an inherent technical safeguard as compared to traditional records. The information is in machine-readable code rather than in a form that anyone can read. Although many can interpret machine readable codes, this does provide at least some protection.

Technical safeguards are directed, first, at preventing unauthorized access to the protected data and, second, at detecting the occurrence of such access. A number of techniques are available to prevent unauthorized access, ranging from the coding of signals on communications lines to the restriction of access. Restricted access can take the form of user-supplied codes, physical keys which can be inserted in the terminal device, and callback systems where the user dials the system and then hangs up, allowing the computer to call back and assure that at least the access is coming from the correct location. One approach to user-supplied codes consists of the computer system supplying the user with a random number, to which the user applies a transformation, known only to him and the computer, and returns the resultant transformed number to the computer. The computer compares the returned number to the result of the transformation which it has applied, and proceeds accordingly. The detection of unauthorized accesses may involve the provision of an automatic audit trail of inquiries, random audits of programs, and the detection of abnormal system requests, either statistically or by details of the requests themselves.

Technical safeguards must be applied during the initial design of the system and not as afterthoughts. In general, sufficient safeguards must be installed to raise the cost of unauthorized access to the system beyond the potential value to be derived from that access. Technological protection can always be broken, if the misuser is sufficiently determined. We can, however, design systems where the risk and the cost to the misuser are very high.

11.6 Conclusion

Although science must be free to proceed according to its own dictates, it is entirely appropriate that the directions of technology be questioned. In the United States today we are surrounded with the litter of self-interested technical decisions made largely by industry, but also by government. The typical technological decision is made by balancing the pluses and minuses to the interests of the agency, with little or no consideration of the broader social effects. As a consequence we have a virtual smorgasbord of pollutions—air, water, sight, noise—we have a morass of urban problems that seem almost beyond solution, we have blighted areas such as Appalachia, and the list goes on and on.

This same basic problem exists with computer systems. So far, decisions have been made with little attention given to social aspects. Although we should be concerned about the social effects of individual computer systems, the greatest cause for alarm lies in the evolution of computer systems. It is entirely possible that the social impact of an evolved network of computer systems will be far greater than the sum of impacts of the individual computer systems operating separately.

The problems associated with the social effects of computers are as appropriate subjects of general concern as are the other social impacts of technology. However, computer systems and the problems they generate are not easily understood either by the public or by the decision-makers who represent them. Admittedly, computer professionals are not competent social scientists, but they are currently the only ones who are capable of asking the significant questions. Thus, although it is inherently dangerous to give technologists a key role in the evaluation of technology, we currently have little choice in the case of computers. Computer professionals simply must take an active role in developing an awareness of, and evaluating the social implications of computer systems. No one else can do it.

The House Committee on Government Operation has taken a valuable first step toward engaging public concern. Although the hearings of the Special Subcommittee on Invasion of Privacy were not particularly well directed or enlightening, they were at least aimed in the right direction. Perhaps the Committee on Government Operations should establish a permanent subcommittee on the general use of computers in government. This subcommittee could be given the authority to review all present and proposed computer applications with the responsibility of assessing both operational and social implications.

Exercises

1. List the major problems faced by the world today. In what ways have computer systems contributed to these problems? In what ways might computer systems contribute to the solution of these problems?

2. To what extent should the systems analyst attempt to evaluate and modify the social impact of the systems he designs?

3. Prepare a list of the numbers by which you are identified.

4. What difficulties would be encountered in converting to a single identification number for each individual to be used by all businesses and government organizations? Lay out a general plan for such a conversion.

5. Suggest a national program that would prepare the citizenry to deal with vastly increased leisure.

6. Select several courses in your major field and suggest ways in which the use of computers might supplement or support the course contents.

7. Should the individual have an absolute "right to privacy"?

8. Prepare a catalog of all the information that is recorded about you, such as military, medical, and employment records. If this information were centralized how accurate a picture would it provide of you as an individual? Do you feel that this centralization would be a threat to your personal privacy?

9. Develop an argument in favor of an "instant referendum."

12 Trends and Projections

Undoubtedly, there will be startling breakthroughs in computers and data processing within the next few years. Specific breakthroughs and innovations clearly cannot be described in advance, but some areas have more innovation potential than others. We can identify points at which innovation is badly needed, points at which the economic reward for innovation will be high. In addition, we can identify current trends and examine the implications if these trends continue. We will not attempt to forecast specific developments nor project specific magnitudes as, for example, the number of programmers. This last information is obsolete almost as soon as it is written, and such projections are readily found in the current literature.

Possibly the most detectable general trend is a shift from hardware to non-hardware orientation in the industry. The fascination with hardware systems and technology is seemingly being replaced with a more proportionate allocation of attention. Personnel, training, software, and, most important, the conceptual foundations of information systems and their design are now becoming recognized as being of equal, if not greater, importance than hardware.

A concomitant of this trend is a shift in perspective concerning the relation of the computer system to the problem or application area. Until now, problems have usually been adapted to the computer. The computer system was considered a fixed quantity, and the key question was whether the problem was amenable to computer solution or could be restated to be amenable. Application packages became more and more generalized to meet the needs of a wide range of customers. The user was expected to modify his procedures and practices so that he could use the more generally applicable requirements of the package. With the new perspective, the computer system must adapt. The organization and its unique needs are the fixed quantity; the challenge is to mold the computer system into a form that can meet these needs. The trend to increasing adaptability of computer systems will, of necessity, initiate corresponding trends in both hardware and software systems. We will defer discussion of these subsequent trends to the sections dealing with those areas.

12.1 Hardware System Trends

In the past, the major advances in hardware systems have been those of speed and capacity. Cycle times of milliseconds gave way to microseconds, and microseconds became nanoseconds, which in turn have been eroding steadily. The ultimate barrier to speed appears to be the speed of light, approximately 1 foot per nanosecond. The increasing integration of circuitry, which has reduced the length of interconnecting wires, has thus been largely responsible for the increases in speed. With cycle times now in the hundreds-of-nanoseconds range we are obviously approaching the limit of speed performance. In addition, improvements of 100 or even 200 nanoseconds in a cycle time of 750 nanoseconds is nowhere near the relative improvement that was achieved in moving from milliseconds to microseconds. Further increases in speed will clearly be of decreasing importance in the performance of future computing systems.

It seems much more likely that improved performance will result from new concepts of machine organization. Parallelism provides an excellent example of new concepts of organization. Increased throughput and performance is achieved by the parallel (simultaneous) operation of independent but centrally controlled processing units. The ILLIAC IV, developed by the University of Illinois and Burroughs Corporation, includes 64 such processing units and is thus capable of performing as many as 64 computations simultaneously.

The cost of computer hardware systems has been another area of major improvement. Cost reduction since the early 1960s has been substantial and seems likely to continue. This is significant for the many potential application areas that are not economically feasible now. The computing needs of small social and economic units such as the household and the elementary school fall into this category. Continued reduction in the cost of computing should drastically expand the impact area of the computer.

Central Processing Unit The division of functions between hardware and software promises to be a significant area of change in the years ahead. Continuing gains in large-scale integration will decrease costs, so that functions such as file management, telecommunication management, and data searching techniques can be implemented in hardware rather than software in the future. A likely means of implementing these *hardwired* functions will be via *microprogrammed control storage*. Fixed or read-only microprogrammed control storage has been used for some time, and little change in technology will be required to hardwire additional functions. It is even technically possible to build additional functions to suit the particular needs of individual users. But manufacturers are understandably reluctant to customize because of the virtually insurmountable barrier to standardized software support which results. Microprogrammed control storage, with both fixed and writable sections, is a compromise solution. The writable portion (variable microprogrammed control storage unit) would be available for those functions that meet the users' unique requirements, while the fixed unit would contain standardized functions. The functions contained in the variable unit are frequently called *firmware*.

It is also possible that future computer systems will consist of multiple central processing units, if not complete computer systems, with each one dedicated to a specific function or task. Such arrangements have been described as hierarchical computer systems, and tasks could be divided by function or application or both. A computer system could, for example, contain one processor dedicated to peripheral unit control, one for communications, one for data management, one for processing, and one to coordinate the rest. A hierarchy based on application might consist of a number of small computer systems monitoring or controlling various segments of a process and feeding a larger computer system, which directs the activities of the entire process and in turn passes information to a computer system with the primary function of supporting the decision-making process.

Finally, from the nature of the most recent developments and in view of the almost disastrous consequences of sweeping technological changes in the past, it seems likely that future development of central processing units will be evolutionary instead of revolutionary. Future CPU designs should be sufficiently modular and flexible to accommodate technology advances gracefully.

Input/Output Systems   Getting data into and out of the computer system has always been a weak link in the data processing chain. The disparity in speed between a card reader, magnetic tape unit, or printer operating in milliseconds and the CPU operating in microseconds has been a significant obstacle to optimum performance.

Progress is being made with a number of different approaches. Card equipment, however, is not one of these. We seem to have reached at least a temporary dead end in the improvement of card devices. Although a drastic improvement in card devices is conceivable, the present trend is toward the development of an array of different devices and techniques.

Keyboard data entry systems are a significant development. These systems range from simple key-to-tape and key-to-disk arrangements to systems with small processing units to edit, reformat, collate, and sort incoming data. In the system illustrated in Figure 3.15, for example, up to 64 stations can record on disk simultaneously. A single disk can hold up to 24 hours of keyed input. The prepared data produced by these systems is then passed to the main processing computer system ready for immediate use. The labor of translating from human-readable to machine-readable form via a keyboard is still necessary, but the process has become integrated rather than being a series of distinct and loosely related steps. Data is keyed directly to a machine-processable medium, so there is no need for a card-to-tape or a card-to-disk function. In general, keyboard data entry systems minimize the handling and thus the errors contained in incoming data.

Source-data collection systems extend this integration process by one major additional step. The devices that are used obviate the need for keyboard translation of data from human-readable to machine-readable form. Possibly the most common device in this category is a cash register that is equipped for point-of-sale recording in some machine-readable fashion. As a sale is rung up on the cash register, the pertinent information is simultaneously recorded on paper tape, for example. More significantly, the cash register may be on-line to the computer system and the data transmitted directly to it. In either case, the possibility of an error in transcription at the keying step is eliminated.

Optical character recognition (OCR) devices are almost certain to offer significant new capabilities in the future. The most important of these capabilities will be that of accepting data generated by non-computer and non-computer-oriented sources. In particular, OCR devices will be capable of accepting both handwritten and hand-printed as well as typewritten input. This is actually a form of source data collection, in that the original documents will be submitted directly to the system, without being transcribed.

The touch-tone terminal is a promising data collection device. A touch-tone telephone itself may be used as a terminal (as we described in Chapter 3) or a special touch-tone keyboard may be attached. In either event the user dials the computer system and transmits tone-coded data from the keyboard to communications equipment that converts the data to digital form and passes it on to the computer system. If the computer system is equipped with audio response capability, the computer system may then respond to the sender over the telephone. Information in digital form is passed to the audio response unit and is converted to a verbal message, which is transmitted over telephone lines to the telephone receiver. The touch-tone terminal is a very low cost device, requiring little training or even explanation to potential users. The increasing use of touch-tone telephones means that this terminal capability will become almost universally available. This in itself will create new applications.

Recording data on microfilm is another potentially important development in input/output systems. Not only is this process faster than printing by several orders of magnitude, but it is much easier to store and a virtually unlimited number of copies can be produced. This flexibility could well produce a major breakthrough in input/output systems.

Besides the specific areas mentioned above, developments are likely to occur in remote terminal equipment, particularly remote input for batch processing, and in cathode-ray tube devices. In the latter case, a decrease in cost will make CRTs a feasible choice for many applications.

Storage In addition to increases in speed, it is reasonable to expect continued increases in storage capacity. Although, as we discussed earlier, increases in speed are likely to be less significant than in the past there seems to be no approaching limit to storage capacity. Whether increases will arise from current lines of development or from entirely new technology, we are likely to see substantial increases in both high-speed and secondary storage capacity. This will be a significant development, for a surprising number of applications and potential applications are "storage-bound." Applications involving information retrieval, for example, are rather primitive primarily because of the lack of sufficient storage capacity.

Computers now simply do not have sufficient room to store an optimum amount of information on a given subject, and so we content ourselves with indexes and abstracts rather than a full range of material.

Technologically the use of semi-conductor memories has seemingly set the course of development for some time to come, although a number of other promising possibilities are in the research stage. Semi-conductor memories seem capable eventually of producing cycle times of less than 10 nanoseconds and of reducing the physical size of high-speed storage dramatically.

Possibly the most significant conceptual development is that of a storage hierarchy, in which the various storage devices are organized according to speed, so that the fastest device interfaces with the central processing unit and also services the majority of the work load. The first reference to a unit of information causes the transfer of a block of information from a slower-speed device to the high-speed device, and subsequent references to the information are to the fast device only. The effective memory speed averaged over all operations thus tends to be closer to the speed of the fastest device than to the speed of the slower devices. This concept solves the problem of the memory paradox that the cycle time and access time of storage vary directly with the physical capacity of the storage. To have a very large storage capacity, the user had to resign himself to proportionately lengthy access and cycle times. With the advent of storage hierarchies this need no longer be the case.

Minicomputers The trend toward increasing use of minicomputers such as the one illustrated in Figure 12.1 is well established. The term *minicomputer* has been

Figure 12.1 Honeywell Series 200m Model 115/2 ini-computer.

defined in various ways but generally refers to a physically small, very low cost, general purpose computer, with relatively limited storage capacity and speed and limited input/output capability. Thousands of these devices have already been installed, and some writers predict annual shipments in the tens of thousands within the next few years. Minicomputers offer a great deal of flexibility to the user organization because additional CPUs can be added as necessary.

Minicomputers will be an essential element in the development of hierarchical computer systems. Many users today are dedicating low-cost minicomputer systems to single functions or tasks. A single system is programmed to perform a specific task such as inventory control and then is simply allowed to sit in a corner and grind away at this task without interruption and in relative isolation from other systems. This approach also limits the extent of a given failure by the compartmentalization of functions.

12.2 Software System Trends

Software development continues to be a "cottage" industry. Each software "craftsman" or group of craftsmen is busily turning out new articles of the craft largely in isolation from his fellow workers. The overall result of this process is confusion. There is very little standardization, and both quality and performance are low. It is reasonable to expect improvement in this situation. At a minimum, quality and reliability will improve simply because computer users demand it. Available software will be made more reliable, easier to use, and less costly. In addition, basic software modules may be developed, to be used as components of larger software structures. Today, for the most part, each software unit is built in its entirety from the bottom up, and this has obviously involved a great deal of duplicated effort. The basic software modules could be developed once, standardized, and then made available for use as basic elements of many different software packages.

Easier-to-use programming languages will most likely be developed. These languages will be constructed so as to be readily usable by nonprofessional programmers, specifically the end user of the required information. If, for example, the sales manager needs a special report, he or one of his subordinates will be able to construct a program quickly to satisfy the need. A language such as we are describing will have to use terminology that is readily interpretable by the user. The terminology will, in fact, have to be a subset of the terminology normally used within the application area. The language must also have powerful debugging features, including highly explanatory syntactical diagnostics and some form of logic checking. Other developments in programming languages will be simpler and more powerful languages for data management, a universal language, and new concepts of the division of function between language and hardware.

12.3 Personnel Trends

The demand for all levels of data processing personnel is virtually certain to grow throughout the foreseeable future. This will not be the wild growth that the industry experienced during the 1960s, however. The present demand for selectivity in both skills and quality is likely to continue. Users are not simply looking for programmers; they are looking for COBOL programmers with two years or more of OS/360 experience and, most important, a proven production ability. Entry-level positions will be available, but landing one will depend on qualifications other than simply surviving a sixteen-week technical course. The individuals' potential for development will be an important consideration in the filling of entry-level positions.

In programming there will be a pronounced shift in the skills demanded. The days of the application programmer are numbered. Application programmers are a stopgap solution to a temporary problem. Until now, programming has been too complex to expect the end user to be able to efficiently perform his own duties and programming as well. A programmer with an adequate knowledge of computers, some skill in programming, and a very weak knowledge of the application area was able to perform a passable service in supplementing the end user's skills. The result, however, is far from optimum, simply because the programmer lacks the intimate knowledge necessary to meet the user's needs adequately. The answer is to make the programming process so simple that the end user can meet his own needs.

We are not predicting the demise of programmers in general—only the problem or application programmer as a distinct occupation. There will be a greater need for what we now call systems programmers. To utilize the computer system effectively, the end user will have to work within the framework of a comprehensive and complex basic information system structure, including an extensive and readily usable data base. This framework will demand many programmers with high skill levels. Viewed from another perspective, we are really predicting a general upgrading of the skill levels of programming demanded. The development of this basic information system structure will drastically increase the skill levels demanded of systems analysts also. Even today, this skill level increase is being recognized by the creation of a new occupation category that deals with the more general information needs of the organization. This category, sometimes called information analyst, is a consulting activity concerned more with the underlying philosophy and nature of the overall information structure than with the design of specific subsystems.

Finally, the amount of professionalism within the fields of computers and data processing is sure to increase. The boom era is over, and the general trend is in the direction of more responsible behavior. Furthermore, the public in general and management in particular are more knowledgeable and less awed by computer technology. The old imperiousness will no longer work.

Exercises

1. Describe a potential application of computers that is presently infeasible because of current speed limitations on computer hardware systems.

2. Describe a potential application of computers that is presently infeasible because of current limitations on input/output capability of computer hardware systems.

3. Describe a potential application of computers that is presently infeasible because of current limitations on storage capacity of computer hardware systems.

Appendix A

IBM 029 Card Punch

This appendix provides a brief introduction to the IBM 029 card punch.

On-off Switch. This switch is located on the right side of the front of the cabinet *under* the keyboard table. The card punch is *on* when the switch is *up*.

Program-Unit Switch. In the middle of the unit above the keyboard is a small window. Beneath the window is a V-shaped switch that should be *set to the right.*

Switch Panel. Six toggle switches are located directly above the keyboard. The switch labeled *print* should be in an *up* position so that the characters being punched into the card will be printed at the top of the card also. The other five switches should be *off* or *down.*

Card-Column Pointer. A numbered drum and pointer are located inside and at the bottom of the window described above. The numbers on the drum correspond to card columns, and the pointer points to the number of the column that is in position to be punched.

Input and Output Hoppers. Blank cards are placed in the input hopper, which is located on the top right of the unit. The punched cards are stacked in the output hopper, which is located on the upper left side of the unit.

Keyboard. The keyboard of the 029 card punch is similar to that of a typewriter in both appearance and operation. All characters are uppercase, however. The bottom character on a key is punched by depressing the key, while the upper character on the key is punched by simultaneously depressing the **NUMERIC** key and the key in question. The bar at the bottom of the keyboard produces a blank column in the card and corresponds to the space bar on the typewriter.

In addition to the alphabetic, numeric, and special characters the following keys are useful:

FEED. Feed one card to the *preregister* station.

REG. Move a card from the preregister station to the *punch* station.

REL. Release a card from the read or punch station. (After a card has been punched it moves left into the read station.)

DUP. Duplicate the card columns of the card in the read station into the card in the punch station.

ERROR-RESET. Release a jammed keyboard.

The following procedures may be followed on the IBM 029 card punch:

A. Punch One Card
 1. Depress the *FEED* key.
 2. Depress the *REG* key.
 3. Punch the required information into the card by depressing the appropriate character keys and the NUMERIC key as necessary.
 4. Depress the *REL* key twice.

B. Duplicate Portions of a Card
 1. Depress the *FEED* key.
 2. Insert the card to be duplicated into the read station through the slots provided.
 3. Depress the *REG* key.
 4. Depress the *DUP* key in order to duplicate the desired portions of the card. Any character or blank may be punched in columns not duplicated.
 5. Depress the *REL* key twice.

Appendix B

Bibliography

Computer Hardware System

Elementary

Hellerman, Herbert, *Digital Computer System Principles*. New York: McGraw-Hill Book Co., 1967.
Murphy, John S., *Basics of Digital Computers*, revised second edition (3 vols.). New York: Hayden Book Co., 1970.
Stone, Harold S., *Introduction to Computer Organization and Data Structures*. New York: McGraw-Hill Book Co., 1972.

Advanced

Foster, Caxton C., *Computer Architecture*. New York: Van Nostrand Reinhold Co., 1970.

Katzan, Harry, Jr., *Computer Organization and the System 370*. New York: Van Nostrand Reinhold Co., 1971.
Lefkovitz, David, *File Structures for On-Line Systems*. New York: Spartan Books, 1969.
Maley, Gerald A., and John Earle, *The Logic Design of Transistor Digital Computers*. Englewood Cliffs, N.J.: Prentice-Hall, 1963.

Programming

Elementary

Bohl, Marilyn, *Flowcharting Techniques*. Chicago: Science Research Associates, 1971.
Farina, Mario V., *Programming in Basic: The Time-Sharing Language*. Englewood Cliffs, N.J.: Prentice-Hall, 1968.

Forsythe, Alexandra I., Thomas A. Keenan, Elliott I. Organick, and Warren Stenberg, *Computer Science: A First Course*. New York: John Wiley and Sons, 1969.

Murrill, Paul W., and Cecil L. Smith, *An Introduction to Fortran IV Programming: A General Approach*. Scranton, Penn: International Textbook Co., 1970.

Runn, Donald L., *An Introduction to COBOL Computer Programming for Accounting and Business Analysis*. Belmont, Calif.: Dickenson Publishing Co., 1966.

Walker, Terry M., *Introduction to Computer Science: An Interdisciplinary Approach*. Boston: Allyn and Bacon, 1972.

Advanced

Chapin, Ned, *360 Programming in Assembly Language*. New York: McGraw-Hill Book Co., 1968.

Donovan, John J., *Systems Programming*. New York: McGraw-Hill Book Co., 1972.

Katzan, Harry, Jr., *Advanced Programming: Programming and Operating Systems*. New York: Van Nostrand Reinhold Co., 1970.

Sammet, Jean E., *Programming Languages: History and Fundamentals*. Englewood Cliffs, N.J.: Prentice-Hall, 1969.

Walker, Terry M., and William W. Cotterman, *An Introduction to Computer Science and Algorithmic Processes*. Boston: Allyn and Bacon, 1970.

System Analysis and Design

Elementary

Clifton, H. D., *Systems Analysis for Business Data Processing*. New York: Auerbach Publishers, 1969.

Lott, Richard W., *Basic Systems Analysis*. New York: Canfield Press, 1971.

Orilia, Lawrence, Nancy B. Stern, and Robert A. Stern, *Business Data Processing Systems*. New York: John Wiley and Sons, 1972.

Advanced

Martin, James, *Design of Real-Time Computer Systems*. Englewood Cliffs, N.J.: Prentice-Hall, 1967.

Sharpe, William F., *The Economics of Computers*. New York: Columbia University Press, 1969.

Shaw, John C., and William Atkins, *Managing Computer System Projects*. New York: McGraw-Hill Book Co., 1970.

Applications

Elementary

Bobrow, Davis B., and Judah L. Schwartz (eds.), *Computers and the Policy-Making Community: Applications to International Relations*. Englewood Cliffs, N.J.: Prentice-Hall, 1968.

Borko, Harold (ed.), *Computer Applications in the Behavioral Sciences*. Englewood Cliffs, N.J.: Prentice-Hall, 1962.

Bowles, Edmund A. (ed.), *Computers in Humanistic Research*. Englewood Cliffs, N.J.: Prentice-Hall, 1967.

Head, Robert V., *A Guide to Packaged Systems*. New York: Wiley-Interscience, 1971.

Meadow, Charles T., *Man-Machine Communication*. New York: Wiley-Interscience, 1970.

Weiss, Eric A. (ed.), *Computer Usage/Applications*. New York: McGraw-Hill Book Co., 1970.

Advanced

Dutton, John M., and William H. Starbuck, *Computer Simulation of Human Behavior*. New York: John Wiley and Sons, 1971.

Evans, George W., II, Graham F. Wallace, and Georgia L. Sutherland, *Simulation Using Digital Computers*. Englewood Cliffs, N.J.: Prentice-Hall, 1967.

Feigenbaum, Edward A., and Julian Feldman (eds.), *Computers and Thought*. New York: McGraw-Hill Book Co., 1963.

Kelly, Joseph F., *Computerized Management Information Systems*. New York: Macmillan Co., 1970.

McLeod, John, *Simulation: The Dynamic Modeling of Ideas and Systems with Computers*. New York: McGraw-Hill Book Co., 1968.

Sackman, Harold, *Computers, System Science, and Evolving Society: The Challenge of Man-Machine Digital Systems*. New York: John Wiley and Sons, 1967.

Impact

Burke, John G., *The New Technology and Human Values*. Belmont, Calif.: Wadsworth Publishing Co., 1968.

Crosson, Frederick J., and Kenneth M. Sayre (eds.), *Philosophy and Cybernetics*. New York: Simon and Schuster, 1967.

Martin, James, and Adrian R. D. Norman (eds.), *The Computerized Society*. Englewood Cliffs, N.J.: Prentice-Hall, 1970.

Pylyshyn, Zenon W. (ed.), *Perspectives on the Computer Revolution*. Englewood Cliffs, N.J.: Prentice-Hall, 1970.

Sprague, Richard E., *Information Utilities*. Englewood Cliffs, N.J.: Prentice-Hall, 1969.

Taviss, Irene (ed.), *The Computer Impact*. Englewood Cliffs, N.J.: Prentice-Hall, 1970.

Whisler, Thomas L., *Information Technology and Organizational Change*. Belmont, Calif.: Brooks/Cole Publishing Co., 1970.

Index

Accumulator, 95
ACL (Artificial computer language), 95
Address:
  actual, 78, 79
  effective, 93
  register, 68
  symbolic, 78, 79, 95, 100
Aiken, Howard G., 72
ALGOL, 79
Algorithm, 10, 84
Analog computer system, 70
Analytical engine, 71
Applications (see Computer applications)
Arithmetic and logic unit (ALU), 68
Artificial computer language (ACL), 95

Artificial intelligence, 7
  artistic applications, 14
  computer-assisted instruction (CAI), 8
  conversation, 11
  game playing, 10
  problem solving, 11
  semantic information retriever (SIR), 11
Assembler, 78
Assembly language, 78, 100
Atlanta Falcons Club, Inc., 158
Atlantic Steel Co., Inc., 147
Authority, centralization of, 193 (see also Social impact)
Automatic sequence controlled calculator (Mark I), 72
Automation, 170, 177, 178

Autonomy, individual loss of (see Economic impact, job structure)

Babbage, Charles, 70
Base number system (see Radix)
Batch processing, 145
Bertalanffy, Ludwig von, 116
Binary coded decimal (BCD), 51
Binary number system, 45–47
Bit, 47
Block data, 59
Blocking factor data, 60
Business:
  concentration (see Economic impact)
  small, 183
Byte, 42

Index

Card (*see* Punch card)
Card processing devices, 20
Card punch (IBM), 19, 215–216
Card reader (*see* Input/output devices)
Carriage control character, 104
Cathode ray tube (CRT), 37
Central processing unit (CPU), 22, 65, 67
Chaining, 57
Character, 42
Checkless cashless society, 164
COBOL, 105–111
COGO, civil engineering simulation language, 81
Commands, 67
Compilation, 79
Compiler, 79, 112
Complex calculator, 72
Computer applications, 145
  batch application, 147
  batch processing, 145
  business application, 146
  business integration, 164
  computer utility information, 163
  data banks, 165
  football application, 158
  medical application, 153
  politics, 193
  small business, 184
Computer-assisted instruction (CAI), 8
Computer hardware system, 5
  costs, trends of, 207

Computer (continued)
  electronics, 6
  resources, 82
Computer invasion of privacy, (*see* Social impact, privacy)
Computer operator, 5
Computer output microfilm, 35
Computer process control, 173
Computer science, 41
Computer system, 2, 3
  analog, 70
  central processing unit (CPU), 65
  dangers, 197
  evolution, 70, 202
  fear (*see* Fear)
  functions, 22
Computer system design (*see* Systems analysis and design)
Computer system environment, 3
Computer system on-line applications, 151
  on-line processing (*see* On-line processing)
  personal data service, 163
  scientific computation, 146
  time sharing, 162
  voter information, 194
  voting simulation, 193
Computer utility, 163, 184
Conceptual model, 122, 132
Conditional transfer command, 99
Control clerk, 5

Control element, 67
Controls, auditing-accounting, 140
Conversation (*see* Artificial intelligence)
Cybernation, 170
Cycle time, 206

Data, 41
Data acquisition and representation devices (*see* Input/output devices)
Data banks:
  literature retrieval, 166
  NCIC, 165, 166
  social, 166
Data base (*see* Data organization)
Data collection system, 27
Data collection techniques, 132
Data organization, 55
  data base, 58
  data base management systems, 58
  documentation, 138
  fields, 56
  files, 56
  hierarchy of data elements, 56
  random organization, 57
  sequence within files, 56
  sequential organization, 57
  specifications and layout, 140
Data processing, 20
  departments, 4
  management, 118

Index

Data storage devices (*see* Storage devices)
Data storage, 58
Debugging, 83, 112
Decentralization, organization, 178
Decimal number system, 45
Decision making, 183
Dehumanization (*see* Social impact)
Delta Airlines (*see* Flight control system)
Design alternatives, 140
Design concept, 123
Difference engine, 70
Direct access storage, 61
Disk storage, 61
Documentation:
   algorithm design, 85
   existing system, 130
   specifications, 137
Document-flow analysis, 132
Documents, 81
Dossiers, 200
Dunn, Edgar S., Jr., 199

EBCDIC (*see* Extended binary coded decimal interchange code)
Eckert, J. Presper, 73
Econometric models, 184
Economic impact, 169–184
   collective bargaining, 177
   competition, 183

Economic (continued)
   economic control, 184
   employment, 170
   job structure, 174
   management, 180–182
   organization, 178
   skill requirements, 176
Editing, 31
EDSAC (electronic delay storage automatic calculators), 77
EDVAC (electronic discrete variable computer), 77
Effective address (*see* Address)
Employment impact (*see* Economic impact)
ENIAC (electronic numerical intergrator and calculator), 73
Equipment off-line (*see* Off-line systems)
Equipment, peripheral (*see* Input/output devices)
Equipment selection, 125
Evolution of computer systems, 70
Extended binary coded decimal interchange code (EBCDIC), 51, 67

Fear, economic, 189–191
Feasibility study, 147, 119–129
Field, 56
File, 56
File security, 140

First generation computers, 73, 74
Firmware, 207
Fixed point number, 67
Flight control system (Delta Airlines), 151–153
Floating point number, 67
Flowcharting, 84, 85, 177
Flowchart symbols:
   annotation, 88
   arrow, assignment, 89
   arrow, replacement operator, 104
   connector, 87
   decision, 87
   flowline, 88
   input/output, 86
   predefined process, 88
   processing, 86
   terminal, 87
Foreign policy, 194
Format, 104, 105
FORTRAN, 76, 79, 80, 102–105
Fourth generation computers, 74
Functional integration, 179
Function flowchart, 132

Game playing (*see* Artificial intelligence)
General problem solver (GPS), 14
General system theory, 116
Giantism, concentration in business, 188

Index

GPSS simulation language, 81
Grady Memorial Hospital, 153–158

Hardware selection, 125
Hardwire functions, 207
Hexadecimal number system, 45, 48, 50
Hierarchical computer system, 207, 211
High-speed storage, 65, 66
Hollerith coding, 43
Hollerith, Dr. Hermann, 43, 73
Howell, Gordon C., 95

IBM machines:
   360 system, 74, 80
   370, 74
   650, 77
   701, 73
   704, 78
   705, magnetic core memory, 74
Illiac IV, 206
Implementation, 126, 127, 141
Indexing, 93
Information, 41, 42
Information sources, 131
Information systems, 8, 19, 41
Input/output control system (IOCS), 101

Input/output devices, 19, 20, 22
   card reader, 23
   cathode ray tube (CRT), 37
   channels, 39
   computer output microfilm (COM), 35
   input devices, 23
   key to tape (or disk), 31
   light pen, 38
   magnetic ink character recognition (MICR), 25
   magnetic tape, 60
   optical character recognition, 25
   output devices, 34
   page search readers, 37
   plotter, 35
   printer, impact type, 34
   printer, nonimpact type, 34
   remote terminals, 31
   special-purpose devices, 27
   tape reader, 24
   touch tone telephones, 31
Instruction counter, 68
Instruction format, 77, 95
Instruction register, 68
Instructions, 67
Intelligence (*see* Artificial intelligence)
International affairs, 194
International information systems (*see* Social impact)
Inter-record gap, 60
Interrupt, 39

Interviewing, 132
Iterative process (looping), 93

Job control languages, 82

Keyboard data entry systems, 208
Key punch, 19
Key punch operator, 5

Languages:
   application-oriented, 81
   development, 211, 212
   higher level, 76
   job control, 82
   problem-oriented, 81
   procedure-oriented, 112 (*see also* ACL, ALGOL, Assembly language, COBOL, COGO, FORTRAN, GPSS, PL/1, RPG, Simscript, SNAIL)
Leibnitz, Gottfried Wilhelm von, 70
Light pen, 38
Literal expansion, 46
Literal value, 95
Literature retrieval system (*see* Data banks)
Loading process, 67
Logic chart (*see* Flowcharting)
Logic theory machine, 11
Looping, 93

Index

Machine language program, 76, 77
Machine readable information, 42
Magnetic cores, 66
Magnetic drum, direct access storage, 62
Magnetic ink characters, 25
Magnetic tape storage media, 31
Management, computer impact (*see* Economic impact, management)
Management perspective, 132
Manual procedures, writing (*see* Implementation)
Mauchly, John W., 73
Mazlish, Bruce, 188
Mechanical adding machine, 70
Mechanization, 136, 170
Memory, 65
Message switching centers, 165
Microfilm, input/output, 209
Micro-programmed control storage, 207
Microseconds, 67
Minicomputers, 74
Mnemonic operation code, 77, 100
Modularity, 83
Multiprogramming, 76, 162

Nanoseconds, 67
National Commission on Technology, Automation, and Economic Progress, 171
National Crime Information Center (NCIC), 165, 166
Neumann, John von, 77
Nonexecutable command, 102
Number systems, 42, 45, 46-48
Numeric data, 67

Object program, 79
Obstetrics-hematology clinic, Grady Memorial Hospital, 153
Occupational categories, change of (*see* Economic impact)
Occupations, 5
  computer operator, 5
  control clerk, 5
  key punch operator, 5
  programmer, 5
  systems analyst, 5
Octal number system, 45-50
Off-line systems and devices, 19, 31
On-line processing, 146, 147
Operands, 95
Operation code, 95
Operations department, 4
Optical character recognition (OCR), 208
Order entry system, 147
Organizational structure, 178
Output devices (*see* Input/output devices)
Output per man hour, 172

Overlapping, 39

Parallelism, 206
Pascal, Blaise, 70
Payroll applications, 146
Performance measurement, 134
Performance requirements, 83, 122, 123, 138
Peripheral equipment (*see* Input/output devices)
PL/1, 80, 81
Plotter (*see* Input/output devices)
Primary record key, 57
Primary storage, 58
Privacy (*see* Social impact, privacy)
Problem analysis, 81
Problem-oriented language (*see* Languages)
Problem solving (*see* Artificial intelligence)
Procedure-oriented language (*see* Languages)
Process control, 118
Processing time, 83
Productivity, 172
Professionalism, 213
Program analysis, 112
Program design objectives, 82
Programmer, 5
  general, 67, 77, 79
  selection, 212

Programming, 75
  analysis, 84
  development of languages, 76–81
  problem analysis, 81
  program design objectives and restrictions, 82
  program performance requirements, 83
  resources, 82
Programming, looping, 93
Programming languages (*see* Languages)
Programming standards, 83
Program narrative, 81, 144
Program performance requirements, 83, 84
Punch card, 23, 44, 75, 105
Punch paper tape, 43, 147

Queuing patterns, 135

Radix, 45, 67
Randomizing technique, 57
Random organization, 57
Rationalization, process, 175
Real time, definition, 147
Records, 56
  combined fields, 56
  fixed length, 56
  group files, 56

Records (continued)
  index, 57
  key, 57, 58
  variable length, 56 (*see also* Chaining, Data organization)
Redesign information systems, 21
Referendum, instant, 194
Register, 68
Report format, 140
Report of the Committee on Preservation and Use of Economic Data, 198
Resources, 82
RPG language, 72

SAGE (semi-automatic ground environment), 147
Scientific computation, 146
Secondary storage, 59
Second generation computers, 74
Self-incrimination, 200
Semi-automatic ground environment (SAGE), 147
Semiconductor memories, 210
Sentinel, 99
Sequential organization (*see* Data organization)
Simscript, simulation language, 81
Simulation, 135, 141
SIR (*see* Artificial intelligence)

Skill level, 76
Skill requirements (*see* Economic impact)
SNAIL (student nonassembly instructional language), 95
Social impact:
  anonymity, 197
  definition, 187
  dehumanization, 189, 190
  education, 195
  fear, 189–191
  general, 180
  individual, 189
  international affairs, 194
  international information systems, 195
  leisure, 187, 192, 194
  National Data Center, 198
  political, 193
  privacy, 196, 197, 200
Software system selection, 125
Sorting, 16
Source data collection, 208
Source program, 78
Starting address, 68
Station loads, individual, 135
Station to station survey, 132
Stibitz, George, 72
Storage capacity forecast, 209
Storage devices, 59
  disk, 61
  hierarchy, 62

Storage devices (continued)
   magnetic drum, 62
   magnetic tape, 59
Storage hierarchy development, 210
Storage, high speed, 65
Storage media, 58
Storage word, 66, 67
Stored program, 76
Student nonassembly instructional
   language (SNAIL), 95
Subscript (I), 93
Syllogism, 71
Symbolic assembly program (SAP), 78
Symbolic operation code, 78
Syntactical errors (*see* Debugging)
System, 115
   analysis, automated, 135
   analysis and design (six steps), 117
   analysis redesign, 130
   computer-based information, 116
   design, 139
   documentation of specifications, 137
   feasibility study, 119
   implementation, 142
   initiating study, 121
   redesign, 129

System (continued)
   review and evaluation, 142
   specifications, 135, 136
   staffing feasibility study, 120
   study, 121
System engineering, 116
System flowchart, 81
System objective, 131
System requirements (*see* System,
   specifications)
System restrictions, 136
Systems analysis and design, 4, 81, 117
Systems analyst, 5, 81, 118–142
   authority, 118
   design evaluation, 141, 142
   design responsibility, 140
   qualifications, 118
   responsibility, 118
   system requirements, 136
System simulations (*see* Simulation)

Technology and the American
   Economy (report), 171
Thinking, capability of, 16
Third generation computers, 74

Threshold techniques, 130
Time sharing, 162
Touchtone terminals, 209
Tracks, 62
Trends and projections, 205
   control processing unit, 207
   hardware systems, 206
   input/output systems, 208
   minicomputers, 210
   personnel, 212
   software, 211
   storage, 209
Turn around time, 146

Unbundled services, 125
Unconditional transfer, 99
Universal automatic computer
   (UNIVAC), 73

Voting simulation, 193

Whisler, Thomas L., 176

QA
76
C589

FEB 20 1975